The CIVIC DEAL

The
CIVIC
DEAL

Re-Empowering
Our Great Republic

RICHARD STRINER

PERICLES INSTITUTE

Washington, D.C.

LIBRARY OF CONGRESS CATALOGING-IN-PUBLICATION DATA

Striner, Richard, 1950–
    The civic deal : re-empowering our great republic / Richard Striner.
        p. cm.
    Includes index.
    ISBN 0-9675462-0-6 (alk. paper) — ISBN 0-9675462-1-4 (pbk. :
    alk. paper)
    1. United States—Politics and government. 2. Liberalism—United
    States. 3. Conservatism—United States. I. Title.

JK2265.S77 2000
973—dc21   99-050092

*This book is dedicated
in friendship and gratitude
to Jay Griswold*

Contents

Foreword

☆ ☆ ☆

T HE CIVIC DEAL REACHES OUT TO THOUGHTFUL AMERICANS
across party lines and across the philosophic spectrum. Richard Striner asks us to re-examine our ideas about many public issues: our expectations of government, our understandings of the
terms "conservative" and "liberal," our conventional wisdom regarding
economic policy. It shows how some of America's greatest leaders borrowed wisdom from both the conservative and liberal traditions — leaders such as Abraham Lincoln, Theodore Roosevelt, and Franklin Delano
Roosevelt. At a time when confidence in government is eroding, *The
Civic Deal* offers a vision of America's future in which this bipartisan
legacy is restored.

The intention behind this book is as old as some of the historical
writing of ancient Rome and the Civic Humanism of the Italian Renaissance: the conviction that historians have a duty not only to study
the past in an accurate and conscientious spirit but also to *interpret* our
past in a manner that guides us in the present and the future. Whatever
our conclusions about Richard Striner's message and recommendations,
it is a healthy sign for our democracy when historians write spirited
books that address public policy issues, especially when their points of
view transcend the partisan and ideological conventions of the moment. Among its other attributes, *The Civic Deal* is strikingly independent.

While the policy prescriptions of *The Civic Deal* present a challenge to some notions that are dominating public life right now, the
historical background materials are rife with interpretations that are

also unconventional: Striner's portrait of Lincoln, for example, as a brilliant risk-taking strategist rather than a somber, if eloquent, "moderate"; his demonstration of the links between the programs of Herbert Hoover and Franklin D. Roosevelt; his account of the Keynesian antecedents of the Eisenhower highway program; his reminder of the large and ambitious environmental agenda of Richard Nixon.

In an age of sound-bites, oversimplifications, and pop cynicism, a spirited but scholarly call for heroic expectations in public life is refreshing. *The Civic Deal* is a challenge to all of us to rediscover some lessons that Americans learned but forgot over time. If the "legacy of Lincoln and the Roosevelts," as Striner refers to it, has served the United States before, there is no good reason why the legacy cannot be revived to serve us again.

A philosopher once noted that convictions are like prisons: once espoused one is committed to defend them. *The Civic Deal* challenges commonly held convictions and thus frees us to act on the best of historic bipartisanship.

REP. CONSTANCE A. MORELLA (R-MD)

Preface

☆ ☆ ☆

THIS BOOK IS AN INTERPRETATION OF AMERICAN HISTORY that seeks to *change* contemporary history. It is a challenge to various destructive stereotypes about government — stereotypes that have been fouling our public life and diminishing our national greatness. It seeks to reveal the importance in our history of a bipartisan legacy of governmental stewardship that resulted from a synthesis of conservative and liberal ideas: a political and ideological reconciliation handed down from Abraham Lincoln to Theodore Roosevelt to Franklin Delano Roosevelt. It argues that the rediscovery of this powerful but dormant heritage is vital to our future.

This reading of American history leads to a policy formulation, the Civic Deal. The term is designed to recall both the "Square Deal" of Theodore Roosevelt and the "New Deal" of Franklin D. Roosevelt while linking both of these programs to a new consensus that might be built around civic necessities to which thoughtful conservatives and liberals should be able to respond. The program of the Civic Deal would acknowledge the validity of conservative insistence on public safety while acknowledging the validity of liberal arguments for well-conceived public works. These themes become linked as the basis for a new reciprocity: opportunity, through training and jobs in rebuilding our public infrastructure, combined with a much tougher ethic toward violent crime.

Training and jobs in exchange for safer streets: a venture in enlightened economic and civic self-interest that is worthy of a great nation. It is practical and achievable, notwithstanding our preoccupation

xi

with budget-balancing — a preoccupation that the book will place in better historical perspective. It could also be inspirational. It could revive the American hope for benign and democratically founded order in our chaotic world, and it would look to the government ordained and established by ourselves to sustain that order.

This book will challenge the prevailing approaches to "centrism" by those who seek to transcend conservative-versus-liberal dialectics. Most of the self-styled centrists of the 1990s have preached a doctrine of "devolution" or localization. But *The Civic Deal*, while recognizing the worth of local governance, will make the case that Americans cannot afford an either-or choice between localism and nationalism. Robust local governance must often be supplemented with vigorous federal action in order to meet the challenges of our times.

The Civic Deal will de-escalate the feud between conservatives and liberals by showing the Republican and conservative (as well as the Democratic and liberal) antecedents of "big government" activism. By analyzing American political history in light of the growth and subsequent erosion of the bipartisan heritage of Lincoln and the Roosevelts, it will give Americans a very different perspective from which to interpret recent history and current events, and to formulate programs for the future.

Some important disclaimers are in order. *The Civic Deal* is intended not as a micro-specific policy guide but rather as a broad conceptual foundation for further development. In the area of public safety, for instance, *The Civic Deal* advocates an *ethic* toward violent crime without advancing elaborate prescriptions for dealing with such issues as parole, the insanity defense, or "jury nullification." Likewise in economic policy, *The Civic Deal* urges an expansive definition of wealth, along with an expansive approach to investment, as a *principle* of capitalist thought with antecedents as varied as the legacies of Alexander Hamilton and John Maynard Keynes.

The Civic Deal's scholarly apparatus is based wherever feasible on primary-source citations from published compilations of public papers and letters rather than on indirect citations from secondary sources or the footnotes of others. Relevant scholarly literature is discussed on a selective basis in extended footnotes, but only when such discussions illuminate the book's major arguments. The historiographical implications of *The Civic Deal* should be obvious to colleagues within the historical profession. This book is conceived within the broad Civic Humanist tradition as an old-fashioned synthesis of scholarship and commentary.

At critical junctures of the book I engage in speculation pertaining to the possible outcomes if players in historical crises had chosen very different courses of action. Such a practice is easy to abuse. It can lead to what some dismiss as "counterfactual history." But I believe that in responsible hands it can also be essential to our understanding of the contingent nature of life and the historical process. To make real sense of history, we must judge the actions of historical participants in light of our understanding of what their *options* were. Classicist Donald Kagan has contended that "all true historians engage in this practice, with greater or lesser self-consciousness." To give a pertinent example, we can obviously never *know* precisely what Lincoln would have done if he had lived to complete his second term. Yet we can profit not only from the knowledge that American history *would* have been drastically different in some respects, but also from the *poignancy* of what might have been as we interpret the trajectory of Lincoln's extraordinary statecraft down to the moment when its dynamism stopped forever. An expansive sense of what *might have been* conveys a greater sense of what *can be*. *The Civic Deal* is offered without apology as a contribution to the ongoing efforts of scholars to offer a genuinely "usable past."

Profound thanks are in order to James M. McPherson, David Grimsted, James MacGregor Burns, Louis Jacobson, David Brooks, Craig Donegan, Judith R. Joseph, Herbert E. Striner, and Edward L. Jaffee for their helpful suggestions on various portions of the text. Personal thanks are in order to Jay Griswold, Ernest L. Scott, Richard B. Berryman, George S. Wills, Benjamin Lamberton, Robert Harrison, Kenneth Mandel and the board of directors of the Pericles Institute for their crucial support in the creation of this maverick essay. Above all, I am grateful to my wife Sara, my parents, and my family for their love and confidence.

The
CIVIC
DEAL

Chapter One

☆ ☆ ☆

Give Me Liberty, Not Chaos

I N 1910, AFTER LEAVING THE PRESIDENCY, Theodore Roosevelt delivered an important speech to a group of Civil War veterans in
Kansas. The philosophy of government pervading this speech flies
directly in the face of today's conventional wisdom. The Republican
Roosevelt contended that Americans should "work in a spirit of broad
and far-reaching nationalism when we work for what concerns our
people as a whole." The American people, he said, were demanding a
"New Nationalism" because of the "utter confusion that results from
local legislatures attempting to treat national issues as local issues." In
cases "where the whole American people are interested," Roosevelt concluded, "the betterment which we seek must be accomplished, I believe, mainly through the National Government."[1]

Millions of Americans today are in a mood that is vastly at odds
with such views. Theodore Roosevelt's Republican Party is dominated
by leaders who assert that "big government" messes up virtually everything it touches and that power should rest with localities and private
citizens. Columnists and radio commentators ridicule the bureaucratic
"nanny state" and its "tax-and-spend" behavior. Libertarian think tanks
and laissez-faire economists encourage us to view "government" as almost a weird and alien force. When Americans think about Theodore
Roosevelt, they typically think of the soldier at San Juan Hill, seldom of
the social theorist who lectured Congress in 1908 about the "mutual-

ism, the interdependence of our time," or who argued in his *Autobiography* that while "a simple and poor society can exist as a democracy on the basis of sheer individualism . . . a rich and complex industrial society cannot so exist."[2]

But the Republican Roosevelt's forgotten social vision holds the key to America's future as a world power. A significant degree of active stewardship by our national government has repeatedly been (and must continue to be) a source of the moral worth, social cohesion, and economic strength of this nation. The widespread cliché that governmental action *inherently* tends toward bureaucracy and repression is simplistic and wrong. The purveyors of this cliché are not only staining the legacy of leaders like Abraham Lincoln and Theodore Roosevelt but threatening a resource upon which America's greatness continues to depend.

This is not a "liberal" tract. It is an essay in history and policy that stands outside of the conservative-liberal feud in order to resurrect a lost milieu of statesmanship that drew from both conservative and liberal ideas. It is not an argument for over-reaching government that tries to "do everything." It is rather a case for governmental actions that are vital to the health of our Republic, actions that local governments and the private sector cannot be expected to provide in the manner that we need.

This book will make the case for four related propositions: (1) the minimal-government doctrines embraced by conservatives since the late nineteenth century are fraught with danger; (2) neither conservatism nor liberalism provides a satisfactory program or social philosophy for our times; (3) the various recent attempts to build a "centrist" option for "reinventing government" through localization cannot meet the challenges confronting our society; (4) our history provides us with a bipartisan heritage that harmonizes conservative and liberal insights to furnish our nation with a government worthy of a first-class power. All four propositions will be considered in the first chapter of this book;

much of the balance of the book will develop Proposition Four, the lost legacy of stewardship whose retrieval is essential to our nation's future.

PROPOSITION ONE:

THE MINIMAL-GOVERNMENT DOCTRINES EMBRACED BY CONSERVATIVES ARE FRAUGHT WITH DANGER

T HE HISTORY OF ANARCHISM, THE UTOPIAN BELIEF that humanity can live without government, is beyond the scope of this study, since respectable American opinion regards this creed with contempt. But the libertarian belief that the functions of government can be kept *minimal* is one of the most passionately held convictions of our time. An idea whose modern roots can be traced to the seventeenth and eighteenth centuries, the doctrine of laissez-faire — the minimal-government maxim of the French Physiocrats — was central to early liberal thought but then was taken up by conservatives in the nineteenth century.

Both the history of laissez-faire and the histories of modern conservative and liberal thought contain peculiar twists and turns. A number of conservative preferences in social policy — crime control and the anti-abortion agenda, for instance — continue to depend upon police or statist regulation, and these conservative proclivities exist in awkward juxtaposition to conservative attacks on government. Yet the ever-growing power of laissez-faire ideology in conservative thought is unmistakable. The insistent conservative promotion of "pure" unregulated enterprise can be traced from Victorian "Social Darwinism" (the creed of "survival of the fittest") through the Coolidge version of laissez-faire in the 1920s through the Liberty League's denunciation of the New Deal to the post–World War II conservative crusade against "statist collectivism." After the Goldwater movement in 1964, the conservative anti-government attitude became re-energized and re-empowered, both financially and intellectually, by the founding in the 1970s of well-endowed libertarian institutes and think tanks. Today, having built upon its breakthrough in the Reagan years, this conservative libertarian movement remains a significant and influential force in American politics. In the wake of the congressional elections of 1994, the president of the laissez-faire Cato Institute exulted that "Americans are looking for politicians to leave them alone, not to presume to be able to solve their problems for them."[3]

This is a message that resonates powerfully in the American mind. The cult of individualism is a part of the American mythos that will probably thrive as long as the United States exists. Americans return perennially to the vision of Jefferson's first inaugural address, in which the third president called for a "wise and frugal government, which shall restrain men from injuring one another, which shall leave them otherwise free to regulate their own pursuits of industry and improvement, and shall not take from the mouth of labor the bread it has earned."[4] Which of us cannot respond to the simplicity of this vision? Which of us cannot attest to the glory of self-reliance in pursuit of worthy goals? We revel in our personal pursuit of happiness, as (within reason) we should.

The problem is that individualism *by itself* is simply inadequate as the basis for creating civilized communities or for sustaining the wealth and might of a great nation. When Jefferson became president, the United States was functioning already under its *second* Constitution, since the first one — the Articles of Confederation — had proven too weak. While Jefferson was sympathetic to the creed of minimal government when he assumed the presidency, he found himself increasingly unwilling to adhere to the strict laissez-faire position. In fact, in his final message to Congress, Jefferson urged the legislative branch to give serious consideration to the expenditure of federal funds for "the improvement of roads, canals, education, and other great foundations of prosperity and union under the powers which Congress may already possess or such amendment of the Constitution as may be approved by the states."[5] Jefferson's secretary of the treasury, Albert Gallatin — initially an advocate of frugality and balanced budgets — laid out a large and ambitious agenda for federally sponsored public works as a guide for Jefferson's successors. The challenges of building the nation had proven too great to justify a permanent restriction of the scope of government. A century later, Theodore Roosevelt had come to the conclusion that the "laissez-faire doctrine" could "be applied, if anywhere at all, only in a primitive community under primitive conditions."[6]

It is ironic, of course, that many of today's prevailing doctrines turn the outlook of Theodore Roosevelt on its head. It is now the idea of *national governance* that tends to get labeled as "primitive" — as a formula for inefficiency and waste — in contrast to all of the bright "new ideas" that will supposedly flourish when the dead weight of "government" is lifted from the backs of entrepreneurs. The choice we are offered by libertarian think tanks and radio "personalities" is one that pits the image of a domineering yet befuddled "nanny state" against the image of liberating enterprise.

And yet it was the federal government of Theodore Roosevelt's time that was regarded as liberating and heroic when it interceded in the marketplace to keep contaminated food products from the shelves of grocery stores. And so our estimation of the need for "big government" depends — does it not? — on the nature of the situations that Americans face in the course of changing times. It is obvious that "big government" has weaknesses and dangers, from the extreme danger of totalitarianism to the mundane but depressing ways of the bureaucratic mind. It is obvious that governmental regulations can get out of hand. But the alternative of minimal government has failed on the few occasions in modern times when people have attempted to put it to the test. That is why the "pure free market" exists hardly anywhere on earth: every major industrial nation where capitalism thrives (even Britain under the legacy of Thatcherism) employs a mixture of the public and private sectors.[7] The mixture is needed for the reason that Theodore

Roosevelt discerned: industrial societies break down as soon as people really try to live according to the creed of "fend for yourself." This would hardly need to be proven today if memories of life in the 1930s had not been softened with the passage of time.

Because the legacy of Franklin D. Roosevelt provides such a flashpoint for left-versus-right disputation, consider some stark facts about the situation in the 1930s that transcend both political party and political ideology. The Great Depression was the latest in a series of up-and-down convulsions that were known as the "boom and bust" cycle of the market. In the nineteenth century a series of financial panics — in 1819, 1837, 1873, and 1893 — were followed by depressions, each one being worse than the one that preceded it. As these economic chain reactions ripped their way through society — as financial panic was followed by contraction of credit, reduction of factory output, layoff of workers, and shrinkage of consumer purchasing power — the results could be powerful enough to punish millions who were guilty of no economic misjudgments. In the case of the Great Depression of the 1930s, the scope of this punishment was greater than anything the American people have experienced before or since. By 1933 there were almost thirteen million people out of work, most of them through no fault of their own.[8] This was roughly a fourth to a third of the full-time workforce. Millions of middle-class families lost their homes and their savings and then moved to shacks at the city dump. Demand for consumer goods was desperate, and yet the "market" (in purchasing power) was shrunken catastrophically by the onset of poverty on such a scale. In any case, the start-up money to re-open closed factories was draining away as the banking system began to collapse in early 1933. By 1933 the American economy was operating at little more than *half* of its 1929 volume.[9]

Let us stop right here for the moment — let us *not* entertain a discussion of the New Deal. Instead, let us put today's free-market ideologists on the spot. Taking these people at their word, one has to conclude that the attackers of the "nanny state" would have recommended that the government should have done *nothing* to revive the economy in 1933. One has to conclude that their faith in the free market would be such that they would forbid any steps by government to ease the suffering of millions and to counteract the risk of an upheaval that might have overthrown democratic institutions. *If* this is true — *if* this is an accurate reading of today's libertarianism in a worst-case setting — then the free market theorists should make it contractually clear to the American people that in times of economic disaster they must absolutely fend for themselves. They should also make it clear to the American people how to fend for themselves if there are insufficient jobs. But if this is *not* true — if this is in fact a distortion or exaggeration of libertarian free enterprise prescriptions — then libertarians should stop oversimplifying modern life, since they very well *might* go along with "big government" intervention if *enough* individuals are suffering. Either way, the laissez-faire people have some tall explaining to do.

Let us now compare the condition of America's economy on the eve of the New Deal — industrial output reduced by half, the full-time workforce reduced by a fourth, the greatest industrial nation in the world reduced to a pathetic and shambling victim — to the condition of the U.S. economy ten years later as America's exertions in World War II approached their zenith. Again, let us *not* make reference to the New Deal. World War II provides a much handier and more unifying case in point, since regardless of party or ideology most Americans look back upon our role in the Second World War with patriotic pride. In World War II the American industrial cripple of the early 1930s transformed itself into an economic powerhouse that outproduced all of its Axis enemies in weapons and war materiel. The gross national product rose from $100.4 billion in 1940 to $213.4 billion in 1945.[10] The United States achieved a level of industrial superabundance in World War II that was staggering, and government made it happen. Federal expenditures soared from $13.3 billion in 1941 to $34 billion in 1942, $79.4 billion in

1943, $95.1 billion in 1944, and $98.4 billion in 1945.[11] Individual, corporate, and excise taxes covered only $109.7 billion of federal spending during World War II — the rest was raised through borrowing.[12] In 1945 the national debt ($258.7 billion) was actually greater than the gross national product ($213.4 billion).[13] And yet the federal government went on to finance the GI Bill — which sent over two million veterans back to college and graduate school, producing hundreds of thousands of engineers, doctors, teachers, scientists, and businessmen while providing tremendous housing benefits for veterans that stimulated a major construction boom — and, later, to initiate the Marshall Plan for rebuilding war-devastated Europe.

By the standards of today's libertarians, much of this would have to be described as a colossal "failure" by the "nanny state" to "balance the budget" and "live within its means." But it certainly didn't seem that way to millions of Americans a half century ago. By the middle of the 1940s, the generation whose experience encompassed both economic extremes — the rotten stagnation of the Great Depression and the surge of miraculous productivity that accompanied total mobilization of the nation's resources — left its policy verdict on the comparison. The verdict took the form of the Employment Act of 1946, which vested the federal government with permanent responsibility for maintaining high levels of employment. No return to laissez-faire was to be permitted, even after the Republicans came back to power. Not only was President Eisenhower quick to reassure the American voters in that regard, but one of the greatest public-works efforts in American history — the Interstate Highway System — was commenced in the Eisenhower years.

It bears noting that the Interstate Highway System resulted in part from Eisenhower's pledge to avert another depression — to avert what he called "another 1929." In 1956, journalist Robert J. Donovan recounted in his semi-official chronicle *Eisenhower: The Inside Story* the Republican deliberations in response to a recession in 1954:

The President informed the Cabinet that he had asked [Arthur F.] Burns to co-ordinate reports from the various departments and agencies on their plans for public-works projects. It would be essential, he said, to have planning advanced sufficiently to insure that men would be put to work quickly. Too often, he said, preliminary planning, testing, and surveys delay start on work. . . . Projects actually under way, he noted, gave the government flexibility in speeding them up or stretching them out, as conditions required.[14]

Such were the sorts of economic concerns which, combined with *bona fide* transportation planning, led to the inauguration of the Interstate Highway System, announced to the public by Vice President Nixon in 1954 and then enacted by Congress in 1956. This tremendous undertaking by government was launched at a time when the ratio of national debt to gross national product was comparable to what it has been in the 1990s.[15]

In light of all this, the tantrum of today's libertarians could well be costly for America. As a great industrial nation we continue to depend upon our national government to ward off economic depressions, and to tide us over with unemployment compensation if our corporate employer happens to "downsize" abruptly. We also depend upon the government to help us when floods and tornadoes smash our homes. We depend upon the government to keep toxic wastes and carcinogens away from ourselves and our children. We depend upon the government to sponsor scientific research into the causes of cancer and its cures. We depend upon the government to give us every one of the roads and bridges and flood-control projects that a superpower ought to have. Or would we rather be a third-class power?

That is what could happen in the next century, according to strategic and defense analyst Edward N. Luttwak, if we do not wake up about things like our deteriorating infrastructure. The alarm has been sounding for years: back in the early 1980s, the authors of a study undertaken for the Council of State Planning Agencies contended that "America's public facilities are wearing out faster than they are being replaced," and that "in hundreds of communities, deteriorated public facilities threaten the continuation of basic community services such as fire protection, public transportation, water supplies, secure prisons, and flood protection."[16] Since then, the situation became even worse: infrastructure spending in the 1980s failed to keep pace with the accelerating stress upon aging public works. Luttwak's 1993 analysis found that in the previous ten years "the burdens placed on . . . infrastructures have increased much more than the amounts spent to improve them. As a result, from sewage systems to interstate highways, many U.S. infrastructures are now deficient in quality or quantity or both."[17] During the Bush administration, the Department of Transportation acknowledged that "much of the highway infrastructure is nearing the end of its economic service life and needs major rehabilitation or replacement. For example, according to Federal Highway Administration statistics, 23 percent of the 575,000 highway bridges in the United States are structurally deficient and another 19 percent are functionally obsolete."[18]

These concerns were echoed and amplified by Wall Street financier Felix G. Rohatyn. This senior partner at one of America's premier investment firms argued in 1992 that Americans "have not invested adequately" in either the "public facilities to provide the infrastructure required by a modern industrial society" or the "human capital to provide all Americans with the education and training to fill the available jobs." Rohatyn warned that to fill these gaps and stay competitive in global terms, Americans must realize that "a more active role for government is an absolute necessity." Otherwise, the future will promise "an eroding standard of living for most Americans."[19] Similar warnings re-echoed through the 1990s until Congress attempted to remedy the lag in infrastructure spending through the 1998 "highway bill."

But at best, this measure was a stopgap. Transportation reinvestment runs in six-year cycles, and the members of Congress who supported this action were excoriated by free-marketeers and "balanced-budget hawks." Will the free-marketeers have control when the current cycle ends?

As a dry rot of dinginess, danger, and chaos spread over American life at the close of the twentieth century, the libertarian zealots made enormous progress in convincing Americans that government — the "nanny state" — has been the source of most of our ills. It is easy enough to find examples of ill-founded action in governmental programs and projects. But it defies common sense to believe that pure commerce and nothing but commerce can be trusted by itself to provide our children with a nation and society worth living in. If our politicians continue to indulge themselves in the platitudes of laissez-faire — if they continue to strive with hilarious gusto to uninvent the legacy of Theodore Roosevelt — they should pause to consider what would happen if the powers of government are shrunk to the point of near-paralysis, either through a balanced-budget amendment or through comparably misguided action, and then our accumulating problems keep building — and building — and building. Will any of these people be around to receive what they deserve if a smash-up happens?

PROPOSITION TWO:
NEITHER CONSERVATISM NOR LIBERALISM PROVIDES A SATISFACTORY PROGRAM

THE AMERICAN PEOPLE HAVE PROFOUNDLY MIXED FEELINGS with regard to the conservative-liberal feud. Some Americans revel in the "take no prisoners" war between the ideologies: they eagerly join the political tribe of their choice and then scream out their tribal loyalty with bumper-sticker slogans. But other Americans are tired of being forced to choose between conservative and liberal doctrines that strike them as flawed. They are tired of being whipsawed back and forth between the sorts of propositions that George Orwell once dismissed as "the smelly little orthodoxies which are now contending for our souls." They are looking for a better course of action.

Many of us — if we are honest with ourselves — can probably admit that we are wearied by the shrillness and dogmatism characteristic of this ideological war. The case can be made that the sickness of conservative-liberal warfare is far more destructive to our society than many of our other vexations. And the sickness of the war is a direct result of the sickness of the ideologies themselves. Both of the creeds are now deplorably encumbered with foolishness.

Since liberal values are especially unpopular now, it is easiest to begin by diagnosing liberal failures. The liberals have been in deep trouble for decades because of the widespread belief that the moral compassion of the liberal conscience has gradually become distorted and unreliable. Take a representative example: the visit to Khomeini's Iran by former Attorney General Ramsey Clark in the summer of 1980. In the depths of the Iranian hostage episode, as terrorists played their sadistic game with the lives of American civilians, the former attorney general of the United States took a trip to Iran and proclaimed that Khomeini's revolution was a "miracle for the century." After delivering a mild and sensitive lecture on the wrongness of hostage-taking, he offered himself as a substitute hostage if Iran would only negotiate. When this offer of personal martyrdom elicited no response from the terrorists, the former attorney general offered to lead an investigation of American imperialism if the hostages were released. All of this took place in the midst of the 1980 presidential campaign, and all of it was richly documented in contemporaneous press accounts.[20]

We Americans are certainly no angels, but we should never have to grovel in the face of outrageous behavior by people who are also far from angelic. Clark groveled — and his antics were symptomatic of more than just the liberal "post-Vietnam syndrome." They were symptomatic of a moral gullibility, a failure to insulate one's sensitive compassion from the fraud of aggressors who claim to represent the downtrodden. The widespread doubt about the soundness of contemporary liberal instincts in this regard is one of the principal reasons why liberal credentials have become such a liability in presidential politics. In a world full of dangerous gangster regimes, American voters are reluctant to entrust the presidential office to anyone who suffers from naiveté, from neurotic guilt, or from squeamishness regarding power.

In domestic politics, liberals have suffered from comparable problems relating to public safety. Once again the problem is the issue of compassion gone wild. Take the matter of crime and mental illness. Does a single month elapse without the appearance in the press of yet another account of an atrocious murder committed by a mental patient who had just been released after being pronounced "cured" by a hopeful, compassionate, and (let us say the word without hesitation) liberal public health system? It goes without saying that the torture of mental illness deserves all the mercy and assistance society can give. But society has some rights too. Who would possibly advocate the release of a psychotic like Charles Manson to some form of out-patient therapy? Clearly, our own rights to life, liberty, and the pursuit of happiness must override the claims to liberty of someone who is criminally insane. And yet maniacs without the notoriety and visibility of Manson are released all the time by a lenient judicial and public health system that is quite prepared to play Russian roulette with the lives of our innocent loved ones.

As violence and savagery erode the very basis of America's social compact — for how can we call ourselves a civilized society when safety for the peaceable citizen cannot be taken for granted? — it is hardly surprising that "liberal compassion" has scant appeal any longer. The tragedy here is that the liberal conscience has changed our world for the better in innumerable ways. The victims of exploitation, the victims of discrimination, and even the victims of rotten luck deserve consideration and assistance from any society that claims to be decent. And yet the prevalence in our world of unspeakably vicious behavior does establish limitations beyond which our leniency and our forgiveness should not extend. The point is that the valuable qualities of the outlook we call "liberal" have finally become too formulaic, too unreliable, and in some respects too gullible to command the support of American majorities any longer.

But the truly insufferable thing about conservative-liberal dialectics is that many of the conservative policies offered as antidotes to the moral confusions of liberalism are causing even greater confusion and disintegration in American life.

Instead of replacing the liberal values they attack with unifying themes that promote social cohesion, conservatives revel in the slash-and-burn politics of religious fundamentalism. What they do for public safety by advocating tougher sentences and adequate prisons they undermine by opposing the measures recommended by law-enforcement officials to keep guns away from lunatics and criminals. They pander to our lust for property rights while attacking the zoning and land-use laws that in many ways *protect* our property rights by preventing obnoxious neighbors or aggressive developers from doing something trashy next door to the land that we own. In other words, today's conservatism — so-called — does not *conserve*. While conservatives love to appropriate the symbols and rhetoric of patriotism in their cultural war against liberals, they cannot even be trusted to save our patriotic shrines from degradation.

Just a decade ago, for instance, Manassas battlefield was threatened when a pushy developer tried to build a 1.2 million-square-foot regional shopping mall — with some two hundred stores and a parking lot to accommodate upwards of four thousand cars — right next door to the federal battlefield park. Indignant citizens protested that a solemn shrine where American soldiers had fought and died was about to be reduced to a sideshow in a gaudy shopping carnival. Congress intervened at the last minute, and the character of this battlefield shrine was protected by federal action, specifically a forced sale of the land in question under eminent domain. But as usual, many conservatives opposed this act of conservation. They revealingly refused to conserve. They were absolutely willing, by the lights of their orthodox market-worship, to sacrifice the civic solemnity of a national battlefield shrine to market-driven vulgarity. Indeed, Milton Friedman, one of the most dogmatic advocates of "pure" free enterprise, once challenged the very existence of national parks of any kind. "If the public wants this kind of activity enough to pay for it," Friedman said, then "private enterprises will have every incentive to provide such parks."[21]

It is easy to imagine the character that such private entrepreneurial wilderness or heritage "parks" would possess — *if* the sites in question survived the ferociously competitive counter-pressures for commercial redevelopment. It is all too easy to imagine the power of the lumber and strip-mining interests that would swiftly vie with any would-be purveyors of wilderness recreation for the use of our national parks and forests if federal ownership should cease. If Friedman's proposition were put to national plebiscite — if, to use Friedman's slogan, the American people were "free to choose" whether to sell off the national parks — is there any doubt which way the American majority would vote? They would almost surely vote to protect the national patrimony that conservationists like Theodore Roosevelt fought so hard to protect.

The tragedy of late twentieth-century conservatism is that it lacks the positive ethic of social cohesion that it had (at its best) in past centuries. While the conservative quarrel with liberalism is sometimes well grounded, especially when it comes to public safety, conservatives have little to offer that promotes a healthy society. True, they offer more jails to increase public order, along with some impressive invocations of western moral values. But otherwise, all is fragmentation — fragmentation in the form of religious divisiveness, of money-making in the old deregulated spirit of "buyer beware," of tax relief that benefits the wealthy more than anyone else, and of unrestrained provision of guns and armaments to anyone, sane or lunatic, with money.

Such, then, are the nonsensical choices we are offered by the ideologies of late twentieth-century conservatism and liberalism. If we find ourselves put off by the chaotic meanness of the right, then we are forced to indulge the disastrous naiveté of the left. As E. J. Dionne, Jr. lamented in 1991, "the false choices posed by liberalism and conservatism make it extremely difficult for the perfectly obvious preferences of the American people to express themselves in our politics."[22] It is not surprising, therefore, that a small but significant number of Americans have sought to move beyond the left-versus-right dialectic — to liberate themselves from this absurd set of choices and chart another course for themselves.

The "communitarians," for instance, under the leadership of sociologist Amitai Etzioni, have called for a new social balance of rights and responsibilities in order to bond our communities into a mature reciprocity.[23] The message (so far) has not resonated extensively, perhaps because "communitarian" conjures up misleading visions of 1960s hippies and communes. Related in some respects to the communitarians, but far more consequential for politics and policymaking, have been the so-called "New Democrats." These self-styled "centrists" have sought to move the Democratic Party toward a mainstream position on issues like public safety. The Clinton administration was dedicated to this search for a "third way," for a "New Covenant" that would end the conservative-liberal rat race and unify Americans. The result has been problematical for a number of reasons.

Some of the problems must be laid at the doorstep of Clinton himself. In a great many cases, his blunders gave his policies a bad name, and this happened well before the Lewinsky affair blighted his second term. The fumbling in foreign policy, the misjudgments in strategy and timing, the presence of embarrassing blatherskites like Dr. Jocelyn Elders — all of this repeatedly ruined Clinton's image of "centrism." It gave right-wing saboteurs a perfect opportunity to pillory Clinton as another incompetent "liberal" and to link his leadership failures with their own stereotypical view of "big government." The resulting conservative trash campaign blighted almost every attempt by Clinton to put national stewardship to use for centrist purposes. The profoundly conservative — and conserving — side of such programs as Clinton's youth service corps became hopelessly lost amid the right-wing din about "liberal government." In savaging the Clinton health-care plan, a right-wing strategist exhorted the faithful with the following candid pep talk: "This is the liberal attempt to prove government works. . . . If we let him [Clinton] succeed in this last gasp of liberalism, we don't deserve to rule in the future."[24] As Anthony Lewis of the *New York Times* observed, the right-wing "campaign to destroy President Clinton" derived from "a larger effort to turn Americans against the whole idea of government."[25]

There was another important reason for the failures of the New Democrat centrists. Many of these people should be called *de*-centrists, since they subscribe — through the slogan of "Reinventing Government" — to the notion that governance is best carried out through decentralized or localized programs. Such people had a very strong voice in the councils of the Clinton administration, and their rhetoric all too frequently played into the hands of Clinton's enemies. By surrendering the moral high ground of nationalism, by joining with the opposition in bad-mouthing most forms of national-scale initiative, the New Democrats botched a historic and precious opportunity. A post-mortem on their failure is essential to reviving our lost heritage of stewardship.

PROPOSITION THREE:

THE NOTION OF "REINVENTING
GOVERNMENT" THROUGH LOCALIZATION
CANNOT MEET THE CHALLENGES
CONFRONTING OUR SOCIETY

IN THEIR BOOK *REINVENTING GOVERNMENT*, David Osborne and
Ted Gaebler argued that "decentralized institutions" are generally "more effective" and "more innovative" than centralized ones:
they "generate higher morale, more commitment, and greater productivity." Consequently, these authors claimed, "unless there is an important reason to do otherwise, responsibility for addressing problems
should lie with the lowest level of government possible."[26] These doctrines had a powerful impact on the Clinton administration. They
formed the basis for recommendations from the Progressive Policy Institute (PPI), a New Democrat think tank that Clinton helped found in
the late 1980s. Osborne's chapters in *Mandate for Change* — PPI's multi-
author recipe book on public policy — alleged that "centralized systems are too slow, too cumbersome, and too rigid," and that "today, a
bias for state and local action makes sense" because of the "imperative
to decentralize."[27] In this spirit, Vice President Gore launched a project
for "reinventing government," contending that "we need to decentralize" in order to "make our government smaller and smarter."[28]

It is hard to take exception to initiatives that seek to "cut red tape"
and pare down bloated bureaucracies. When government becomes incompetent, superfluous, or stale, we have every right to "reinvent" it,
whether by restructuring its programs, decentralizing them, or by de-
ferring the activities in question to the private sector. But it behooves
us to be selective in this "reinventing," since American history provides
us with scores of examples of much-needed actions that could only
have happened through strong federal leadership. Without centralized
national power, for instance, the disgrace of American slavery might

well have survived beyond the mid-nineteenth century. Emancipation did not come about through decentralized or localized methods. Neither did the civil rights and voting rights reforms of the mid-twentieth century. It took federal marshals and FBI agents to overpower local sheriffs who were members of the Ku Klux Klan. In the areas of natural resource conservation and historic preservation, it defies common sense to believe that our national parks, or our national battlefield shrines like the one at Manassas, would have been protected from "development" by local initiatives. Prince William County, Virginia, gave its blessing to the previously cited development project next to Manassas battlefield until Congress intervened and put a stop to it. A subsequent proposal for a Disney theme park close to the battlefield was also supported by Prince William County officials. It was stopped by a coalition of Civil War buffs, local preservationists, professional historians, and national organizations such as the National Trust for Historic Preservation.

Even if local officials are innocent of sleaziness or stupidity, certain environmental challenges are bigger than they can handle. In general, our vast but fragile ecological systems cannot be protected on a piecemeal, decentralized basis. Take the multi-state expanse of the Chesapeake Bay: protection of the Chesapeake watershed depends upon a clumsy jurisdictional give-and-take between the policies of Maryland, Virginia, Pennsylvania, and the District of Columbia. Only the efforts of a federal agency — EPA — have brought a semblance of co-ordination.

Consider the effects of our state and local bidding wars to bring about corporate relocations. Robert Reich has observed that in their "furious auction" to attract big companies, state and local governments vie with each other to cut back corporate taxes, thereby stripping themselves of important resources for education and infrastructure at the very moment when the theorists of localization would saddle them with greater tasks in these areas.[29] Consider the reasoning of writer Louis Jacobson, who has argued that "some government duties range easily across state borders and thus are best attacked by a single authority, rather than a patchwork. Criminal telemarketers or quack physicians, for instance, can already escape prosecution by slipping undetected into another state; widening such escape routes by nixing federal standards might needlessly complicate enforcement."[30]

Consider local struggles with organized crime. Would any sane person insist that our local governments should be our primary line of defense against regional or national patterns of mob criminality? Do we not "call the Feds" right away if we discover that our local elected officials are taking bribes from the Mafia? Consider the crisis of random street crime. The Brady Law, overwhelmingly supported by local police across the country, is based upon *national* background checks to identify violent criminals who migrate from city to city.

Consider the food and drug inspections that protect us from garbage in our hamburgers. An exposé of contaminated food that caused a national scandal in 1906 was confirmed by an undercover federal probe that was ordered by Theodore Roosevelt The drug Thalidomide caused horrid birth defects in the sixties until a courageous inspector at the Food and Drug Administration blew the whistle. Do we really want to entrust such things to state or local oversight? How much risk do we really want to take in the United States?

Years ago, the political scientist Robert A. Dahl observed that the complexity of modern life makes a preference for any single level of governance impossible. "The commune, neighborhood, city-state, the region, the nation-state — none can possibly be, by itself, a satisfactory basis for authority." Dahl argued that a number of "stages of government fitting together rather like the components of a Chinese box are necessary if 'the people' are to 'rule' on matters important to them, whether a neighborhood playground, water pollution, or the effective prohibition of nuclear war."[31] "The people" — despite their current weakness for anti-government rhetoric — continue to demand a truly vigorous degree of governance, whether at the local, state, or federal level, or through some combination of them all. We want police protection and traffic management and zoning regulation to protect our quality of life. We want national leadership when national problems affect us as individuals. We want national protection from the vast economic chain-reactions that we cannot control. We hold the federal government responsible for guaranteeing prosperity, and in times of recession we blame the incumbents and throw them out of office.

We abhor "big government" in theory, but we certainly want it on the job when another Love Canal is unearthed below the neighborhood we thought was safe. We want federal disaster money when the damage from a hurricane or avalanche exceeds our insurance coverage. We want Uncle Sam to stand by his promise to protect our life's savings if the local S&L goes bankrupt. We do not want to hear that we will get our money when and if the U.S. budget can be balanced. We want our money — period.

If our local officials let us down, then we complain to the Feds. If our mayor caves in to developers who want to obliterate historic buildings and construct an overpowering project, we find ourselves some lawyers, nominate the historic buildings to the National Register of Historic Places (U.S. Department of the Interior), and then attempt to sue our city government for failing in its duty to protect our environment and heritage.

In short, we want the Feds when we need them — and such are the complexities of modern life that we need them often.

Very little of this came through in Clinton's message as a New Democrat. True, he emphasized the need for national health care reform, and he started a national youth service corps with a modest amount of fanfare. But the force of these initiatives was often cancelled out by the constantly reiterated promises to "shrink bureaucracy." Perhaps Clinton did this believing it would undercut the right-wing libertarians, pre-empting their vote-getting issue. But the effect was precisely the reverse: it enhanced their influence and worsened their belligerence. By degrading or at least undervaluing the federal government's reputation, the New Democrats' attempt to build a constructive and enduring legacy during the Clinton administration collapsed in a shambles.

The next opportunity to revitalize national stewardship might be years in the future; the national mood remains corroded with significant cynicism. But moods change, and cynicism sometimes wears itself out in its own corrosion. When Americans are ready to listen again, they may well be receptive to the work-ethic value of programs like the Job Corps and national service corps, especially when linked to the challenge of rebuilding our infrastructure. The benefits of such action could extend beyond the economic sphere; they could help to redeem our society. Even James Pinkerton, a former Bush administration staffer — he was one of the people who thought up the Willie Horton gambit in the 1988 election — observed not long ago that "Clinton is right when he says, 'Work organizes life.' So it's tragic that the administration hasn't followed up with a New Deal style Civilian Conservation Corps to get disorganized youth off the streets before they get into trouble."[32]

We are living at a time in American history when violence and the lust for grotesquerie are near-pervasive forces in our culture, especially the culture of youth. We are living at a time when decent citizens are forced to confront the fury of people like the red light runners who act as though whatever interferes with ME deserves to be wiped away or out. Especially in times like these, is there not a case to be made that activities fostering a greater sense of national community — a sense of cultural cohesion that affirms decent values on a national basis — can assist in the work of rebuilding those values at the local and family level? Is there not a case to be made that the characterization of "government" as the source of all our ills is fueling the disintegration of the civic culture? By the constant maligning of "government," do we not tend to fray the bonds that unite us through a sense of mutuality and law into one society? Theodore Roosevelt understood this, and most of our citizens understand it too when the issues are articulated properly.

Notwithstanding our attraction to government-bashing and the lore of individualism, Americans still retain a strong devotion to the value of national community. We are also receptive to values that harmonize conservative and liberal insights.

In spite of the dogmas that have spoiled so much of the conservative and liberal traditions, each of the traditions has lingering elements of wisdom, useful not only on the grand scale of history but also in our own everyday lives. For all of the liberals' persistent neurosis and wishful thinking, something magnificent endures in a legacy that links the visions of Jefferson and Paine with the struggles and exertions on behalf of "the underdog" ever since. And there is something enormously valuable as well in the conservative tradition at its best, something that puts the brakes upon the liberal spirit when its longings are too naive. As the ironies of history unfold — as the ugly side of human nature recurrently frustrates utopian visions — a grim sort of comfort can be had from the old-fashioned insights of John Adams, from the eloquent warnings of Edmund Burke, and from the civilized astringency of Samuel Johnson. At their best, the conservative and liberal sensibilities help us do justice to important sides of our ambiguous human nature; they help to delineate the light and shadow of our complicated moral existence. Each is incomplete without the other.

At the level of everyday matter-of-factness, most of us live in a manner that balances a "liberal" hopefulness and a "conservative" toughmindedness. We live in the everyday presumption that most of our fellow citizens are fairly decent people most of the time, but we also avoid dark alleys. We revel in the joyous tidings of Christmas as we fervently pray that we remembered to lock the door to the car. We raise our children to be friendly and gregarious, all the while training them in elementary forms of watchfulness and self-protection. We do not self-consciously regard ourselves as the bearers of conservative or liberal doctrines as we go about practicing these principles of everyday sense. But they lead us to policy preferences that synthesize conservative and liberal values. What most of us want in public life, at least in the moments when we know our own minds, is a *balance* of liberty and governance, of personal freedom and public regulation, with the regulators fully accountable to us, the people. What most of us want is political leadership inspiring enough to make us strive for the common good but grounded in a shrewd understanding of human nature at its worst as well as its best.

In the late 1990s, the American people have *not* really known their own minds. Many were seduced — at least before the shock of the Oklahoma bombing — by the pleasure of blowing off steam with the anti-government screamers. But the American majority appears to be turning upon the screamers since national problems continue to fester and market forces fail to solve them. As this happens, we have another chance to break out of the conservative-liberal impasse. We will have it in our power to break down the structures of conservative and liberal thought, to salvage the elements of wisdom from each, while discarding what is spoiled and dogmatic. We can then put the pieces back together in a manner that gives our nation what it needs. The New Democrats tried to do something like this, but they failed because they misunderstood the dynamics of our Republic. They undervalued national governance in generating national cohesion and morale. But American history provides us with a heritage — a bipartisan heritage — that does reconcile the conservative and liberal traditions in order to provide us with inspiring national governance. Let us call this heritage the legacy of Lincoln and the two Roosevelts.

PROPOSITION FOUR:

WE HAVE A BIPARTISAN HERITAGE OF STEWARDSHIP THAT UNIFIES CONSERVATIVE AND LIBERAL VALUES

I N 1909, THE CRITIC AND JOURNALIST HERBERT CROLY wrote a classic study of politics. Published in the afterglow of Theodore Roosevelt's presidency, this important book, *The Promise of American Life*, praised the presidential leadership of Roosevelt and credited him with resolving an old political feud — one that derived from the age of the Founding Fathers when Alexander Hamilton and Thomas Jefferson clashed in the 1790s. By using Hamiltonian means (the use of an active national government) to achieve Jeffersonian ends (the well-being of ordinary Americans), Roosevelt taught the American people a priceless lesson, Croly proclaimed.[33]

We have heard a great deal of the "original intent of the Founders" from people like Antonin Scalia and Edwin Meese, but the furious disputes of the early Republic reveal that the Founders could be deeply polarized. The clash in the 1790s between the Hamiltonians and Jeffersonians was the first explicit example of conservative-liberal dialectics in American history. While the sources of conservative and liberal thought could be traced all the way to antiquity, the two traditions took distinctive shape in the age of the French Revolution — the age that crystallized earlier political patterns into the "left-versus-right" configuration.

In their reactions to the French Revolution these two American factions showed extremely divergent views of human nature and its social possibilities. The Hamiltonians reacted to the radicalism of the French Revolution with fear and loathing, while the Jeffersonians reacted with sympathy and hope. Hamiltonian and Jeffersonian governance clashed as well: Hamilton's brand of conservatism led to an activist approach toward government, while Jeffersonian liberalism showed an early affinity for laissez-faire. "I own I am not a friend to a very energetic government," Jefferson wrote to Madison in 1787; "It is always oppressive."[34] Hamilton disagreed vehemently. In *The Federalist* #70 he stated that "energy in the Executive is a leading character in the definition of a good government."[35]

It is certainly a major curiosity of modern history that conservatism and liberalism eventually *exchanged* (to a certain extent) these philosophies of governance. They did *not*, however, exchange their distinct social outlooks.

While conservative and liberal ideologies evolved, there was a recurrent tendency in American history to unify the best conservative and liberal insights by harmonizing Hamiltonian and Jeffersonian politics. Croly showed outstanding perception in pointing out the way in which Theodore Roosevelt used the Hamiltonian power of the national government to help Mr. Jefferson's "common man." But this achievement had begun even earlier. By the 1810s, a number of political leaders like Henry Clay sought to reconcile Hamiltonian and Jeffersonian principles. Clay's "American System" entailed the creation of extensive public works — as Jefferson himself had suggested in his last message to Congress. But the first real success in using Hamiltonian means to serve Jeffersonian ends was achieved by Lincoln (a protégé of Henry Clay) and the early Republican Party of the 1850s and 1860s.

The Republican Party of the Civil War era created what some have called a "blueprint for modern America" by using and expanding the powers of the federal government to deliver important services to highly diverse constituencies.[36] Republicans created the land-grant college system; they passed the Homestead Act to assist American farmers; they enacted a program of financial assistance to promote the development of transcontinental railroads, thereby investing in industrial infrastructure; they even created one of the first social welfare agencies in American history: the Freedmen's Bureau, created by Congress with Lincoln's approval in 1865 to smooth the transition from slavery to freedom through humanitarian assistance. Lincoln said in the 1850s that "the legitimate object of government is to do for the people what needs to be done, but which they can not, by individual effort, do at all, or do so well, for themselves."[37]

In this instinctive preference for activist government, Lincoln was clearly a Hamiltonian. But he was also a champion of Jeffersonian egalitarianism: he took Jefferson's maxim that all men are created equal and forged it into an anti-slavery weapon of surpassing power. "All honor to Jefferson," Lincoln proclaimed in 1859 — the man whose text for the Declaration of Independence had articulated principles that would serve as "a rebuke and a stumbling block" to resurgent oppression.[38]

This blending of Hamiltonian activism and Jeffersonian idealism carries major implications for conservative and liberal thought. For if we ask ourselves whether Lincoln was "conservative" or "liberal," we are forced to conclude that he was *both*. The liberal side of Lincoln is easily discerned. In 1857 Lincoln said that when the Founders agreed to Jefferson's assertion that all men are created equal "they meant to set up a standard maxim for free society which could be familiar to all, and revered by all, constantly looked to, constantly labored for, and even though never perfectly attained, constantly approximated, and thereby constantly spreading and deepening its influence, and augmenting the happiness and value of life to all people of all colors everywhere."[39] What statement could be more in tune with modern liberal sensibilities? And yet this liberal quality in Lincoln — which came through so clearly in his folksy stories and his common touch — was balanced by a grim and conservative recognition of the ugly side of human nature. "Slavery," said Lincoln in 1854, "is grounded in the selfishness of man's nature, opposition to it in his love of justice. These principles are an eternal antagonism."[40]

An *eternal* antagonism — one that would forever preclude a naive faith in the future. Though slavery was one of the clearest manifestations of the human tendency to do unto others precisely what we wish to avoid having done to ourselves, it was far from the last one to surface in the course of history. Lincoln chided the complacent in 1854 that we "cannot repeal human nature."[41] We cannot repeal the side of human nature that revels in degrading and dominating others. We cannot repeal the side of human nature that proclaims, in the words of George Fitzhugh — an antebellum advocate of slavery — that "some were born with saddles on their backs and some were born booted and spurred to ride them — and the riding does them good."[42] We cannot repeal the oppressive side of human nature, but we can *govern* it.

Here is the conservative side of Lincoln, the Lincoln who was able to look unflinchingly at human evil and call it evil. In Lincoln's first inaugural address he referred to the "better angels of our nature"; in his second inaugural address he invoked a more sombre American tradition — a tradition handed down from the Puritans. He spoke of the punishment inflicted on a wayward people for indulging the evil of slavery so long — the great purgation, the ordeal by fire, for our failure to deliver on the promises left by Jefferson. A mighty scourge of war, Lincoln said, had been whipping the American people. And,

> if God wills that it continue, until all the wealth piled by the bond-man's two hundred and fifty years of unrequited toil shall be sunk, and until every drop of blood drawn with the lash, shall be paid by another drawn with the sword, as was said three thousand years ago, so still it must be said "the judgments of the Lord, are true and righteous altogether."[43]

There is something in this passage that makes us avert our eyes and hasten with relief to the more familiar and comforting passage that follows, the one in which Lincoln's promise of malice toward none and charity for all does its soothing work. But there is something *bracing* in the grim side of Lincoln — something that strengthens us to live in this age of brutality without illusions and without despair.

In Lincoln's view, the mission of government is stewardship —

assisting the creative side of human nature while controlling the human lusts to degrade the lives of others. In 1864 Lincoln said that one of the primary social imperatives was the mission of protecting the liberty of the sheep from the liberty of the wolves.[44] The challenge of doing this while preserving a government of, by, and for the people was for Lincoln a task that every free society must face and take in stride.

From these precepts emerged a political synthesis that was crucial to the leadership of two major twentieth-century presidents, one of them Republican and one of them Democratic: the Roosevelts. Theodore Roosevelt was consciously seeking to revive the Lincolnesque tradition in Republican politics. He praised the activist leadership of Lincoln again and again. In his *Autobiography*, he said that "men who understand and practice the deep underlying philosophy of the Lincoln school of American political thought are necessarily Hamiltonian in their belief in a strong and efficient National Government and Jeffersonian in their belief in the people as the ultimate authority, and the welfare of the people as the end of government."[45]

Like Lincoln, Roosevelt refused to sentimentalize human nature; like Lincoln, he summoned up themes from the Puritan past. In a 1907 address, "The Puritan Spirit and the Regulation of Corporations," he proclaimed that "the Puritan was no Laodicean, no laissez-faire theorist. . . . The spirit of the Puritan was a spirit that never shrank from regulation of conduct if such regulation was necessary for the public weal; and this is the spirit which we must show today whenever it is necessary."[46] A year later, in his final message to Congress, Roosevelt observed that "every new social relation begets a new type of wrongdoing — of sin."[47]

If there appears to be too much draconian blood and iron in Theodore Roosevelt's outlook, we must remember that these sermons from the "bully pulpit" were far from an electoral turn-off. They were a tonic for the national mood. They conveyed the presence of someone at the helm who would take responsibility. Ebulliently "progressive,"

Theodore Roosevelt combined no-nonsense governance with brilliantly appealing and magnetic qualities. His balanced view of human nature led him to advocate a social reciprocity conveyed by the motto of his presidential program, the "Square Deal."

A great many followers of Roosevelt's Square Deal — Progressive Republicans like Harold Ickes — crossed over party lines to participate in the "New Deal" of his younger Democratic fifth cousin, FDR. The ideological polemics of the past fifty years have all but blinded us to the links between the politics of the "Republican Roosevelt" and the later "Democratic Roosevelt." But FDR grew up idolizing his older cousin, and so the Republican legacy that harmonized conservative and liberal values was handed down (via Theodore Roosevelt) from Lincoln to Franklin D. Roosevelt. It remained fundamentally intact as it crossed party lines. Once again, Hamiltonian action was provided for the "common man."

It is very important to observe that Franklin Delano Roosevelt expressed the wish to transcend the conservative-liberal feud on a number of occasions. In his re-election campaign against Alf Landon in 1936, he declared that "liberalism becomes the protection of the far-sighted conservative. 'Reform if you would preserve.' I am that kind of conservative because I am that kind of liberal."[48] In the throes of the greatest economic emergency in the history of the United States, FDR was striving to repair and adapt the American social order — to keep the private property system from being overthrown, and to do this by repairing its flaws. He told a Hearst reporter in 1935 that "I am fighting Communism, Huey Longism, Coughlinism, Townsendism. I want to save our system, the capitalist system."[49]

The sources of FDR's program were deeply bipartisan: many of the New Deal measures like old-age pensions and unemployment insurance could be traced to the "Bull Moose" platform offered by Theodore Roosevelt in 1912. And of course the candidate of 1912 — the Republican Roosevelt who said that "only by the exercise of government can we exalt the lowly and give heart to the humble and the downtrodden" — had once been the introverted boy whose imagination was captured in the 1860s by the liberating work of Mr. Lincoln's soldiers.[50]

FDR quoted Lincoln recurrently in the course of the Second World War. Like Lincoln, he combined a warm and reassuring nature with implacable will as he confronted evil. For all his blithe optimism, FDR was also the indignant warrior who led the American people in a total and unconditional struggle, in a fiery war to the death, against the Nazi savages and everything that they and their predatory Axis partners represented. James MacGregor Burns and others have reflected on this interplay of traditional conservative moral themes regarding human nature in FDR's nominal "liberalism." "During the war years," according to Burns, "Roosevelt became interested in Kierkegaard, and this was not surprising. The Danish theologian, with his emphasis on man's natural sinfulness, helped explain to him, Roosevelt said, why the Nazis 'are human, yet they behave like demons.'" But while confronting the demonic in human nature, Roosevelt's natural serenity endured; Burns has said that "if his loving references to his Hyde Park home were not revealing enough of his sense of identity and roots, his habit all through his presidency of reducing policies and programs to terms of home and family would have betrayed his thinking; thus the Good Neighbor policy, the Big Four constables or policemen." Through it all flowed "Roosevelt's most important single idea — the idea that government had a positive responsibility for the general welfare. Not that government itself must do everything, but that everything practicable must be done. Whether government does it, or private enterprise, is an operating decision dependent on many factors — but government must insure that something *is* done."[51]

If contemporary pundits and broadcasters view this bipartisan heritage with scorn, they are blind. For in the legacy of Lincoln and the Roosevelts exists an extraordinary model for a politics of balance and coherence — for a balanced view of political dynamics and a balanced view of human nature — that can give us back a leadership philosophy befitting a great power. Regardless of party loyalties, and regardless of the way in which Americans reflexively identify their ideological preferences, a vast number of American citizens have waited for the better part of a generation for this kind of leadership to be restored. At the end of the century Americans have grasped at ephemeral "covenants" and crudely destructive "contracts." They have waited in vain for a new social compact that gives them back national stewardship. They have waited in vain for a worthy political "deal" to be offered to them. They should not have to wait any longer.

THE CIVIC DEAL

HOW CAN WE BEST PUT THE LINCOLN-AND-ROOSEVELT achievement to work for ourselves? The civic deal that would make the most sense for our nation comes down to five prescriptions:

1.

WE MUST CONTINUE TO INVEST IN A PROGRAM OF INFRASTRUCTURE REBUILDING ON A SCALE THAT IS WORTHY OF OUR STATUS AS A SUPERPOWER.

Felix Rohatyn has observed that "the most competitive economies in the world today are backed by the highest levels of infrastructure investment," noting that Taiwan embarked upon a six-year plan investing $600 billion in public infrastructure while Germany has invested $1 trillion in rebuilding the former East Germany. Until recently, America was falling behind; and while the 1998 transportation bill was a significant step in the right direction, its momentum must be sustained. The benefit in up-to-date public facilities will swiftly carry over to the private-sector economy. Rohatyn and economists such as David

Alan Aschauer have stated that for every dollar of public infrastructure investment, an additional fifty cents of private investment is generated.[52] Investment in our own bricks and mortar will create new wealth, new jobs, and new power for our Republic.

2.

WE MUST INVEST IN OUR HUMAN CAPITAL, NOT ONLY BY CREATING
NEW PUBLIC WORKS JOBS BUT THROUGH UPGRADING THE SKILLS OF
THE WORKFORCE SIMULTANEOUSLY.

In the Reagan years, a federally sponsored but independent study of the government's most prominent job training program — the Job Corps — found that the program succeeded so well at turning welfare recipients into fully employed taxpayers that the corps returned about a dollar and a half for every federal dollar that it spent.[53] It is a scandal that the Job Corps is still not funded at a level that approaches its potential for rescuing the underclass. And for middle-class workers displaced by corporate down-sizing, or locked into jobs with a stagnant income, a great public works campaign with appropriate skills retraining would eliminate much of the free-floating anger and frustration that are still poisoning our politics. M.I.T. economist Rudiger Dornbusch has said that "we need a comprehensive skill-building program ranging from Head Start and apprenticeships to ongoing training of the labor force and retraining of displaced workers. . . . No investment in the economy commands a higher return. Skeptics argue that such schemes never work, but if they work in Germany, why can't we make them work here?"[54]

3.

AS MUCH AS POSSIBLE, THE PUBLIC WORKS OF NATIONAL SCOPE
SHOULD BE DELIVERED BY THE FEDERAL GOVERNMENT.

One of the precepts for "reinventing government" alleges that the federal government should "steer, but not row." *This is not always true.* One major reason why the anti-government feeling today is so strong is that the federal government's actions are *too indirect* a great deal of the time — too subtle by half. The benefit of federal programs is not getting through to the American people. Consequently, many federal workers feel a deep demoralization, which can lead to wishy-washy management. And this, in turn, will breed anti-government ridicule. Even high-salaried and high-profile government scientists are suffering from bad morale. Robert C. Gallo of the National Cancer Institute announced his intention to leave federal service with the observation that "government scientists used to be the golden boys, but those days are over. Government is the bad guy today."[55] Ronald C. Moe of the Congressional Research Service has observed that "the executive branch is today . . . an institution that has been poorly led and managed by Presidents for three decades and that presently functions under great stress."[56] If we beat it into people's minds that they are nothing but bureaucratic drudges, is it really so surprising when they act like bureaucratic drudges?

How different things were at the beginning of the twentieth century. Historian John Milton Cooper, Jr. has said that Theodore Roosevelt imbued "public service with a prestige unknown since the early days of the American republic."[57] Henry L. Stimson (later FDR's Republican secretary of war during World War II) told Yale alumni at a class reunion in 1908 that when he left private legal practice for federal service his "first feeling was that I had gotten out of the dark places where I had been wandering all my life, and got out where I could see the stars and get my bearings once more."[58] What was true at the beginning of the twentieth century could be true again: so much of public service comes down to a matter of morale and public perceptions. It is not just a question of *what* the federal government does but also *the manner* in which it is done, for better or for worse. Dramatic symbolism and even occa-

sional pageantry can play a very salutary role in our culture. Consequently, the numerous benefits of federal stewardship deserve to be *visible as such*. The message got through in the days of Franklin D.
Roosevelt's PWA and TVA: in the powerhouse of TVA's Fontana Dam
— the highest dam east of the Rocky Mountains — visitors passed along
a row of gleaming dynamos and saw, emblazoned at the top of a skylit
wall, the following words: "Built for the People of the United States of
America."

The principle is ancient. Classicist Donald Kagan has said that in
the fifth century B.C. one of the central purposes of Pericles' Acropolis
building program in Athens — the Parthenon was its supreme archi-
tectural achievement — was the civic and symbolic purpose of making
"the greatness of Athens tangible and visible to all." Even as Athenians
gloried in the benefits — the creation of jobs and prosperity which,
according to Plutarch, were both deliberate objectives of Pericles —
they gloried in something greater; Kagan has said that "they were caught
up in the magnificence of the structures they were building" and that
"they understood that the buildings would be a memorial to their democracy."[59] Cohesion in public life to a certain extent depends on a
sense of something worthy, something at times magnificent, at the center of our common culture.

More than two thousand years after Pericles, Alexander Hamilton
stated in *The Federalist* #27 that "the more the operations of the national authority are intermingled in the ordinary exercise of government, the more the citizens are accustomed to meet with it in the common occurrences of their political life, . . . the further it enters into the
objects which touch the most sensible chords and put in motion the
most effective springs of the human heart, the greater will be the probability that it will conciliate the respect and attachment of the community."[60]

4.

PUBLIC WORKS SHOULD BE FURNISHED THROUGH A SOCIAL COMPACT
THAT LINKS THEM TO PUBLIC SAFETY.

A consensus based upon this new Civic Deal would bring as many wayward or suffering people as possible into the compass of American community life. It would offer a deal that would link individual assistance to the needs of the overall community. It would reach out to the poverty-stricken with proven governmental initiatives like the Job Corps, programs that strengthen individual values and social commitedness. It would offer a clear alternative to drugs, dependency, and crime through the culture of jobs and family and neighbors. It would tackle our society's staggering backlog of physical and social needs with *esprit de corps,* and with the following proviso: that in light of the Civic Deal's offer of assistance, anyone who chooses to reject the civic culture by engaging in the molestation of the innocent, anyone who breaks the social compact in favor of the ways of predatory violence, will be taken off the streets without a twinge of neurotic guilt and without the assurance of easy, formulaic parole for murderous offenses. In restoring public safety, we could re-establish the basis for balanced justice, a justice dispensed in the knowledge that a valiant effort has been made to provide for the legitimate needs of all citizens. There will be no more excuses for predation. Public works in exchange for safe streets: the Civic Deal.

5.

WE MUST DO EVERYTHING REQUIRED IN ORDER TO PAY FOR THIS
NECESSARY PROGRAM NOW.

It is time for Americans to unify around the proposition that whatever is demonstrably necessary in our public life is a *necessity* — it *must* be provided. The public works and the worker retraining that we need as an industrial superpower should be regarded this way. So should the law enforcement and detention facilities we need for public safety. We are not broke, and we can pay for the things that we need if they are truly essential. There are several ways that we can do this. Revenue can be raised from an increase in gasoline taxes such as Rohatyn and others have been recommending for years. But if gasoline taxes represent too much of a sacrifice, there remains a very different option.

Here is some shocking heresy: it is time to calm down about the budget —regardless of deficit or surplus conditions — and spend what our national priorities require. It is time to get over our taboo about government borrowing and turn our backs upon the "balanced budget" fanatics. We have seen already that the costs of winning World War II created national debt that makes the current situation look trifling. We have seen that the government went on to spend additional billions for national necessities, even while the ratio of national debt to gross national product was similar to what it is today.

And the world did not come to an end. The economy boomed in the 1950s and revenue came streaming back to the government from prospering citizens and businesses.

In 1992 a group of dozens of distinguished economists, including several winners of the Nobel Prize, recommended an increase in short-term federal borrowing to reinvest in things that our nation needs: in rebuilding the infrastructure and upgrading the skills of the workforce. These economists argued that deficit spending to invest in our long-term prosperity and productivity is very different from deficit spending that is misdirected. The sort of borrowing that fuels (or helps to create) a healthy and expanding economy should never be confused with the borrowing that drains an economy. It all depends on how the borrowed money is *used* — what it *creates*.[61]

Is this not the way in which our businesses and families behave with regard to credit? What intelligently managed business forbids it-

self from raising capital by going to the bank or the bond market —
thus engaging in deficit finance? What budgetary logic prohibits a family
from taking out a mortgage or a car loan? To be sure, successful families pay off the mortgage eventually, but then the next generation goes
"in debt." And it is not the end of the world — it is a miracle of capitalism. It helps us do necessary things when we *need* to, and thus to get
ahead in our lives. So why should the government that serves us be
different when it comes to our public investments? Hamilton argued,
in *The Federalist* #34, that "there ought to be a CAPACITY" in the national government "to provide for future contingencies as they may
happen; and as these are illimitable in their nature, it is impossible safely
to limit that capacity."[62]

BALANCING THE BUDGET: AMERICA'S
FISCAL NEUROSIS?

NOTWITHSTANDING THE LEGACY OF ALEXANDER HAMILTON,
multitudes of people believe that the federal budget should
be balanced and that large and ambitious new programs
are dependent on a budgetary surplus. Opinion makers, from the president and Congress to editors, pundits, and reporters, take the balanced-
budget proposition for granted. The idea of a government that "lives
within its means" sounds fine — and why should it not? Warnings that
"fiscal extravagance" could spoil our future and slow our economy are
legion. A whole generation has been raised to believe that we have been
"living beyond our means."

But economists are deeply divided on the balanced-budget proposition. Indeed, our consensus on balancing the federal budget may prove
to be a passing cultural fixation — a fetish that will strike posterity in
much the same way that we regard such obsessions of the past as the
constitutional amendment that brought Prohibition. It is time to con-

sider that our current fiscal doctrines are closer than many would imagine to the thinking that dominated national councils in the days of Herbert Hoover. By the 1950s and 60s, this orthodoxy was an object of widespread derision. But today it is back, and its seductive common-sensicality — ironically at odds with the common-sense experience of millions of American families and corporations — has created a climate that could lead us into policies that vitiate our economic interest.

Much of the passion for balancing the federal budget is based upon economic folklore, upon simple-minded adages that *sound* so convincing that they seem irrefutable. The sing-song logic of conventional wisdom assures us that only finaglers or fools believe in "spending what you don't have." We dread the bitter prospect of "sinking ever further into debt." The very term in question — debt — sounds pejorative.

On the other hand, when we succeed in securing a *loan* to launch a daring new business venture, we bask in visions of prosperity.

It is obvious enough that our folklore is wildly inconsistent on the subject of *borrowing*. The obvious fact is that borrowing money may be wise or foolish, creative or destructive, depending on the fate of the enterprise. It makes little sense to congratulate yourself for your "success in securing a loan" if you spend the money stupidly. Conversely, it is pointless to chide yourself for "sinking into debt" if you invest the borrowed money in brilliant money-making projects. This is kindergarten stuff. Every banker understands it, every corporate executive who raises new capital by going to the bank or the bond market understands it, and every family that ever got ahead in life by "going into debt" through a mortgage or a car loan understands it.

Nonetheless, we have now become convinced that for the federal government to go on borrowing money is somehow wrong. We are told that "we cannot keep doing this forever": to do so would "burden the children." We are told that we will drive ourselves "bankrupt" or "broke" if we do not become "fiscally responsible."

We are told a lot of other things as well: that interest rates are driven up by federal deficit spending, and that private-sector borrowing can be "crowded out" of the money market by the Feds. We are told that the tax-paying public is overburdened by interest on the national debt. But the fear that accumulated federal deficit spending will "bankrupt" the country is a fear that surpasses all others. We fear that we are "running out of money," it would seem. There is "only so much to go around," people figure, and if Uncle Sam keeps borrowing more and more of it, anyone can see that the results will be catastrophic.

But how many of our citizens truly understand the extraordinary way in which our money supply is created? How many of them comprehend that the gold standard is gone — that the only real limits to the government's ability to print more money are the limits we set for ourselves through our laws and our policies? How many Americans understand that *our nation's money supply can expand*? Or that our money supply is to a certain extent *created through a never-ending series of loans* — deficit spending — by the public and private sectors? If this sounds strange, consider: deficit spending is the use of borrowed money, and Federal Reserve Notes represent *loans* by Federal Reserve Banks to other banks which then proceed to make *loans* to people who will spend this borrowed money for goods and services. Indeed, every time a bank makes a loan it "creates new money" through the paradox of our system of "fractional reserve banking." This paradox is so important that a brief description is in order.

In their explanation of the process, economists William J. Baumol and Alan S. Blinder acknowledge that while "many bankers will deny that they have any ability to 'create' money," such people are fooling themselves. "Because it holds only fractional reserves, even a single bank can create money," these economists insist, and there is definitely "some hocus-pocus in the process."[63]

To understand the paradox, forget about the paper apparatus — forget about dollar bills and think about money as a generator of economic *energy*. Case in point: a customer opens a bank account, depositing $100. The bank is required to keep a certain percentage "on reserve" — let us say twenty cents on the dollar, for the sake of simplicity — and the rest can be used to make loans. Hence $20 of this customer's account must remain on reserve, while the other $80 can be lent to other customers, some of whom deposit it in other banks, where the process continues.

Question: if the depositor's money is *in* the bank — since anytime he asks for his $100 he can have it instantaneously — is the $80 drawn from his deposit and lent to other people a part of *the very same money* as the $100, since all of it *derives* from the same $100 that the customer can have on demand? Or is the $80 "different" money? Remember that *even if the bank account is closed* — the depositor gets back his $100 in full — *there is still $80 on loan out there* that is recorded in ledgers and electronic pulses: $80 on record that is instantly convertible to cash through the writing of a check or through an automatic teller transaction with a plastic card.

Almost any economist will tell you not only that the $80 represents a new infusion in the money supply but also that so long as Uncle Sam protects American citizens through FDIC deposit insurance, this expansion of money through the strange metaphysics — through the book-keeping sleight-of-hand — inherent in our system of fractional reserve banking is an economic miracle. Indeed, this expansion of money through a never-ending process of loans involves the *power to create new wealth,* to make investments that will call goods and services to life that would otherwise not exist.

In other words, deficit spending — what we do when we spend borrowed money — can *expand our nation's supply of money;* it can also *create prosperity* if the borrowed money is put to good uses that expand the economy.

To return to the metaphor of energy, different forms of money — like catalysis in physics — can convert potential energy to active and kinetic energy. When enough of the electronic pulses or the pieces of paper that constitute money are channeled in certain directions in the form of investment capital, we — real people — will create real products and services that would not have existed otherwise. If others choose to purchase these products and services, the revenue will give us the purchasing power to buy *other* products, and the money that we pay for such products will give others the wherewithal to buy still *other* products, which create more jobs for *other* worker-consumers — jobs that might not have existed otherwise.

Again, this would seem to be elementary stuff, but we should not take the process for granted. Our modern economy is a wonder of mind over matter, a prodigy resulting from centuries of capitalist thinking at its most advanced. Audacious thinking that invests borrowed money in productive projects has gradually raised the American standard of living for the general populace to levels that have seldom existed for long in many centuries of economic scarcity.

That is why a national consensus existed by the 1950s and 1960s on behalf of continued deficit spending by the federal government: the spending was perceived as a way to channel powerful new investments into the economy. The generation of Americans who comprised the adult population included scores of people who could never forget the comparison of economic life in the 1930s and the 1950s — in the years before and after World War II. They remembered the Great Depression, when America's economy was crippled and scarcity prevailed, and they could look all around them to see the great post-war comparison of luxurious abundance. It was World War II — and not the New Deal — that made the difference for our economy. It was World War II that all but ended the Depression era's blight of unemployment, transforming our nation from an economic cripple to a superpower so mighty that it out-produced all of its Axis enemies. We have seen that the economic *tour de force* of World War II was produced by deficit spending on a scale so massive it defies comparison. As we have seen, the national debt (the year-after-year accumulation of deficit spending) was greater in 1945 than the gross national product.

If that were the case today, the conventional wisdom would surely conclude that the end of the world was approaching. We would probably conclude that we were "strapped," bereft of resources. We would cut governmental spending to the bone. We would pinch every penny, practice rigid frugality, find every possible method of sacrificing and "doing without." But nothing of the kind occurred after World War II. To the contrary: America spent more money than ever on far-sighted forms of investment and public works. We spent money for the GI Bill and created the Marshall Plan; we built the St. Lawrence Seaway and commenced the Interstate Highway System. And all the while our nation's "debts" kept increasing: year after year in the 1950s and 1960s, our national debt grew apace.

But America's economy was growing much faster than the increase of national debt. So what was the financial problem? *There wasn't any problem*: all that mattered was Uncle Sam's ability to pay off securities like U.S. Savings Bonds when they matured. And that was easy, because Uncle Sam was constantly selling new bonds as he paid off the old ones. The system has continued ever since.

But as our infrastructure spending diminished in the 1970s and afterwards, our productivity dwindled. Notwithstanding the transient economic "booms" of the 1980s and late 1990s — the latter in many ways reminiscent of the evanescent, stock-driven boom of the 1920s — America's economic health became pathetic when compared to the 1950s.[64] The sad truth of the matter is that deficit spending in recent years has not been channeled sufficiently in ways that could have broadened prosperity for all working Americans. Thousands of families have found that it takes two incomes to equal the standard of living that their families enjoyed with a single income in the 1950s.[65] Corporate down-sizing and organizational under-staffing are the mode — and yet the president and Congress are hoping that the private sector will create the vast number of jobs that we need as we attempt to phase out welfare. That could be a very serious problem. Meanwhile, we need to consider all the thousands of middle-class people who may be "downsized" out of employment. The true rate of unemployment — as distinct from the rate that most public officials invoke — must include the sort of people who have reached the point of embittered despair where they have given up. The most widely touted unemployment figures don't count such people at all. But there is reason to believe they are out there, subsisting in a makeshift, demoralizing world of dysfunction and anger.[66]

They could once again be part of the workforce. Beyond the necessities of infrastructure reinvestment, the case can be made for much higher levels of investment in a broad range of national necessities, from military readiness to prison construction to environmental protection. Productive work that could generate jobs and salaries is needed across the board. But our elected leaders and policymakers are locked in a mind-set of scarcity and grinding retrenchment: we must "live within our means," we are told, we must practice "fiscal discipline" and prioritize our "limited resources." We must veritably uninvent ourselves as an economic superpower so that columns of figures in a balance sheet may be correlated just *so*.

Does it really have to be this way? Just as families and banks consider mortgages based upon the long-term issues that determine a family's ability to gain and generate wealth, should we not view the issue of federal deficit-spending (including the issue of what percentage of our taxes pays interest on the national debt) as entirely dependent on the question of *what public spending is producing* in the real-life economy? Again, recent economic studies have suggested that an adequate level of investment in public infrastructure stimulates approximately fifty cents of private-sector money for every federal dollar. A booming economy investing in the physical necessities that generate national power along with the human potential of energetic citizens means greater prosperity, profits, and earning power, which in turn would boost federal revenues. As economist Robert Eisner, the former president of the American Economic Association, has argued,

> As we grow richer, we can indeed afford more of everything. And we can grow much richer still. More and more businessmen and economists are recognizing that our potential for growth is significantly greater . . . if we do not have government policies — budgetary or monetary — to hold down that growth. Rather than insisting willy-nilly on budget balancing, we should invest more.[67]

Almost all of the formulaic arguments used to make the case against federal deficit spending are based upon variations of the economic scarcity model. We are told that excessive borrowing by Uncle Sam until recently was "crowding out" loans to the private sector. But if a strong and expanding economy tends to expand its own supply of money through the process of fractional reserve banking, it follows that the right kind of federal borrowing applied through the right kind of public investments could stimulate — rather than inhibit — the private sector. Economists Baumol and Blinder have argued that "if government deficits succeed in their goal of raising production, there will be more income and therefore more saving. In that way, *both* government *and* industry can borrow more."[68] By the same token, the complaints that federal deficit spending leads to higher interest rates beg some obvious practical questions: interest rates on money to be borrowed by *whom* and to pay for *what*? There are national necessities — like highways and aircraft carriers — beyond the scope of private-sector action. Hence government must pay, and if higher taxation is out of the question, then government must borrow the money.

Interest rates will fluctuate according to a number of variables, not least of all decisions of the Federal Reserve Board. And the monetary policies adopted by the board will vary according to a range of issues, not least of all concern about inflation. But none of these issues by itself requires balancing the federal budget. The budget, like monetary policy, must always be responsive to the needs of the real-life economy.

This issue should not be regarded as a matter of conservative-versus-liberal ideology. It is more fundamental than that: it is nothing less than the health of our capitalist system, and the public-private devices of banking that we use to achieve prosperity.

The crusade to balance the federal budget forces Uncle Sam to meet an arbitrary standard of accounting that most of our families, most corporations, and the great majority of states in this Union would regard as completely ridiculous. Forty-seven of America's fifty states break their budgets into capital and operating segments: they balance their *operating* budgets but they finance their big-ticket capital items through the sale of long-term bonds — through deficit finance. The same holds true of corporations, and (by virtue of the special way in which we finance the acquisition of items like a car or the purchase of a home) American families. Our elected leaders and opinion makers are telling us we have to force Uncle Sam into a straight-jacket. They are pushing us into a kind of economic primitivism that few of them — when you come right down to it — understand.

We are playing this game for very high stakes indeed: a century of superabundant new wealth or a world of diminished expectations. While austerity thinking will produce austerity, the expectation of abundance can deliver very real abundance. It is time to reconsider the conventional wisdom, time for us to challenge the economic dogmas with the force of economic logic. In the world of economics, what you can envision — depending on the happenstance of natural and human resources — may become what you get, for better or for worse. What we need is a powerful America.[69]

OUR CHALLENGE

Will a leadership arise with the audacity and vision to deliver that powerful America? Conservative and liberal follies may continue to haunt this nation for a very long time, and our next opportunity to break with these patterns could elude us for years on end. But we deserve to see a politician try it. We deserve to see the faces of conventional polemicists when someone has taken up the challenge. We deserve to see the legacy of Lincoln and the two Roosevelts — the legacy of democratic stewardship empowered by the great Republic — made good once again in our land. Will the current generation live to see it?

Chapter Two

✩ ✩ ✩

Classical Liberals, Tory Reformers, and the Achievement of "Father Abraham"

CONSERVATIVE AND LIBERAL TRADITIONS amount to evolving clusters of ideas. This point needs very strong emphasis in light of the furious struggles over doctrinal purity that rage among the ideologists. The meanings of conservative, liberal, and radical have altered according to changing variables — variables such as economic interests, religious beliefs, reactions to change, and convictions regarding human nature. But while perfect definitions are elusive, significant patterns of ideology can be sketched to some degree. And one of the most striking patterns is this: conservative and liberal doctrines regarding the proper role of government were once the reverse of what they are today.

Conservatism and liberalism, as terms and articulated creeds, are modern developments. But their antecedents and sources can be traced through millenia. It is possible to see a dim foreshadowing of left-versus-right dialectics, for instance, in the struggles between the "many" and the privileged "few" in classical antiquity: in Plutarch's account of the "democratic" and "aristocratic" factions in ancient Athens, in Livy's account of the struggles between plebeians and patricians in early Rome, and in the violent confrontations of the later Roman Republic between "populares" — reformers like Tiberius and Gaius Gracchus who sought to help the lower classes — and the wealthy defenders of the status quo whom contemporaries dubbed "optimates," the self-proclaimed "worthies."

Later, out of medieval Europe, there emerged a pervasive outlook that could be called proto-conservative, a wary view of human nature combined with belief in hierarchic control and social continuity. "O, when degree is shaked," warned Shakespeare's version of Ulysses in *Troilus and Cressida* — when control maintained by upper-class "degree" and rank is overturned — "the enterprise is sick. . . ."

> Then everything include itself in power,
> Power into will, will into appetite.
> And appetite, an universal wolf,
> So doubly seconded by will and power,
> Must make perforce an universal prey
> And last eat up himself.

Without governance, warned countless moralists, the wolfishness of human nature would be unleashed with appalling results. Hence regulation — by the aristocracy, by the church, and to some extent by the state — was inherent in proto-conservative European thought on the eve of American colonization. Some of its principles were brought to America by groups such as the Puritans. As Perry Miller, one of the deans of New England Puritan studies, pointed out years ago:

> The lone horseman, the single trapper, the solitary hunter was not a figure of the Puritan frontier; Puritans moved in groups and towns, settled in whole communities, and maintained firm government over all units. Neither were the individualistic businessman, the shopkeeper who seized every opportunity to enlarge his profits . . . neither were these the typical figures of the original Puritan society. Puritan

opinion was at the opposite pole from Jefferson's feeling that the best government governs as little as possible. . . . They would have expected laissez-faire to result in a reign of rapine and horror.[1]

Suspicion of human nature, of course, does not lead automatically to a creed of regulation. By the end of the seventeenth century, the fear of human nature and its lust for power would be used by English Whigs as one of the justifications for *limiting* the monarchy's power. Yet a fundamental linkage of fears about human nature and a preference for social regulation would continue to shape conservative-tending ideas through the nineteenth century. As historian Roland Stromberg stated in *European Intellectual History Since 1789,* "British and European conservatism has been an enemy of laissez-faire" until recent times.[2] Especially after the French Revolution, European conservatives emphasized vigorous regulation by the state. At its most repressive, this counter-revolutionary governance assumed the form of authoritarian monarchy.

The rise of liberalism occurred in the seventeenth and eighteenth centuries, even though the term itself was not in widespread political use until the 1800s. One of the central liberal principles was insurgency against regulation: liberals strove to *liberate* the social process. Stromberg has said that while "there were several strains in early modern liberalism, not always in exact agreement with each other . . . they all tended to agree broadly on a negative conception of the state, on something approaching laissez-faire as an ideal."[3] Many have associated this early liberal antipathy to regulation with the economic needs of the rising middle class — with the entrepreneurial spirit of the bourgeoisie, a spirit that demanded opportunities for social mobility. Yet there was another dimension to the ethos of liberalism beyond acquisitiveness: an idealistic view of human nature that associated open opportunity (free labor and free markets) with higher forms of human fulfillment (free speech and freedom of conscience). At its most passionate, liberal idealism entertained millennial and world-redemptive visions.

Reinhold Niebuhr's allusion to the tell-tale utopian longings in the liberal mind — the "general liberal hope of redeeming history," as he put it — can be validated by examining the rhetoric of such early liberal-tending figures as Thomas Paine, who told Americans in 1776 that "we have it in our power to begin the world over again."[4] At first Paine accepted traditional views about the "fallen" state of humanity. "Government," he acknowledged in *Common Sense,* "like dress, is the badge of lost innocence; the palaces of kings are built upon the ruins of the bowers of paradise."[5] But by the 1790s Paine abandoned all doubts about human innocence. People are naturally good, he asserted in 1791, and evils are the fault of government. "Man, were he not corrupted by governments," Paine argued in *The Rights of Man,* "is naturally the friend of man, and . . . human nature is not of itself vicious."[6] The moral was obvious: dispense with regulation and the natural beauty and harmony of human nature would flourish as never before. Historian Eric Foner has said that Paine "transformed the language of an impending millenium into the secular vision of a utopia in the New World."[7]

In the Old World (especially in Britain), the laissez-faire creed of liberalism would become well established by the mid-nineteenth century. In the 1850s British Whigs began to call their political organization the Liberal Party. According to historian R. K. Webb, "most Victorian liberals were convinced individualists" whose "distrust of the state" was corollary to their belief "that the free play of enlightened self-interest in an aware citizenry would bring about the millenium."[8]

It was determined Tory dissent from this faith in a laissez-faire millenium that brought out a positive and benevolent side of conservative regulation in Britain. Precisely because of their distrust of human nature, Tories urged humanitarian action by the state to rectify injustices arising from the market. As Stromberg has pointed out, conservatives such as Samuel Taylor Coleridge

believed in government regulation of manufacturers, government aid

to education, the duty of the state to enhance the moral and intellectual capabilities of its citizens in all sorts of positive ways. Conservatism abhorred, and was set over against, the individualism of the "liberals".... It can be related to the rural squirearchy, was certainly not
equalitarian or levelling . . . but was deeply humanistic and more likely
than liberalism to support governmental welfare measures for the
poor. The leading hero of factory reform and other humanitarian
measures in early industrial England was the Tory, Lord Shaftesbury.
The Coleridge tradition passed to such writers as John Ruskin, who
described himself as a "violent Tory of the old School," and violently
denounced the materialistic and unprincipled society of industrial
England. It also passed to Benjamin Disraeli and his conception of a
democratized Conservative Party leading the way to social reform on
behalf of the workers.[9]

However one interprets this phenomenon of Tory reform — as a genuine expression of noblesse oblige or as a calculated ploy to defuse revolutionary ardor by proving that the system would respond to lower-
class grievances — the fact remains that the modern welfare state was
to some extent the creation of conservative minds.

Such were the lost worlds — so strange according to the standards of today's political orthodoxies — of liberal laissez-faire and the
conservative welfare state in nineteenth-century Britain. But in America,
the development of conservative and liberal doctrines was far more
complicated and ambiguous.

· II ·

ONE OF THE RECURRENT ISSUES IN AMERICAN political history is debate about the Founders' "intent." The early national era was a time of intellectual ferment, and many of
the Founders were eclectic thinkers. Some of them changed their minds
about crucial issues; some of them differed with each other to the point

of intermittent hostility. Historian Forrest McDonald has said, with regard to the Framers of the Constitution, that "it is meaningless to say that the Framers intended this or that the Framers intended that: their positions were diverse and, in many particulars, incompatible. Some had firm, well-rounded plans, some had strong convictions on only a few points, some had self-contradictory ideas, some were guided only by vague ideals. Some of their differences were subject to compromise; others were not."[10]

It is nonetheless possible to find common themes in the Founders' world-view. Most of them shared a hatred of arbitrary power derived from English whiggism. Most of them agreed with the principle of creating a balance of political forces to prevent excessive power from accumulating anywhere. Some of them believed in the ancient theory of Polybius that the perfect political system should incorporate elements of rule by "the many" (the democratic principle), rule by "the few" (the aristocratic principle), and rule by "the one" (the executive/monarchical principle). Supposedly, such a system of counterpoised forces would safeguard the liberties of all. Some of the Founders dismissed this particular theory but subscribed to more general visions of political balance.

One of the most adroit American practitioners of balanced politics was James Madison. In the 1780s Madison worked to strengthen the national government in order to control the chaos and "mob rule" that he perceived in state and local politics. In the 1790s he tilted in the other direction and sought to counterbalance national governance by reinforcing state power. The purpose of Madison's tilting and shifting was to counteract the ever-shifting flow of human mischief. "If men were angels," he explained in *The Federalist* #51, "no government would be necessary." But since men are not angelic, the task of the statesman was first to "enable the government to control the governed; and in the next place oblige it to control itself." In Madison's view, the development of checks and balances would help maintain governmental self-control; he hastened to add that "a dependence on the people" would always remain "the primary control on the government."[11] But his forth-right assertion that government should also "control the governed" reflected his belief that human nature could not be trusted anywhere — neither in the governmental process nor among the general populace. Such were the views of the putative "Father of the Constitution."

Though the Constitution would eventually rise to the status of a sacred text, some of its Framers regarded it with doubt or at least ambivalence. Madison expressed private fears that because the Constitutional Convention rejected his proposal to give Congress a veto power over state laws, "the plan should it be adopted will neither effectually answer its national object nor prevent the local mischiefs which every where excite disgusts agnst [sic] the state governments."[12] George Washington confided to a relative that even the supporters of the Constitution did "not contend that it is free from imperfections," and that "if evil is likely to arise there from, the remedy must come hereafter."[13] Madison's notes from the convention revealed Hamilton's confession that "no man's ideas were more remote from the plan than his own were known to be."[14] Jefferson — in Paris on diplomatic business — expressed mixed feelings when the Constitution reached him. He urged the addition of a Bill of Rights, while consoling Madison that "no society can make a perpetual constitution" and that the document should probably be overhauled from top to bottom on a regular basis. "Every constitution," he asserted, "and every law, naturally expires at the end of 19 years," which Jefferson determined was the span of a human generation.[15] Such was the instability of the constitutional consensus of 1787–88. It was against this background that left-versus-right dialectics began to emerge among the Founding Fathers.

When the first party system developed in the 1790s, the proto-conservative belief in hierarchic governance was almost instinctive for many prominent members of the emergent Federalist Party. One of the most fervent "High Federalists" was Fisher Ames of Massachusetts. According to one biographer, Ames supported "political and social dominance by a business-minded upper class closely allied to a strong government." Ames believed in strong governance because he was "fearful of the democratic excesses in an embryonic republic."[16] "Our country," he lamented in 1803, "is . . . too democratick for liberty. What is to become of it, he who made it best knows. Its vice will govern it, by practising upon its folly."[17] Three years later, his attitude was more extreme: "Our disease is democracy. . . . [O]ur very bones are carious, and their marrow blackens with gangrene."[18] In far milder terms, such views were also present in the outlook of Alexander Hamilton, the Federalist Party's premier intellectual leader. Hamilton feared the caprices of the democratic multitude. According to Madison's notes from the Constitutional Convention, Hamilton attacked "the amazing violence & turbulence of the democratic spirit."[19] He proposed that the president and Senate be elected for life to check the "vices of democracy."[20]

Yet while Hamilton distrusted the multitude, his view of the upper-class business elite was far from trusting or complacent. In the *Report on Manufactures* that Hamilton prepared in 1791 pursuant to his duties as secretary of the treasury, he said it was essential for the "activity of speculation and enterprise" to be "properly directed" by government in order to be "made subservient to useful purposes." "If left entirely to itself," he warned, the spirit of enterprise "may be attended with pernicious effects."[21] As early as 1782 Hamilton had ridiculed the notion "that trade will regulate itself" as "one of those wild speculative paradoxes, which have grown into credit among us, contrary to the uniform practice and sense of the most enlightened nations."[22]

Importantly, Hamilton believed in a positive as well as a negative role for government's involvement with business. Forrest McDonald has emphasized Hamilton's belief in governmental action not only "when the 'avarice of individuals' threw trade in channels inimical to public interest" but also "when desirable enterprises might otherwise not be undertaken for want of sufficient private capital, or when unexpected causes thwarted a prosperous flow of commerce."[23] Hamilton envisioned America's growth into a mighty industrial republic. He championed a partnership of government and business through a modernized banking and monetary system, financial measures to foster industrialization, and public works — roads and canals — for improvement of transportation. In his *Report on Manufactures,* Hamilton contended that the facilitation of "inland Navigation" was "one of those improvements, which could be prosecuted with more efficacy by the whole, than by any part or parts of the Union," and asserted "the power of the national Government to lend its direct aid, on a comprehensive plan."[24] In furthering these aims, Hamilton interpreted the Constitution in broad terms; he said that the general welfare clause gave Congress tremendous discretionary power, and that "whatever concerns the general Interests" should be "within the sphere of the National Councils as far as regards the application of money."[25] President George Washington supported this program, both in overall terms and in key legislative provisions.

But Jefferson's views — at least before his presidential years — were inimical to Hamilton's vision of heroic government. Jefferson detested industrialization; he placed his hopes for America's future in virtuous and self-sufficient tillers of the soil. Moreover, as we have seen, he regarded "energetic government" as inherently "oppressive." His minimal-government preference became more impassioned in the 1790s. In 1798 he privately espoused "a single amendment to our Constitution . . . taking from the federal government the power of borrowing."[26] Two years later he proclaimed to another correspondent, "Let the General Government be reduced to foreign concerns only, and let our affairs be disentangled from those of all other nations, except as to commerce, which the merchants will manage the better, the more they are left free to manage for themselves, and our General Government may be reduced to a very simple organization, and a very inexpensive one; a few plain duties to be performed by a few servants."[27]

It is not at all fanciful to view these pronouncements as signs of classical liberalism: the spirit of crusading liberation, of faith in the overall goodness of human nature if freed from regulation. It was the spirit of laissez-faire — the spirit of Jefferson's friend and ally Thomas Paine. Allow free speech, free expression, free trade, and all would be well. Years later, looking back upon the birth in the 1790s of his Democratic Republican Party, Jefferson mused that "the cherishment of the people then was our principle, the fear and distrust of them, that of the other party."[28] This "cherishment of the people" extended even to indulgence of occasional rebellion: "I hold that a little rebellion now and then is a good thing," Jefferson wrote to Madison in 1787, "and as necessary in the political world, as storms in the physical."[29] By the 1790s such rhetoric became rather risky. The crisis of the French Revolution made the Hamilton-Jefferson enmity a full-blown episode of left-versus-right confrontation. The resulting party strife approached hysteria before it subsided.

The feud began in 1791 when Madison decided for a number of reasons that Hamilton's program — the program of his old collaborator in the writing of the *Federalist* papers — was going too far. Accordingly, Madison joined with Jefferson in arguing for constitutional "strict construction." But the simmering dispute began to escalate wildly in 1793, when revolutionary France — invoking the Franco-American treaty of 1778 — invited the United States to join in its "war of all peoples against all kings." Conservative-tending figures such as Hamilton, Washington, and John Adams were reluctant to ally themselves with the likes of Robespierre, whereas liberal-tending figures such as Jefferson continued to emphasize the positive aspects of France's revolutionary struggle. Before long, "Democratic Societies" had been established in a number of states to foster sympathy for revolutionary France. The crisis of the French Revolution made the issue of left-versus-right dialectics explicit for the Founding generation: the Founding Fathers began to take sides in a foreign conflict with overtones of class war. And in the course of declaring their sympathies, Americans began to regard one another as surrogates for foreign villains — as allies of the Jacobins or as partisans of crown and aristocracy. "The French Revolution," said Madison in 1799, "has produced such a ferment and agitation in the world, and has divided it . . . into such violent parties, that nothing depending on opinion, nor much even on facts, is received without a strong tincture from the channel through which it passes."[30]

The situation worsened in 1794 when rebellious Pennsylvania farmers refused to pay a federal tax on whiskey. Hamilton immediately warned that a "large and well organized republic can scarcely lose its liberty from any other cause than anarchy, to which a contempt of the laws is a high road."[31] Washington decried the "lawless and outrageous conduct" of the rebels. He declared that "this insurrection is viewed with universal indignation and abhorrence; except by those who have never missed an opportunity by side blows, or otherwise, to aim their shafts at the General Government." He also declared that "I consider this insurrection as the first *formidable* fruit of the Democratic Societies."[32]

Washington and Hamilton took personal command of the troops that put down the "Whiskey Rebellion," and Washington denounced the "self-created societies" which, in his opinion, had fomented this sedition.[33] Jefferson (privately) responded in kind: he told Madison that supporters of the administration were crypto-monarchists who "must be perfectly dazzled by the glittering of crowns and coronets, not to see the extravagance of the proposition to suppress the friends of general freedom," namely the "democratical societies, whose avowed object is the nourishment of the republican principles of our Constitution."[34]

The polarization grew worse after Washington retired from the presidency and was succeeded by John Adams. Tensions with France were increasing so drastically that war seemed highly probable. In 1798 the Federalists in Congress passed repressive laws — the Alien and Sedition Acts — against "internal enemies," laws that were blatant violations of the Bill of Rights. The acts were directed not only at French agents but also at the members of Jefferson's fledgling Democratic Republican Party, men who would now be threatened with jail for "libellous" attacks on administration policy. Some complained and appealed to George Washington in his retirement at Mount Vernon, but Washington had no sympathy either for the "mad and intoxicated" French or for "*their* party," which he called "the curse of this country."[35] Federalists, in short, had come to view Jefferson and his party as Jacobins in all but name, and Jefferson returned the insult by claiming the Federalist assault upon the Bill of Rights was the work of monarchists. He lamented in 1799 that the "monocrats had so artfully confounded the cause of France with that of Freedom, that both went down in the same scale."[36] He told Elbridge Gerry that he feared a new Federalist attempt to effect a "transition to a President and Senate for life, and from that to an hereditary tenure of these offices, and thus to worm out the elective principle" in the United States.[37]

So much for the "original intent of the Founding Fathers." The Founding generation was as much degraded by ideological warfare as we are today. The spiteful and vicious feuding continued for the better part of fifteen years after Jefferson won the presidency in 1800. By the end of the War of 1812, the Federalist Party had lost: it dwindled and died. Its audacious genius, Hamilton, had been sent to his grave already by the dueling pistol of Aaron Burr. Jefferson's Democratic Republicans — now called "Republicans" for short — constituted the only American political party by the early 1820s.

But something remarkable had happened to Jefferson in his presidential years: he quietly became a convert to some of Hamilton's program. In his second inaugural address he cautiously suggested a program of federal grants for internal improvements to be financed by import duties. He expanded the suggestion to encompass education in his final message to Congress. He authorized Albert Gallatin, his secretary of the treasury, to prepare a report on roads and canals. The Gallatin Report, delivered to Congress in April 1808, called for a magnificent network of inland waterways and highways. Gallatin estimated the cost of the program at $20,000,000. "The general utility of artificial roads and canals is at this time so universally admitted," Gallatin said, "as hardly to require any additional proofs." There were many circumstances that "naturally check the application of private capital and enterprise to improvements on a large scale"; hence it was likely that the "General Government alone can remove these obstacles." The result would repay the investment, not only in functional terms but through its strengthening of national cohesion. "No other single operation, within the power of Government, can more effectually tend to strengthen and perpetuate that Union which secures external independence, domestic peace, and internal liberty," Gallatin concluded.[38]

While the Gallatin Report was prepared for use by subsequent administrations, Jefferson himself, before his retirement, approved an advance installment on the plan: the National Road from Cumberland, Maryland to Wheeling, Virginia, that Congress authorized in 1806. Jefferson signed the legislation. While die-hard believers in minimal government and strict construction would assail this Jeffersonian apostasy, Jefferson appeared nonchalant. "I know . . . that laws and institutions must go hand in hand with the progress of the human mind," he told a correspondent in 1816. "As that becomes more developed, more enlightened, as new discoveries are made, new truths disclosed, and manners and opinions change with the change of circumstances, institutions must advance also, and keep pace with the times."[39]

In their presidential years, both Jefferson and Madison supported the establishment by Congress of a national university, an idea that George Washington had championed in the 1790s. Madison argued, in his second annual message to Congress, that a "seminary of learning" should be "instituted by the National Legislature" since a "well-instructed people alone can be permanently a free people" and that a national "temple of science" could "strengthen the foundations. . . of our free and happy system of government."[40] In his retirement, Madison acknowledged the degree to which both he and Jefferson had embraced Hamiltonian-tending measures — but like Jefferson, he invoked the mitigation of changing circumstances, observing that "the Republican party has been reconciled to certain measures & arrangements which may be as proper now as they were premature and suspicious when urged by the Champions of federalism."[41]

The times seemed propitious for a politics of "Hamiltonian means for Jeffersonian ends." While Jefferson and Madison both urged amendment of the Constitution to establish an unassailable basis for public works on a national scale, a number of rising politicians — Henry Clay, John Quincy Adams, and young John C. Calhoun — justified public works through broad construction of the Constitution and regarded the idea of a constitutional amendment as a needless delay. Clay proposed a unified "American System" in which a dynamic and activist government would harmonize the needs of the country's diverse regions and sections. "All the powers of this government," Clay declared in 1824, "should be interpreted in reference to its first, its best, its greatest object, the Union." And in that regard, he said, "we believe that the government incontestibly possesses the constitutional power to execute such internal improvements as are called for by the good of the whole."[42] But a second party system developed in the 1820s and 1830s, and the old Hamiltonian-Jeffersonian division reasserted itself.

After his election to the presidency, John Quincy Adams attempted to implement something like Clay's "American System." Congress had passed a General Survey Act in 1824 to update the Gallatin Report and pave the way for public works funding. A related piece of legislation vested the U.S. Army Corps of Engineers with the responsibility for improving the nation's river and harbor infrastructure. Accordingly, John Quincy Adams recommended a massive public works program in his first message to Congress on November 25, 1825 — a huge outlay for internal improvements, the founding of a national university and astronomical observatory, the creation of a new Department of the Interior, and more. He urged the "cultivation and encouragement of the mechanic and of the elegant arts, the advancement of literature, and the progress of the sciences."[43]

Adams, however, was a maladroit president: at best, he was tactlessly honest. Historian George Dangerfield has said that his manner played into the hands of enemies who promulgated the "rumor that 'all Adamses are monarchists'" and suggested "that if the first presidential Adams had signed the Alien and Sedition Acts, the second had even stronger views about consolidation and central government."[44] The enemies of Adams were implacable. They included men who believed that his very election to the presidency was a swindle. Four candidates — Adams, Clay, William Crawford, and Andrew Jackson — campaigned in 1824, and the election was thrown into the House of Representatives. Clay gave Adams his support and was swiftly rewarded with the post of secretary of state. Jackson and his followers condemned this "corrupt bargain" and launched an incessant campaign to pillory Adams as a haughty, domineering aristocrat. The fact that the Adams program corresponded with some very early stirrings of aristocratic Tory reform in Great Britain did little for Adams's popularity, and Congress reacted to the public works proposals of the Adams administration in a meager fashion. Jackson triumphed in the election of 1828. Adams would later be elected to the House of Representatives, lamenting that his program, if adopted in full, "would have afforded high wages and constant employment to hundreds of thousands of laborers," and that "every dollar expended would have repaid itself fourfold."[45]

Upon his election, Jackson's ideas about public works were unclear. But he quickly endorsed laissez-faire and regarded himself as the guardian of older, more pristine Jeffersonian verities. He combatively vetoed a number of internal improvement bills, and his struggle with American political leaders who remained committed to the activist "American System" was one of the important features of the rapidly-emerging second party system. Increasingly after 1828, the Jacksonians called themselves "Democrats." Their opponents first called themselves

"National Republicans" but then rechristened their organization the "Whig" Party — in what they hoped was a clever bid to turn the tables on Jackson (the putative champion of the common man) by calling him "King Andrew the First" and claiming that only a new "whiggism" could restrain the power of this quirky, obstructive despot who vetoed measures that the people and their representatives in Congress desired to pass.

After Jackson left office in 1837, a financial panic stunned the American economy. A brief recovery flickered and waned, and then a ruinous depression ensued. The Democratic Party under Jackson's successor Martin Van Buren took no significant action to promote recovery. Many Whigs, however, urged internal improvement projects to put the unemployed back to work. Abraham Lincoln, as a young Whig legislator, advocated programs of this type in Illinois.[46] As historian Lawrence Frederick Kohl has said, "the Whigs believed that the power of government could safely serve the needs of all. . . . This being so, the Whigs sought to create closer bonds between the people and the government."[47] Conversely, the Democratic Party embraced laissez-faire. The slogans of the *Washington Globe* (the journalistic house organ of Jacksonian Democracy) and the *Democratic Review* were respectively the following: "The world is too much governed," and "That government governs best, which governs least."

Yet another factor blighted the chances for governmental stewardship: the growing perception by the slaveholding South that an activist government could fall into the hands of abolitionists. Historian William W. Freehling has said that after the controversy in 1819 and 1820 regarding the admission of Missouri as a slave state, southern leaders began to argue that "The 'general welfare' clause would serve abolitionists as well as road builders."[48] Much of the southern resistance to the tariff of 1828 — and the use of its revenue for internal improvements — was grounded in this perception. James Hamilton, Jr., one of the leading South Carolina "nullifiers," confessed in 1830 that

I have always looked upon the present contest with the government, on the part of the Southern States, as a battle at the outposts, by which, if we succeeded in repulsing the enemy, *the citadel would be safe*. The same doctrines "of the general welfare" which enable the general government to. . . appropriate the common treasure to make roads and canals . . . would authorize the federal government to erect the *peaceful* standard of servile revolt.[49]

John C. Calhoun admitted in the same year that "I consider the Tariff, but as the occasion, rather than the real cause of the present unhappy state of things. The truth can no longer be disguised, that the peculiar domestick institutions of the Southern States . . . [have] placed them in regard to taxation and appropriation in opposite relation to the majority of the Union."[50]

Northern advocates of public works understood the situation; John Quincy Adams explained that "When I came to the presidency the principle of internal improvement was swelling the tide of public prosperity, till the Sable Genius of the South saw the signs of his own inevitable downfall . . . and fell to cursing the tariff and internal improvement, and raised the standard of free trade, nullification, and state rights. I fell and with me fell, I fear never to rise again . . . the system of internal improvement by means of national energies."[51]

When the third party system — today's party system of the Democrats and Republicans — developed in the 1850s and 1860s, it was Lincoln's Republican Party that consummated the Hamiltonian-Jeffersonian reconciliation. According to historian James M. McPherson,

The Republican Party had inherited from its Hamiltonian and Whig forebears a commitment to the use of government to foster economic development through tariffs to protect industry, a centralized and regulated banking system, investment subsidies and land grants to high-risk but socially beneficial transportation enterprises, and government support for education. By 1860 the Republican Party had also pledged itself to homestead legislation to provide farmers with an infusion of capital in the form of free land. Before 1860, the southern-dominated Democratic Party that controlled the federal government had repeatedly defeated or frustrated these measures. During the war, Republicans passed them all: a higher tariff in 1861; a homestead act, a land-grant college act, and a Pacific railroad act providing loans and land grants for a transcontinental railroad in 1862; and a national banking act in 1863. . . . In addition, to finance the war the government marketed huge bond issues to the public and passed an Internal Revenue Act which imposed a large array of federal taxes for the first time, including a progressive income tax. This astonishing blitz of laws . . . did more to reshape the relation of the government to the economy than any comparable effort except perhaps the first hundred days of the New Deal.[52]

Hence, it was Lincoln's Republican Party that successfully healed the most significant rift that had divided the Founding Fathers. And it was Lincoln and his party who would finally eradicate the worst moral flaw within the nation the Founders had created: the flaw of slavery.

· I I I ·

LINCOLN WAS ONE OF THE MOST EFFECTIVE moral strategists the world has ever seen. Gifted with the power to envision the interplay of huge historical forces, he was also skilled in manipulating events, skilled in pushing them as far and as fast in the right direction as circumstances seemed to permit.[53] These are large claims, and there is no shortage of Lincoln detractors to dispute them. Many people these days are inclined to view the radical abolitionists as the heroes of America's freedom struggle, while dismissing Lincoln as a tepid "moderate" who viewed preservation of the Union as the paramount goal and who embraced emancipation only as a means to that end. There can be little doubt that abolitionism was a crucial precondition to the death of slavery. Yet the fact remains that abolitionists by themselves could not defeat the hated institution. Decades of ferment and denunciation only stiffened the defiance of the southern master class. It took a master strategist employing the power of the national government to make America live up to its ideals.

Unlike the abolitionists who called for immediate emancipation in the decades prior to the Civil War, Lincoln hoped to bring about a gradual phase-out of slavery through compensated manumission. As a first step, he and fellow members of the "Free Soil" movement attempted to contain the evil by campaigning for a halt to the westward expansion of slave states. This strategy was derived from the Founding Fathers, who prevented the expansion of slavery into the old Northwest Territory in 1787. Nonetheless, slavery expanded below the Ohio River, and its westward march extended into the Louisiana Purchase. With the admission of Missouri as a slave state in 1820, the institution began to move northward as well as westward.

One of the great questions of the time — indeed, an open question ever since — is the issue of how far slavery might have spread if its advocates had not been challenged. After Texas was admitted as a slave state in 1845, the South was rife with expansionist talk, and the Polk administration's acquisition of the Mexican Cession led to visions of slavery expanded to the western mining and agricultural frontier.[54] There was talk of a second Mexican War, of a conquest of Central America; southern "filibusterers" — a term derived from the Spanish "filibustero," or pirate — sought to foment trouble as a pretext for armed intervention by America. One of these southerners, a Tennessean named William Walker, briefly overthrew the government of Nicaragua and instituted slavery there in 1856. In 1854 an organization called the "Knights of the Golden Circle" was founded in Kentucky. Its purpose was to advocate an empire of slave states encompassing the Caribbean rim, including upper South America — a golden circle of rule by the white master race.[55] The Pierce administration flirted with the prospect of seizing Cuba for slavery.

Even more disturbing than this agitation for a tropical slave empire was the fact that slavery was becoming adaptable to industrial production. Since the 1840s slaves had been used as factory workers in Richmond, Virginia's Tredegar Iron Works, replacing white factory workers who had tried to go on strike.[56] More than one observer has suggested the stark though by no means implausible scenario that slaves might have entered the northern states as chain gangs of rented strikebreakers if the Civil War had been averted.[57] Lincoln himself was firmly convinced that slavery was on its way north — indeed, that was the point of his 1858 "House Divided" speech. "I do not expect the house to *fall*," Lincoln said, "but I do expect it will cease to be divided." Either the opponents of slavery would place it in the "course of ultimate extinction," Lincoln warned, or "its *advocates* will push it forward, till it shall become alike lawful in *all* the States."[58] Already, said Lincoln, pro-slavery settlers were trying to import the institution into Kansas, thanks to Stephen A. Douglas's Kansas-Nebraska Act. Lincoln and his fellow Republicans demanded legislation to prohibit slavery in all remaining federal western lands, but the Supreme Court ruled in its infamous *Dred Scott* decision of 1857 that Congress had no power to pass such a law against "property rights." Only one more step was needed, said Lincoln, for the nationalization of slavery: a second Supreme Court decision ruling that *state* governments also lacked the power to keep slavery out.

As much as any abolitionist, Lincoln viewed slavery as a vicious negation of America's creed — a "cancer," as he put it in 1854, that was eating away at the inalienable rights enshrined in the Declaration of Independence. "Our progress in degeneracy appears to me to be pretty rapid," he wrote to his friend Joshua Speed. "As a nation, we began by declaring that '*all men are created equal.*' We now practically read it, 'all men are created equal, *except negroes.*'" Pretty soon, Lincoln said, Americans might read it as "'all men are created equal, except negroes, *and foreigners, and catholics.*' When it comes to this I should prefer emigrating to some other country where they make no pretence of loving liberty — to Russia, for instance, where despotism can be taken pure, and without the base alloy of hypocrisy [sic]."[59]

Racist Democrats like Stephen Douglas insisted there was no hypocrisy: equality was for equals, said Douglas, and blacks were inferior to whites. The great challenge for Lincoln and the Free Soil movement in the 1850s was the challenge of convincing white racists in the North that the fate of black slaves mattered. In a private memorandum from the period Lincoln jotted down some lines of argument:

> If A. can prove, however conclusively, that he may, of right, enslave B. — why may not B. snatch the same argument, and prove equally, that he may enslave A? —
>
> You say A. is white, and B. is black. It is *color*, then; the lighter, having the right to enslave the darker? Take care. By this rule, you are to be the slave to the first man you meet, with a fairer skin than your own.
>
> You do not mean *color* exactly? — You mean the whites are *intellectually* the superiors of the blacks, and, therefore, have the right to enslave them? Take care again. By this rule, you are to be slave to the first man you meet, with an intellect superior to your own.[60]

In Lincoln's opening speech of the 1858 senatorial campaign against Douglas, he begged his opponent to "discard all this quibbling about this man and the other man — this race and that race and the other race being inferior."[61] But again and again in the Lincoln-Douglas debates, Douglas taunted Lincoln with race-baiting tactics and asked him if he advocated intermarriage of black men and white women, if he advocated race-mixing, if he advocated "mongrel" offspring. Lincoln said that he had never advocated social equality for blacks, a statement that latter-day detractors have seized as proof of his "racism." But was it really racism — or was it rather a compromise dictated by the racism of his audience?

This much is clear: secessionist southerners viewed Lincoln as a "Black Republican," as an abolitionist whose free-soil policies were fatal to southern slavery. With slavery's expansion precluded, it was only a matter of time before enough free states could be added to the Union to constitute a three-quarters majority, sufficient to amend the Constitution and destroy the slave system everywhere. Southern militants did not propose to sit on their hands and let the process begin; as soon as Lincoln won the presidency in 1860 a secessionist convention was called in South Carolina. The convention proclaimed the dissolution of the Union on the grounds that the victorious Republican Party "has announced that the South shall be excluded from the common territory, that the Judicial tribunal shall be made sectional, and that a war must be waged against Slavery until it shall cease throughout the United States. . . . The Slaveholding States will no longer have the power of self-government, or self-protection, and the Federal Government will have become their enemy."[62]

A final attempt was made to stave off war through a sectional compromise on slavery: the Crittenden Plan of December 1860, which would have entertained the possibility of further slavery expansion. Lincoln slammed the door on this surrender of the free-soil platform. He told his fellow Republicans to "entertain no proposition for a compromise in regard to the *extension* of slavery. The instant you do, they have us under again; all our labor is lost, and sooner or later must be done over. . . . Have none of it. The tug has to come & better now than later."[63] It is vital to understand the momentous significance of this action. It made the Civil War a near-certainty, and it also flatly disproves the assertions of those who believe that "Lincoln only wanted to preserve the Union" at the outset of the Civil War. Preservation of the Union was easy: simply appease the South and let slavery continue to expand. But Lincoln refused. He faced the outbreak of the Civil War with not one but *two* non-negotiable and quite inseparable goals: preservation of the Union and a firm prohibition of the further extension of slavery.

The expansion of these preliminary Lincoln war aims to encompass the emancipation of slaves in the rebellious states is a fascinating study in Lincoln's political methods as a moral strategist. He had privately considered such action long before he issued the Emancipation Proclamation in September 1862. As early as January of that year abolitionists were urging him to take such a step; two anti-slavery leaders, William Ellery Channing and Moncure Daniel Conway, called upon him at the White House to make their case. Conway's recollection of the interview is worth quoting at length:

> Mr. Channing having begun by expressing his belief that the opportunity of the nation to rid itself of slavery had arrived, Mr. Lincoln asked how he thought they might avail themselves of it. Channing suggested emancipation with compensation for the slaves. The President said he had for years been in favour of that plan. When the President turned to me, I asked whether we might not look to him as the coming Deliverer of the Nation from its one great evil. . . . He said, "Perhaps we may be better able to do something in that direction after a while than we are now." I said, "Mr. President, do you believe the masses of the American people would hail you as their deliverer if, at the end of this war, the Union should be surviving and slavery still in it?" "Yes, if they were to see that slavery was on the downhill." I ventured to say, "Our fathers compromised with slavery because they thought it on the downhill; hence war to-day." The President said, "I think the country grows in this direction daily, and I am not without hope that something of the desire of you and friends may be accomplished. Perhaps it may be in the way suggested by a thirsty soul in Maine who found he could only get liquor from a druggist; as his robust appearance forbade the plea of sickness, he called for a soda, and whispered, 'Couldn't you put a drop o' the creeter into it unbeknownst to yourself?'" Turning to me the President said, "In working in the antislavery movement you may naturally come in contact with a great many people who agree with you, and possibly may overestimate the number in the country who hold such views. But the position in which I am placed brings me into some knowledge of opinions in all parts of the country and of many different kinds of people; and it appears to

me that the great masses of this country care comparatively little about the negro, and are anxious only for military successes." We had, I think, risen to leave and had thanked him for his friendly reception when he said, "We shall need all the anti-slavery feeling in the country, and more; you can go home and try to bring the people to your views; and you may say anything you like about me, if that will help. Don't spare me!" This was said with a laugh. Then he said very gravely, "When the hour comes for dealing with slavery I trust I will be willing to do my duty even though it cost my life. And, gentlemen, lives will be lost."[64]

"You may say anything you like about me, if that will help. Don't spare me!" How often in American politics have we seen a president encouraging others to besmirch his own reputation — to call him names — in order to increase public pressure for policies he secretly favors but cannot yet espouse?

In the spring and summer of 1862 Lincoln tested the waters for a demonstration program of compensated emancipation in non-rebellious border slave states like Maryland, Kentucky, and Missouri. Congressional Republicans authorized the funds on a nearly straight party-line vote — most Democrats refused to authorize "taxes to buy negroes" — and Lincoln pleaded with border state delegations to give the plan a try. "You can not . . . be blind to the signs of the times," he exhorted. "To you, more than to any others, the privilege is given."[65] But they were blind. The border state representatives turned him down. Whereupon, mindful of casualty reports coming back from the battlefields in Tennessee and Virginia, Lincoln made the irrevocable decision to issue an Emancipation Proclamation. The sheer pig-headedness of slaveholders, coupled with the escalating battlefield carnage, prompted Lincoln to raise the moral stakes for which so many lives were being lost. If even the offer of money made no impression on slaveowners, then so much the worse for them. The timetable for phasing out slavery would be accelerated. But Lincoln kept the proclamation a secret until the right moment arrived for its release. Many Democrats would surely try to trigger a backlash against a Republican administration that caused the death of white soldiers to free blacks.

In the months between the drafting and release of the Emancipation Proclamation, Lincoln acted as though he had not yet decided on the issue. When the journalist Horace Greeley pleaded for emancipation in a *New York Tribune* editorial, Lincoln seized the opportunity for public reply. In his famous response he positioned himself as a commander-in-chief who was solely devoted to the cause of saving the Union: "My paramount object in this struggle *is* to save the Union, and is *not* either to save or to destroy slavery. If I could save the Union without freeing *any* slave I would do it, and if I could save it by freeing *all* the slaves I would do it; and if I could save it by freeing some and leaving others alone, I would also do that."[66] For years these lines have been read with only minimal comprehension by those who argue that "Lincoln only wanted to save the Union" in the Civil War. But — as we have seen — his entire career in the 1850s belies this proposition. Lincoln rejected the notion of saving a Union that was not *worth* saving: he said he would rather live in Russia if America's sinister "progress in degeneracy" made a mockery of its creed. He killed the Crittenden Compromise for saving the Union because he refused to pay the price of any further appeasement on the issue of slavery expansion. It was, after all, the Lincoln free-soil platform that *caused* the secession crisis in the first place.

No, the famous letter to Greeley is *not* proof that Lincoln "only wanted to save the Union." It is rather a stunning demonstration of Lincoln the tactician: the Lincoln who used constitutional logic and patriotic sentiment to insulate himself against attack by racists, who worked in secret with abolitionists to soften up public opinion for measures that did not yet command majority support, and who posed as undecided on the issue of emancipation when the liberating document was written already, and was waiting in his desk drawer.

Notwithstanding the careful preparation — including statements that newly-freed slaves might be colonized in other lands — a white backlash occurred very quickly. It worsened as the casualty lists from Fredericksburg, Chancellorsville, and other battlefields made "Copperhead" Democrats brazen in attacking "Old Abe the Widow-Maker," the fanatic whose "negro-loving" affinities had shattered the nation. In July 1863 the worst riots in American history turned New York City into a battleground for weeks as draft-resisting whites turned their wrath upon free blacks. Troops from the Gettysburg battlefield had to be rushed to New York to suppress the draft rioters. In the aftermath of this incident — and in the afterglow of some valiant battlefield actions by black troops — Lincoln used the patriotic theme in a reply to a detractor that also merits quoting at length:

> But, to be plain, you are dissatisfied with me about the negro. Quite likely there is a difference of opinion between you and myself upon that subject. I certainly wish that all men could be free, while I suppose you do not. Yet I have neither adopted, nor proposed any measure, which is not consistent with even your view, provided you are for the Union. I suggested compensated emancipation; to which you replied you wished not to be taxed to buy negroes. But I had not asked you to be taxed to buy negroes, except in such way, as to save you from greater taxation to save the Union exclusively by other means.
>
> You dislike the emancipation proclamation; and, perhaps, would have it retracted. You say it is unconstitutional — I think differently. I think the constitution invests its commander-in-chief, with the law of war, in time of war. The most that can be said. . . is, that slaves are property. Is there — has there ever been — any question that by law of war, property, both of enemies and friends, may be taken when needed? And is it not needed whenever taking it, helps us, or hurts the enemy? . . . The war has certainly progressed as favorably for us, since the issue of the proclamation as before. . . . [S]ome of the commanders of our armies in the field who have given us our most important suc-

cesses, believe the emancipation policy, and the use of colored troops, constitute the heaviest blow yet dealt to the rebellion. . . .

You say you will not fight to free negroes. Some of them seem willing to fight for you; but, no matter. Fight you, then, exclusively to save the Union. I issued the proclamation on purpose to aid you in saving the Union. Whenever you shall have conquered all resistance to the Union, if I shall urge you to continue fighting, it will be an apt time, then, for you to declare that you will not fight to free negroes. . . .

Peace does not appear so distant as it did. I hope it will come soon, and come to stay; and so come as to be worth the keeping in all future time. . . . And then, there will be some black men who can re-member that, with silent tongue, and clenched teeth, and steady eye, and well-poised bayonet, they have helped mankind on to this great consummation; while, I fear, there will be some white ones, unable to forget that, with malignant heart, and deceitful speech, they have strove to hinder it.[67]

Can we possibly read this letter as a statement by a racist politician who was only interested in saving the Union, regardless of what it stood for?

As a grim but compassionate magistrate Lincoln wielded the power of his government and its armies to save the continental Union and to liberate millions of oppressed people. His tactics were guided by a pow-erful strategic sense and by an architectonic grasp of the way in which parts relate to whole. "The tycoon is in fine whack," wrote Lincoln's secretary John Hay in 1863. "He is managing this war, the draft, foreign relations, and planning a reconstruction of the Union, all at once. I never knew with what tyrannous authority he rules the Cabinet, till now. The most important things he decides, and there is no cavil."[68]

As Lincoln faced re-election in 1864, he confronted one of the most terrible ordeals of his career. By summer the armies of Grant and Sherman were thoroughly bogged down, and the casualties from the Virginia theatre were horrendous. The offer of a lenient Reconstruction had elicited responses only from a few southern states that were largely under Union occupation anyway. White racists were in full cry, and the Democrats hinted that the rights of the slaveholding South would be upheld when peace negotiations commenced under Democratic leadership: the Emancipation Proclamation would be abrogated and slavery might once again expand. It was against this background that Lincoln pocket-vetoed the Radical Republicans' demanding scheme for Reconstruction, the Wade-Davis Bill. It was also in light of this situation that the Republican national convention chose a southern Democrat as Lincoln's running mate.

But even in August 1864, as he faced the prospect of losing the presidency to a pro-slavery Democrat, the presidential strategist was testing the best-case, as well as the worst-case, eventualities for social reform. He quietly wrote to the occupation Governor of Louisiana suggesting that limited black voting rights should be explored. Meanwhile, the Democratic press continued to excoriate the "negro-loving, negro-hugging worshippers of Old Abe." One Democratic newspaper said that "Abe Lincoln — passing the question as to his taint of Negro blood . . . is altogether an imbecile. . . . He is filthy. He is obscene. He is an animal."[69]

The military successes of Sherman in Atlanta and Sheridan in the Shenandoah Valley reversed the dynamics of the 1864 election, and Lincoln triumphed. The northern mood had changed overnight. "We are Coming, Father Abraham, Three Hundred Thousand Strong," rang the words of Stephen Foster's new song. With military victory approaching, Lincoln joined forces with the Radical Republicans. He played the key role in persuading the outgoing Congress to pass the new Thirteenth Amendment to the Constitution — the amendment killing slavery forever — in January 1865. He signed the Radical Republicans' bill creating a new social welfare agency: the Freedmen's Bureau, established in March 1865. He let stand a military order by Sherman transferring a huge tract of seized plantation lands in Georgia and South Carolina to newly freed slaves on a "promissory" basis that Congress would have to confirm.

Most importantly, on April 11, 1865, he gave a speech on Reconstruction, a speech in which — while urging the retention of the lenient Reconstruction regime that was established in Louisiana — he openly endorsed black voting rights and hinted that he might be receptive to the Radical Republicans' plans for extended occupation. In singing the praises of the new "free-state constitution" adopted in the "heretofore slave-state of Louisiana," he pointed out that it gave "the benefit of public schools equally to black and white" and empowered the Louisiana legislature "to confer the elective franchise on the colored man." Twelve thousand voters in Louisiana had committed themselves to these principles, Lincoln said, and by supporting their efforts "we encourage the hearts, and nerve the arms of the twelve thousand to adhere to their work, and argue for it, and proselyte for it, and fight for it, and feed it, and grow it, and ripen it to complete success. The colored man too, in seeing all united for him, is inspired with vigilance, and energy, and daring, to the same end. Grant that he desires the elective franchise, will he not attain it sooner by saving the already advanced steps toward it, than by running backward over them?"

Nonetheless, said Lincoln, though his "promise is out as before stated" with regard to the Louisiana government, a more demanding Reconstruction policy might be needed. And if so, "as bad promises are better broken than kept, I shall treat this [the Louisiana plan] as a bad promise, and break it, whenever I shall be convinced that keeping it is adverse to the public interest." The South had better realize, said Lincoln, that "so new and unprecedented is the whole case, that no exclusive, and inflexible plan can safely be prescribed as to details and colatterals. Such exclusive, and inflexible plan, would surely become a new entanglement. Important principles may, and must, be inflexible. In the present 'situation' as the phrase goes, it may be my duty to make some new announcement to the people of the South. I am considering, and shall not fail to act, when satisfied that action shall be proper."[70]

Is it stretching credulity to see in this speech the moral strategist once again testing the historical circumstances to determine whether Jefferson's promise of equality could be extended just a bit further? In the audience was John Wilkes Booth. When Lincoln had concluded, Booth turned to his companion and said, "That means nigger citizenship. Now, by God, I'll put him through. That is the last speech he will ever make."[71] The second Lincoln term would be completed by a racist Democrat, Andrew Johnson.

·IV·

AMERICA'S TRANSFORMATION INTO A SLAVE EMPIRE was not averted by market forces, by the interplay of checks and balances, or even by the power of moral protest. Protest was necessary — but only decisive intervention by a genius using every governmental resource at his command prevented the United States from becoming a society worse than South Africa under apartheid. Harry V. Jaffa, an eloquent scholar of political philosophy, has observed that "the totalitarian regimes of the twentieth century provide us with ample evidence" of the ways in which slavery could have been introduced into "the mines, foundries, factories and fields of the free states. . . . It is simply unhistorical to say that such a thing *couldn't* happen because it *didn't* happen. It didn't happen because Lincoln was resolved that it *shouldn't* happen. And nothing but his implacable will made it impossible."[72]

It was Lincoln's will that sustained the proposition that all men are created equal. "It is now no child's play to save the principles of Jefferson from total overthrow in this nation," Lincoln wrote in 1859. "They are denied, and evaded, with no small show of success. One dashingly calls them 'glittering generalities'; another bluntly calls them 'self evident lies'; and still others insidiously argue that they apply only to 'superior races'. . . . This is a world of compensations; and he who would *be* no slave, must consent to *have* no slave."[73]

Lincoln understood that tyranny emanates not only from "crowned heads, plotting against the people" — it can also emanate *from* the people if they let themselves be seduced by the impulse to dominate. Jaffa has said that "a case against the people, as well as for them, was present in Lincoln's thought from beginning to end."[74] This "case against the people" — or, more accurately, this insistence by Lincoln that anyone is capable of acting tyrannically — was present in Lincoln's declaration that the "selfishness of man's nature" eternally challenges his "love of justice."[75] It was present in a wartime speech about the meaning of liberty. The word liberty, Lincoln observed, is sometimes perverted to signify the prerogative of "some men to do as they please with other men. . . . The shepherd drives the wolf from the sheep's throat, for which the sheep thanks the shepherd as a *liberator,* while the wolf denounces him for the same act as a destroyer of liberty."[76] Such were the denunciations of Lincoln's alleged wartime "tyranny" by white supremacists like Booth.

It was Lincoln's achievement to synthesize classical conservative insights regarding the wolfish side of human nature — and the need to use governmental power to regulate it — with classical liberal ideals of opportunity and freedom for all.[77] It was Lincoln's achievement to save Jeffersonian values through the instrumentalities of Hamiltonian nationalism. Historian Phillip Shaw Paludan has said that the "more perfect Union" resulting from Lincoln's presidency "was achieved chiefly through an extraordinary outreach of national authority."[78] The result was the firm prohibition of involuntary servitude enshrined in the Constitution's Thirteenth Amendment.

Of course the early Republican legacy entailed much more than control and regulation: it included positive forms of governmental assistance. The Homestead Act, the Morrill Act creating the land-grant college system, the subsidies for transcontinental railroads, brought long-delayed fulfillment of proposals that Henry Clay and others had advanced years earlier. Moreover, the precedent set by this Republican "blueprint for modern America" wrought a transformation in American constitutionalism, as James M. McPherson has said:

> Nearly all of the first ten amendments to the Constitution apply the phrase "shall not" to the federal government. In fact, eleven of the first twelve amendments placed limitations on the power of the national government. But beginning with the Thirteenth Amendment in 1865 — the Amendment that abolished slavery — six of the next seven amendments radically expanded the power of the federal government at the expense of the states. The very language of these amendments illustrates the point: instead of applying the phrase "shall not" to the national government, every one of them grants significant new powers to the government with the phrase that "Congress *shall* have the power to enforce this article."[79]

But the power would remain largely dormant until another Republican president revived the use of Hamiltonian means for Jeffersonian ends in the twentieth century. The power would remain little used until the revival of Lincolnesque Republican statecraft by President Theodore Roosevelt.

Chapter Three

☆ ☆ ☆

Social Darwinism, Social Gospel, and the World of the Two Roosevelts

I
N 1871, THE ARDENT LINCOLN ADMIRER WALT WHITMAN declared
that "we had best look our times and lands searchingly in the
face, like a physician diagnosing some deep disease. Never was
there, perhaps, more hollowness of heart than at present, and here in
the United States."[1]

What had happened? Clearly, Reconstruction had satisfied no one,
and much of the blame could be laid at the doorstep of Andrew Johnson,
an old Jacksonian Democrat placed on the ticket with Lincoln in 1864
at a time when military stalemate instilled the realistic fear that the
Republicans might lose the election. This short-term tactic left Lincoln's
tasks in the hands of a believer in minimal government and white supremacy, a man who had virtually nothing in common with his prede-
cessor except commitment to the Union and opposition to secession.
The result was the notorious brawl between Johnson and the Radical
Republicans, whom Lincoln had regarded as the morally indispensable
(though at times hot-headed) conscience of the party.[2]

After Lincoln's death, Johnson tried to make very short work of

Reconstruction. He cancelled the military order establishing the "Sherman reservation" of land to be distributed to former slaves. Thereafter, he looked the other way as the ex-Confederate states established second-class citizenship for blacks — indeed, a system of semi-slavery — through the infamous "Black Codes." Under some of these codes, blacks who chose not to work for white employers were arrested as "vagrants" and then forced to work for any white man who paid their fine. Attempts by blacks to assume full citizenship were greeted by mob violence and by terrorism from the newly founded Ku Klux Klan.

When the Congress elected in 1864 convened in autumn 1865 — after a prolonged but at that time customary recess — its members confronted a stark choice: either go along (like Andrew Johnson) with the partial resurrection of slavery, or else intervene using federal power. Congress intervened, and the president resisted every step of the way.

John Wilkes Booth had made certain that Abraham Lincoln's "new announcement to the people of the South" would never be written. Instead of Lincoln, a racist Democrat was now stubbornly ensconced in the White House. In early 1866, Johnson vetoed the bill to re-authorize the Freedmen's Bureau that Lincoln and the Radical Republicans had created the previous year. Congress overrode this veto, and the Freedmen's Bureau continued to provide assistance to former slaves until 1869. Among the other partial successes of "Radical Reconstruction" were the Fourteenth and Fifteenth Amendments to the Constitution — amendments that eventually supplied the constitutional basis for the civil rights revolution that occurred a hundred years later.

Could the civil rights revolution have begun in the 1860s if Lincoln — who had come to support black voting rights and who remained a committed Hamiltonian — had completed his second term? The times were almost revolutionary in the months after Appomattox, and "Father Abraham," the savior of the Union, had begun to work in undisguised partnership with Radical Republicans after his massive re-election victory. The differences between Lincoln and the Radicals were chiefly disagreements involving tactics. Lincoln said in his Reconstruction speech of April 11, 1865, that black voting rights would probably be secured most quickly if Congress built upon existing policies. But he also made it clear that he would switch to stronger measures as soon as events convinced him that tougher policies were needed. And in this regard, who can possibly believe that if Lincoln had lived he would have tolerated the creation of the Black Codes, or the brutality of the Klan?

Johnson did — and for the rest of his term he struggled to prevent the Republicans from intervening on behalf of southern blacks. Crucial years for Reconstruction — years that might have been used by a like-minded President and Congress to build a political consensus for civil rights — were soured in a legislative-executive fight for control of governmental machinery and national policy. By the time that the Republicans finally regained the White House in 1868, the possibility of national consensus on civil rights had largely evaporated. American voters were repelled by the "mess in Washington." And this feeling strongly reinforced the prevailing habits of white supremacy.

Perhaps the best that even Lincoln could have done during Reconstruction would have been to avert the worst alternatives. In any case, Reconstruction began to languish in the early 1870s. Resurgent Klan violence and Democratic chicanery (including ballot box fraud in a number of southern states) hastened its demise, as did charges of "carpetbagger" corruption. Corruption did exist in certain parts of the South under Reconstruction — Louisiana and South Carolina appear to have had the worst of it — and yet in other southern states the situation was dramatically different. Mississippi, for example, had the cleanest government in years under Reconstruction governors James Alcorn and Adelbert Ames.[3]

But corruption in truth became a *national* problem by the late 1860s. The turmoil of Reconstruction was only the beginning of the great unraveling. Ulysses S. Grant — elected president in 1868 — tried to do what he could for southern blacks in his first term. But Republican affairs drifted gradually and inexorably into the hands of political bosses like Senator Roscoe Conkling of New York. Crookedness flourished in the Grant administration, and the president refused (until fairly late in his second term) to see what he did not want to see. A tone of machismo and swagger infected the political mainstream; cynics like Conkling vilified Republican honesty-in-government reformers, all the while shamelessly posing as the true heirs of Lincoln. Conkling called Republican civil service reformers "the man-milliners, the dilettanti and carpet knights of politics." He declared that "parties are not built up by deportment, or by ladies' magazines, or gush."[4] Senator John J. Ingalls of Kansas called the anti-graft reformers political eunuchs; he said they were "endowed with the contempt of men and the derision of women, and doomed to sterility, isolation, and extinction."[5]

What was going on? To some extent there was a cultural backlash going on, a reaction against a generation's worth of moral crusading as well as the wartime years of privation and sacrifice. Amid the nagging ambiguities and problems of Reconstruction, many voters were eager to be let out of "Sunday School," in political terms, to be done with idealistic crusading. America was ready for a binge of self-indulgence, and the taste for lofty ideals was temporarily burned out. Reformers were increasingly satirized as mincing buffoons, as epicene do-gooders who lacked the ruggedness to rise in a "man's world." To make matters worse, reformers were divided among themselves. Radical Republicans were challenged repeatedly by self-proclaimed liberals committed to the proposition that honesty in government could only be delivered through the purity of minimal government. The laissez-faire spirit was increasingly the order of the day, and when another economic depression struck in 1873, the predominant middle-class sentiment appeared to be "root, hog, or die."

A related transformation of values was occurring in conservative culture: its mission of noblesse oblige was draining away. A new and abrasive doctrine of conservative laissez-faire was emerging — a doc-

trine of raw and elemental struggle whose results would be a new social hierarchy based upon dog-eat-dog competition. From its traditions
regarding the need to regulate the wolfish side of human nature, conservatism was being seduced into something of a cult of bully-worship.
This development was already under way by the late 1860s. The source
of its intellectual respectability can be traced to a seemingly unlikely
point of inspiration: transmuted natural science.

In the eighteenth century, natural law had been the static equilibrium described by Newton, the tidy and self-correcting balance of the
"clockwork universe." By the middle of the nineteenth century, natural
law became the system of Darwin, the grand and evolutionary sorting-
out of the "fit" and the "unfit." From the popularized language of Darwinian science there emerged a laissez-faire permutation of conservative thought that historians have termed "Social Darwinism." Richard
Hofstadter, in his classic study of the subject, observed that

> as a phase in the history of conservative thought, social Darwinism
> deserves remark. In so far as it defended the status quo and gave
> strength to attacks on reformers and on almost all efforts at the
> conscious and directed change of society, social Darwinism was
> certainly one of the leading strains in American conservative thought
> for more than a generation. But it lacked many of the signal character-
> istics of conservatism as it is usually found. . . . A body of belief whose
> chief conclusion was that the positive functions of the state should be
> kept to the barest minimum, it was almost anarchical, and it was
> devoid of that center of reverence and authority which the state
> provides in many conservative systems.[6]

The chief intellectual advocate of Social Darwinism was the British
philosopher Herbert Spencer, who had coined the term "survival of the
fittest" in the 1850s well before the publication of Darwin's *Origin of
Species*. Spencer believed that all social interference in the competition
for survival subverts natural law and results in the triumph of the "unfit." Consequently, he opposed public education, public health regula-

tions, and state intervention on behalf of the poor. Interference in the struggle for survival undermines the way in which nature removes the inferior, he said. "The whole effort of nature is to get rid of such, to clear the world of them, and make room for better." Under nature's laws all were put on trial: "if they are sufficiently complete to live, they *do* live, and it is well that they should live. If they are not sufficiently complete to live, they die, and it is best they should die."[7] Spencer did believe that after many years — after eons — of further evolution, society would gradually develop along more "cooperative" lines, but only after the *Untermenschen* had been weeded out of the human species. In the meantime, it was every man for himself.

It bears noting that the social application of Darwinian-sounding principles could result in very different doctrines. In the 1870s, Henry George used the language of progressive "evolution" to challenge social inequalities. He also argued that as species and societies become more complex, the powers of mind must be summoned to adapt to evolutionary change. By the turn of the century, John Dewey was employing what some have termed "Reform Darwinism" to argue that the "fittest" societies are those which promote the greatest teamwork and cooperation. But there is no evading the cultural and intellectual power of the laissez-faire permutation of "Darwinian" social theory. And there is no evading the corrosion it seems to have inflicted on enlightened conservative values.

Spencer's ideas were taken up by Americans such as sociologist William Graham Sumner and lecturer/editor Edward Livingston Youmans, the founder (in 1872) of *Popular Science Monthly*. Sumner blended Spencerian doctrines with the precepts of Malthus and Ricardo. He waged unremitting warfare against reformers in books and essays with titles like "The Absurd Effort to Make the World Over" (1894). Youmans spread a similar message and insisted that every venture in social or political reform was futile. Only the glacial process of biological selection could improve the world; reformers had better defer to the insights of science and cease their meddling, Youmans declared.

Spencer arrived in the United States for a triumphal tour in 1882, and he was feted at Delmonico's with a banquet at which celebrities showered him with praise. Business leaders were particularly taken with his doctrines. Even Andrew Carnegie (in some ways an unusually altruistic employer) reminisced about the effect of reading Spencer. "I remember that light came as in a flood and all was clear. Not only had I got rid of theology and the supernatural, but I had found the truth of evolution. 'All is well since all grows better,' became my motto, my true source of comfort."[8] Many other businessmen preened themselves as specimens of evolutionary fitness — forgetting, in some cases, the Hamiltonian assistance that had strengthened their ventures in the crucial years. But Hamiltonianism was a fading political tradition. The legacy of governmental stewardship diminished to vestigial proportions in the 1870s.

Certain traces of governmental activism lingered. High tariffs (a flagrant violation of the principles of laissez-faire) were kept at the behest of powerful interests. Congress set aside land for the first national park, Yellowstone, in 1872. In 1879 Congress created the Mississippi River Commission, which laid the groundwork for eventual federal involvement in flood-control efforts. The stewardship ideal would also linger in some of the decade's jurisprudence: the Supreme Court's decision in *Munn v. Illinois* (1877) validated governmental regulation of commerce at the state level. Writing for the majority, Chief Justice Morrison R. Waite declared that when "one devotes his property to a use in which the public has an interest, he, in effect, grants to the public an interest in that use, and must submit to be controlled by the public for the common good."[9]

But the currents of Gilded Age politics steadily eroded these stewardship principles. And behind it all was the ignominious demise of

Reconstruction: one of the most grievous symptoms of Gilded Age cynicism was the failure to enforce the recent civil rights amendments to the Constitution. After a brief attempt to protect black voting rights with the Enforcement Act of 1870 and the Ku Klux Klan Act of 1871, the federal government, especially after former Confederates returned to Congress, gradually washed its hands of the matter. Congress also refused to pass legislation introduced in the 1870s to establish a national Bureau of Health, and to regulate interstate railroads.[10] Even Republican reformers were starting to renounce interventionist governance. In the election of 1872, a faction of self-styled "Liberal Republicans" sought to reduce the governmental corruption of the Grant era by means of the classical liberal precepts — that is, by reducing government itself.

By the 1880s, such doctrines were more influential among Republicans. In 1882 a new river and harbor improvement bill had to be passed over Republican President Chester A. Arthur's veto. At the same time, Democrats adhered to their own laissez-faire tradition. Finally, the Supreme Court changed its philosophy: the Justices who voted for the *Munn* decision were gradually replaced in the 1880s by Social Darwinists. The result was the Gilded Age politics of trivial or do-nothing government — of weak and forgettable presidencies — content to let the market resolve social issues.

The market, however, was creating conditions that were rife with turbulence. The post Civil War generation achieved momentous results in its drive to build industrial infrastructure and expand the nation's productivity. Yet the prosperity was, to put it mildly, ill-distributed. A small number of people accumulated fabulous wealth, and the middle class prospered in general. On the other hand, significant numbers of Americans found their position starkly degraded. Farmers suffered a calamitous period of losses and sustained depression in the midst of plenty. The harder they worked, the lower commodity prices fell, and the closer they came to being pushed off the land and into bankruptcy. Their plight was worsened by extortionate shipping rates in parts of the country where railroads enjoyed a monopoly. Tenant farmers of the South, both black and white, were sinking into miserable peonage.

In urban America thousands of unskilled immigrants flooded the labor market, and their working conditions were often squalid. Many worked twelve-hour days and six- or seven-day work weeks. Stygian tenements proliferated. Desperation at times turned violent as workers attempted to strike and found themselves battling company police or the National Guard. The destructiveness of these confrontations escalated, from the war of the "Molly Maguires" in the early 1870s to the great railroad strikes of 1877 and the bloody violence of the Homestead and Pullman strikes in the 1890s. Wherever one's sympathies lay in these labor-management conflicts, there was no escaping the fact that chaotic disruption, with frightening overtones of class warfare, was increasing in America.

From the grassroots came urgent demands for reform. A short-lived attempt to form a third American political party in the early 1890s — the People's or Populist Party — called for a wide-ranging program of economic regulation and assistance from government and scorned the Republicans and Democrats as worse than useless. At the St. Louis conference that founded the Populist Party in 1892 the oratory of the Minnesota writer-politician Ignatius Donnelly bespoke a revolutionary fervor:

> We meet in the midst of a nation brought to the verge of moral, political, and material ruin. Corruption dominates the ballot box, the legislatures, the Congress, and touches even the ermine of the bench. The people are demoralized. . . . The urban workmen are denied the right of organization for self-protection; imported pauperized labor beats down their wages; a hireling standing army, unrecognized by our laws, is established to shoot them down, and they are rapidly disintegrating to European conditions. . . . We charge that the controlling

influences dominating the old political parties have allowed the existing
dreadful conditions to develop without serious effort to prevent or
restrain them.[11]

Though prosperous middle-class Americans might have viewed such
rhetoric as nonsense in 1892, the American economy was crippled by
another depression that was triggered by the Panic of 1893. The next
year an Ohio businessman named Jacob Coxey led an "army" of unemployed men to petition Congress for public works jobs. Their leaders
were arrested.[12] The same year the workers at the Pullman Palace Car
Company went on strike after five cuts in wages without any reduction
in the rents charged for housing in the company town. The Pullman
Strike spread into a general railroad strike, and the federal government
smashed it by sending in troops.

In 1896 the traditionalist leaders of the Democratic Party were
swept temporarily aside by the protest candidacy of William Jennings
Bryan, who excoriated the complacent in both major parties with an
incantation of fury:

> We have petitioned and our petitions have been scorned; we have
> entreated and our entreaties have been disregarded; we have begged,
> and they have mocked when our calamity came. We beg no longer, we
> entreat no more, we petition no more. We defy them![13]

Even this was too equivocal for some. Revolutionary socialism was
spreading. People at both extremes of the continuum of wealth and
poverty spoke of incipient revolution. No less than the 1790s, the 1890s
were a time when apocalyptic visions of class war interrupted the an-
thems of American progress. Such was our political situation just over
a century ago.

· I I ·

THE MOST VISIBLE CHALLENGE TO THE POLITICS of Social Darwinism was the challenge from the grassroots: from the Farmer's Alliances, the labor unions, and the short-lived Populist Party. But a second challenge was gathering force — a challenge in the middle class and intelligentsia — and with voter insurgency it ushered in a major period of governmental activism at the turn of the century.

The intellectual counter-movement against Social Darwinism was catalyzed quickly, and some of its earliest participants were members of the Christian clergy. Devout Christians reacted to "Darwinianism" in radically divergent ways. A number of clergymen like Henry Ward Beecher embraced both Darwinian science and Spencerian social philosophy. In contrast, fundamentalist Christians began a long and embittered campaign against Darwinian influence. Other Christians singled out the Spencerian version of Darwinianism for a moral condemnation that was not fundamentalist at all. The problem for such people was the issue of Christian ethics: if the "fittest" survivor turned out to be a thug, were Christians who professed adherence to the teachings of the Sermon on the Mount to regard the result with equanimity? Repeatedly accused of spreading a hard-hearted and anti-Christian outlook, Spencer protested that charitable acts, when performed on an individual basis, did *not* contradict the laws of survival, but his logic was far from clear. Why was it that haphazard acts of benevolence directed toward supposedly "unfit" people were consistent with natural selection, while more purposeful community action was held to be at odds with natural selection?

Across the denominations in the 1880s spread a movement known as the "Social Gospel," and it preached the extension of Christian charity to community-wide dimensions in industrial society. Ministers such as Washington Gladden among the Congregationalists and Walter Rauschenbusch among the Baptists were leading figures. Social Gospel preaching engendered a wave of altruistic activity. Settlement houses were founded in major cities by the 1890s, and young idealists — young Harry Hopkins and young Eleanor Roosevelt — took time to do service for the poor. At Groton young Franklin Delano Roosevelt absorbed a rendition of the Social Gospel values from the Rector Endicott Peabody. Figures in the business community were also swayed by the Social Gospel teachings. In an essay entitled "Wealth" — it was published as "The Gospel of Wealth" in England — Andrew Carnegie proclaimed in 1889 that it was a sin to die rich, and that those who had triumphed in the struggle for survival should practice noblesse oblige and retire to careers of philanthropy.

The Social Gospel continued to gather strength in the twentieth century. In 1907 Walter Rauschenbusch proclaimed in *Christianity and the Social Crisis* that the "social problem" was the mandatory mission of the church in the industrial era:

> The gospel, to have full power over an age, must be the highest expression of the moral and religious truths held by that age. . . . In our thought to-day the social problems irresistably take the lead. If the Church has no live and bold thought on this dominant question of modern life, its teaching authority on all other questions will dwindle and be despised.[14]

As the Social Gospel developed, a number of critics attacked laissez-faire as an affront not only to Christianity but also to rational social order. Moral abdication through laissez-faire causes social dysfunction and breakdown, such critics declared. These arguments were often combined with the ethical teachings of the Social Gospel.

The association of ideas — laissez-faire as both immoral and inefficient — was not new. Early in the nineteenth century economist Mathew Carey had compared laissez-faire to the practice of a "physician who found his patient in a raging fever and let the disorder take its course, or 'regulate itself.'" While such a doctor would be "deservedly reprobated as unworthy of his profession," said Carey, his conduct would be no more "irrational than that of a statesman, who says the agriculture, manufactures, trade, and commerce of his country" can "regulate themselves" — even if "the interests of the nation" cry out for the sort of stewardship that is as much a "sacred trust" of government as the healing arts are the sacred trust of a physician.[15]

This theme was taken up in the 1880s and 1890s by sociologist Lester Frank Ward, who wrote a series of books and articles in which "pure" natural selection was ridiculed as mindless, and social intervention was justified through pointed analogies. The survival of species, said Ward, is relegated by nature to the vagaries of chance, disease, and disaster.[16] But the human species is protected by the human mind, with its interventionist arts of medicine, agriculture, planning, all of which *harness* the workings of nature. Competition may sometimes improve a species, said Ward, but at other times the judicious *removal* of competition — through protection from natural predators, for instance — can bring about desirable results. Ward proclaimed that in agriculture

> whenever competition is wholly removed, as through the agency of man in the interest of any one form, that form immediately begins to make great strides.... Such has been the case with all the cereals and fruit trees; it is the case with domestic cattle and sheep, with horses, dogs, and all the forms of life that man has excepted from the biologic law and subjected to the law of mind.[17]

Ward's agitation in sociology was paralleled in economics by the work of Richard T. Ely and John R. Commons. In 1886 Ely included in the draft prospectus for the American Economic Association a platform commencing with the following declaration: "We regard the state as an educational and ethical agency whose positive aid is an indispensable condition of human progress. While we recognize the necessity of individual initiative in industrial life, we hold that the doctrine of laissez-faire is unsafe in politics and unsound in morals."[18] Once again, the association of practicality and ethics — "unsafe in politics and un-sound in morals" — revealed the influence of the Social Gospel in the period's academic insurgency. Examples of this influence abounded. Washington Gladden, one of the most prominent clergymen in the Social Gospel movement, was also a participant in the founding of the American Economic Association.[19] Ely's fellow economist John R. Com-mons was the author in 1894 of a book entitled *Social Reform and the Church*. Ely wrote the volume's introduction.

Beyond academia, significant numbers of people were conclud-ing that a new coordination — a new efficiency consistent with higher Christian ethics — was urgently needed in America. The best-selling novel of the era, Edward Bellamy's *Looking Backward* (1888), described a cooperative society replacing the competitive horrors of the day. The book inspired a broad "Nationalist" movement. Leaders in professional and business circles were telling one another that America's social con-flicts had gotten out of hand. Industrialist (and later U.S. Senator) Marcus Alonzo Hanna, for instance, condemned the autocratic behav-ior of his fellow industrialist George Pullman by declaring in the middle of the Pullman strike that "a man who won't meet his men half-way is a God-damn fool."[20] Hanna went on to play a major role in the work of the National Civic Federation, a group of business and labor leaders organized in 1900 to mediate labor-management conflicts.[21]

The 1890s were rife with the fear of social chaos. As the new cen-tury approached, America seemed to be poised at the edge of an abyss. Perhaps the downward slide had begun already, as Americans assailed one another like a gang of savages. Middle-class voters were frightened by reports of typhoid-infected water supplies that private utilities were said to be pumping into schools and homes. They were frightened by reports of adulterated food products from the meat-packing "trusts" of Chicago. They were ready to demand a return to interventionist gover-nance, ready to demand a new civic mutuality — a new dedication to the common good. From the drive to promulgate the newly-composed

"Pledge of Allegiance" to the newly-conceived "City Beautiful" movement — a movement to restore the principles of classical grandeur to
urban design — American culture was pervaded by demands for a worthy and cohesive social order.

Both the Democratic and Republican parties were affected by
America's turn-of-the-century "Progressive Era," an age of vigorous striving to clean up corruption and disorder. Progressive reform entailed
crusades in almost every state to cleanse municipal politics of graft and
expand the electorate's power. It encompassed national campaigns to
abolish child labor, to grant women the right to vote, to guarantee the
purity of food and drugs, and to expand the scope of the federal
government's natural resource protection.

The Progressive Era was also pervaded by the Social Gospel creed.
In 1913 Walter Rauschenbusch hailed the "Christianizing of the social
order," a Christianization that was not fundamentalist. The Progressive
Era's gospel, said Rauschenbusch, was a socially-*applied* gospel:

> I do not mean putting the name of Christ into the Constitution of the
> United States. . . . Jesus himself does not seem to have cared much
> about being called "Lord, Lord," unless there was substance in the
> word. To put a stop to child labor in our country would be a more
> effective way of doing homage to his sovereignty than any business of
> words and names.[22]

Rauschenbush exulted that the values of Gilded Age cynicism seemed
everywhere under attack, that a moral reawakening was everywhere
apparent and ascendant:

> When God wants to halt a proud man who is going wrong, he lets him
> go the full length and find out the latter end for himself. That is what
> he has done with our nation in its headlong ride on the road of
> covetousness. Mammonism stands convicted by its own works. It was
> time for us to turn. We are turning. . . . The same sense of a great
> change comes over any one who watches the life of this nation with an

eye for the stirring of God in the souls of men. There is a new shame
and anger for oppression and meanness . . . a new hope for a better day
that is even now in sight. . . . We talk of the "social feeling" or "the new
social consciousness."[23]

The new "social feeling," however, did not preclude toughness in
reformers. To the contrary: the presidential paragon of the new social
consciousness was an exemplar of soldierly virtues. Gone were the days
when derisive cynics could dismiss reformers as eunuchs. At hand was
the age of President Theodore Roosevelt, the champion of progressive
reform and a self-proclaimed Christian soldier.

The first major figure to occupy the White House since Lincoln's
time (and a military hero because of his exploits in the Spanish-Ameri-
can War), Roosevelt preached a hard and demanding version of the
Social Gospel. Though his foibles of hyper-activity (and occasional
hyper-aggressiveness) would shape his policies for better or worse,
Roosevelt was also driven by deep inner forces to assume the burdens
of the just magistrate. He demonstrated this proclivity in 1902 when he
threatened to send in troops to resolve the anthracite coal strike — not
by putting the strikers in jail in accordance with Gilded Age practice,
but rather by *seizing the mines from their owners* if they didn't come to
reasonable terms.[24] He was the strong champion of the underdog but
he would brook no lawlessness either. He was the marshal in Dodge
City, and every peaceable citizen could expect a "square deal" from him
so long as certain ground rules were observed. He joined the fight for
pure food and drug legislation with righteous fervor after checking out
the allegations of the "muckrakers" with undercover agents.[25] He occupied the front ranks of the natural conservation crusade. He condemned
revolutionary rhetoric but shook his presidential fist at "malefactors of
great wealth" whose behavior provoked revolutionary rhetoric.

His leadership on the issue of adulterated food provides a useful
case study of his methods. Shocked by allegations from the "muckrak-

ers" that ground-up rat meat, the flesh of diseased animals, and rat dung pervaded the products of Chicago meat-packing houses, Roosevelt ordered an investigation by Commissioner of Labor Charles P. Neill and attorney James B. Reynolds. Roosevelt insisted on checking out the facts since he distrusted the principal "muckraker" in this affair — namely, the socialist author Upton Sinclair, whose novel *The Jungle* was published in 1906. Roosevelt's investigators reported to him that conditions in the meat-packing houses of Chicago were actually *worse* than Sinclair alleged. Accordingly, Roosevelt threatened to publicize the scandal himself if recalcitrant congressmen refused to take action. He told the chairman of the House Agriculture Committee that

> I have recently had an investigation made by Commissioner Neill of the Labor Bureau and Mr. J. B. Reynolds, of the situation in Chicago packing houses. It is hideous, and it must be remedied at once. I was at first so indignant that I resolved to send in the full report to Congress. As far as the beef packers themselves are concerned I should do this now with a clear conscience, for the great damage that would befall them in consequence would be purely due to their own actions. But the damage would also come to all the stock growers of this country and the effect of such a report would undoubtedly be well-nigh ruinous to our export trade in meat. . . . I do not wish . . . to give publicity at this time to the report, with the certainty that widespread damage will be caused not merely to the wrongdoers but to the innocent. Nevertheless, it must be distinctly understood that I shall not hesitate to cause even this widespread damage if in no other way does it prove possible to secure a betterment in conditions that are literally intolerable. I do not believe that you will have any doubt on the matter. If you have, I earnestly hope you will see me at once.[26]

The tactics worked, and the meat inspection bill was signed on June 30, 1906. Moral indignation, interventionist governance, and practical calculation had once again thwarted the ever-shifting human propensity for sleaziness and predation.

Over and over Roosevelt declared the necessity of regulating the wolfish energies of human nature as a cautionary note in the social application of Christian values. He likened himself to the Puritan magistrates of old, declaring in a 1907 address on "The Puritan Spirit and the Regulation of Corporations" that the Puritan was

> no laissez-faire theorist. When he saw conduct which was in violation of his rights — of the rights of man, the rights of God, as he understood them — he attempted to regulate such conduct with instant, unquestioning promptness and efficiency. If there was no other way to secure conformity with the rule of right, then he smote down the transgressor with the iron of his wrath. The spirit of the Puritan was a spirit which never shrank from regulation of conduct if such regulation was necessary for the public weal; and this is the spirit which we must show today whenever it is necessary.[27]

In his final message to Congress, Roosevelt observed that "the chief breakdown" in American society derived from "the new relations that arise from the mutualism, the interdependence of our time. Every new social relation begets a new type of wrong-doing — of sin, to use an old-fashioned term — and many years must always elapse before society is able to turn this sin into crime which can be effectively punished at law."[28]

Here was the Social Gospel militant, the new philanthropy tempered with *Realpolitik*. One of Roosevelt's most important achievements as an intellectual in politics was his synthesis of Social Darwinist imagery — ruggedness, "fitness," and struggle — with Social Gospel ethics and "Reform Darwinist" efficiency through social teamwork.

And here, too, was a blending of conservative stewardship with progressive reform. Once again, Hamiltonian means were applied to Jeffersonian ends: Roosevelt repeatedly invoked the legacy of Hamilton and praised the Hamiltonian aspects of Lincoln's leadership. The activist spirit of Republican governance in Lincoln's time was the spirit that

Roosevelt meant to rekindle if he possibly could. John Milton Cooper, Jr. has said that "as a self-proclaimed Hamiltonian, Roosevelt meant to exalt the power and prestige of the federal government. As a self-anointed heir of Lincoln and Civil War Republicanism, he yearned to preserve his party's fidelity to nationalism."[29] The message was appealing to a great many young and progressive Republicans; Henry L. Stimson later reminisced that the elder Roosevelt was "the most commanding natural leader" he had ever known.[30] It was also appealing to Republican survivors of the Lincoln years; John Hay — one of Lincoln's secretaries in the Civil War — told Roosevelt that he was "one of the men who most thoroughly understand and appreciate Lincoln."[31] In 1905 Hay presented Roosevelt with a ring containing strands of Lincoln's hair that had been shorn on the night of the assassination. It was obviously significant that Theodore Roosevelt's father was a social acquaintance of the Lincolns.[32] It was also significant that planning for the Lincoln Memorial in the nation's capital began to take shape during Roosevelt's presidency.

In general terms the Civil War Republicans' "blueprint for modern America" was extended significantly during Roosevelt's years in the White House. The legacy included the Newlands Act of 1902 (a bipartisan measure earmarking funds from the sale of public lands for the construction of dams and irrigation projects in the West), the creation of the U.S. Forest Service, the sequestering of millions of acres of public lands for conservation purposes, and the creation of the Food and Drug Administration. In addition, Roosevelt convened nine commissions to study policy issues involving water power, transportation, natural resource conservation, and rural life.

When Roosevelt retired from the presidency in 1909, the critic and journalist Herbert Croly hailed him in *The Promise of American Life* as a towering figure in American history:

> What Mr. Roosevelt really did was to revive the Hamiltonian ideal of

constructive national legislation. During the whole of the nineteenth
century that ideal, while by no means dead, was disabled by associations and conditions from active and efficient service. . . . Of course
Theodore Roosevelt is Hamiltonian with a difference. Hamilton's fatal
error consisted in his attempt to make the Federal organization not
merely the effective engine of the national interest, but also a bulwark
against the rising tide of democracy. The new Federalism or rather
new Nationalism is not in any way inimical to democracy. On the
contrary, not only does Mr. Roosevelt believe himself to be an unimpeachable democrat in theory, but he has given his fellow-country-
men a useful example in the way in which a college-bred and well-to-
do man can become by somewhat forcible means a good practical
democrat. The whole tendency of his programme is to give a democratic meaning and purpose to the Hamiltonian tradition and
method. . . . More than any other American political leader, except
Lincoln, his devotion both to the national and to the democratic ideas
is thoroughgoing and absolute.[33]

When Roosevelt returned from a year of travels abroad, he acknowledged Croly by using his phrase — the "New Nationalism" — as
the title of a speech to Civil War veterans in Osawatomie, Kansas, a
speech in which he outlined his vision of industrial-age coordination
and morality. "I do not ask for overcentralization," Roosevelt said,

> but I do ask that we work in a spirit of broad and far-reaching nation-
> alism when we work for what concerns our people as a whole. We are
> all Americans. Our common interests are as broad as the continent. I
> speak to you here in Kansas exactly as I would speak in New York or
> Georgia, for the most vital problems are those which affect us all alike.
> The National Government belongs to the whole American people, and
> where the whole American people are interested, that interest can be
> guarded effectively only by the National Government. . . The Ameri-
> can people are right in demanding that New Nationalism, without
> which we cannot hope to deal with new problems.[34]

Roosevelt declared that the age of mass organization had come to stay. While popularly known as the "trust-buster," he was actually in-clined to view anti-trust prosecutions against monopolistic enterprise as a strategy of last resort. The optimal approach, he said, was regula-tion by the government. "Combinations in industry are the result of an imperative economic law which cannot be repealed by political legisla-tion," he asserted in his New Nationalism speech. "The way out lies, not in attempting to prevent such combinations, but in completely con-trolling them in the interest of the public welfare."[35] As he elaborated in his autobiography:

> A simple and poor society can exist as a democracy on the basis of sheer individualism. But a rich and complex industrial society cannot so exist; for some individuals, and especially those artificial individuals called corporations, become so very big that the ordinary individual is utterly dwarfed beside them, and cannot deal with them on terms of equality. It therefore becomes necessary for these ordinary individuals to combine in their turn, first in order to act in their collective capacity through that biggest of all combinations called the govern-ment, and second, to act, also in their own self-defense, through private combinations, such as farmers' associations and trade-unions.[36]

As early as 1905, Roosevelt had told the wealthy members of Philadelphia's Union League Club that "the great development of industrialism means that there must be an increase in the supervision exercised by the Gov-ernment. . . . Such men as the members of this club should lead in the effort to secure proper supervision."[37] "Proper supervision": the conser-vatism of this vision — the instinct to ward off chaos through policies of governance that re-established balance, equilibrium, and order in the body politic and extended the principle of checks and balances to industrial-age dimensions — has not escaped the notice of historians. As John Morton Blum has observed, "those Progressives who shared Roosevelt's views were . . . seeking ways to accommodate American so-cial, political, and economic institutions to advancing industrialism. . . .

[but] they were not seeking to uproot those institutions." Roosevelt "believed in change, but gradual change; change within established institutions; change obtained by adapting, managing, administering."[38]

Roosevelt was restless in retirement, and he was unhappy with the performance of his presidential successor, William Howard Taft. By 1912 he could stand it no longer, and he challenged Taft for the Republican nomination. When Taft's nomination was assured, Roosevelt bolted the Republican convention and formed a third political party, the Progressive (or "Bull Moose") Party. At its convention Roosevelt's followers joined him in a chorus of "Onward Christian Soldiers." Among Roosevelt's younger supporters were Alfred M. Landon, Harold Ickes, Felix Frankfurter, and Dean Acheson.

Taft came in a poor third in the election of 1912; the real fight was the struggle between Theodore Roosevelt and the Democrats' nominee, Woodrow Wilson. While Roosevelt campaigned with his doctrine of "New Nationalism," Wilson offered a Progressive revision of Democratic laissez-faire. While he still expressed some of the traditional Democratic fears about centralized regulation, he also advocated strong governmental leadership in reform activities such as anti-trust intervention to restore competition. Wilson called his program the "New Freedom," and the clash between this program and the "New Nationalism" of Roosevelt was the source of great oratorical drama during the campaign. Replying to a statement by Wilson to the effect that "the history of liberty is a history of the limitation of governmental power," Roosevelt contended that

> so long as governmental power existed exclusively for the king and not at all for the people, then the history of liberty was a history of the limitation of governmental power. But now the governmental power rests in the people . . . and what the people sorely need is the extension of governmental power.[39]

Governmental power was needed, said Roosevelt, to protect the American people from the sort of economic chain reactions that result in involuntary unemployment or impoverished old age. A significant amount of the New Deal legacy was sketched in the "Bull Moose" platform of 1912. In his speech to the Progressive convention, Theodore Roosevelt specifically advocated social security and unemployment compensation. "The hazards of sickness, accident, invalidism, involuntary unemployment, and old age," he proclaimed,

> should be provided through insurance. This should be made a charge in whole or in part upon the industries, the employer, the employee, and perhaps the people at large to contribute severally in some degree. Wherever such standards are not met . . . the workers are in jeopardy . . . and the community pays a heavy cost in lessened efficiency and in misery.[40]

At the height of the campaign, Roosevelt contrasted the Wilsonian program with his own New Nationalist vision in the following terms:

> We are for human rights and we intend to work for them in efficient fashion. Where they can be best obtained by the application of the doctrine of States' rights, then we are for States' rights. Where, in order to obtain them, it is necessary to invoke the power of the nation, then we shall invoke to its uttermost limits that mighty power. We are for liberty. But we are for the liberty of the oppressed, and not for the liberty of the oppressor to oppress the weak and to bind burdens on the shoulders of the heavy-laden. It is idle to ask us not to exercise the power of the government when only by the power of the government can we curb the greed that sits in high places, when only by the exercise of government can we exalt the lowly and give heart to the humble and the downtrodden.[41]

With Taft and Roosevelt dividing the Republican electorate, Woodrow Wilson was elected president with 41.9 percent of the popular vote. Theodore Roosevelt would never hold public office again. Resenting his third-party venture, the Republicans nominated Charles Evans

Hughes in 1916. As the 1920 election approached, the wounds appeared to have healed: Theodore Roosevelt was a strong contender for the Republican nomination. But on January 6, 1919, he died in his sleep at the age of sixty.

· I I I ·

As CONSERVATISM BEGAN TO ABANDON the governmental stewardship ideal — in favor of the Social Darwinist variety of laissez-faire — liberalism moved in the opposite direction, from a free market creed to a tentative embrace of the welfare state. This transformation would prove to be long and difficult, and it would not be completed in the United States until the 1930s. An important harbinger of the change was the 1848 declaration of John Stuart Mill that "the admitted functions of government embrace a much wider field than can easily be included within the ring-fence of any restrictive definition."[42] Historian David Harris has sketched the continuation of the process in Britain, observing that "after Gladstone was gone, the British liberal party became converted to the doctrine of the state as an engine of social betterment."[43] Winston Churchill offered a retrospective glimpse of the transformation, observing that by the final years of the nineteenth century

> the great victories had been won. All sorts of lumbering tyrannies had been toppled over. Authority was everywhere broken. Slaves were free. Conscience was free. Trade was free. But hunger and squalor and cold were also free; and the people demanded something more than liberty. The old watchwords still rang true; but they were not enough. And how to fill the void was the riddle that split the Liberal party.[44]

In America the cumulative impact of Populist demands — the Populists had argued in 1892 that "the powers of the government . . . should be expanded. . . as rapidly and as far as the good sense of an intelligent people and the teachings of experience shall justify" — the ideas of intellectuals like Ward and Ely, and the cross-currents of the Progressive Era forced liberals to question the validity of laissez-faire.[45] Uncertainty reigned in the administration of Wilson, who had pledged himself to the "New Freedom," and was initially ambivalent about regulation. Wilson did, however, champion banking reforms and his initiatives helped bring about the creation of the Federal Reserve system in 1913. Thereafter, his thoughts about regulation changed. He gradually supported the creation of the Federal Trade Commission in 1914, the National Park Service in 1916, and the passage in the same year of the Adamson Act, which established the eight-hour day for interstate railroads.

Wilson's principal focus of concern would of course be foreign policy. Indeed, his major contribution to the governmental stewardship legacy would be the mobilization during World War I — an achievement that suggested the tremendous potential for increasing the nation's productivity through partnerships among government, business, and labor.

In other ways, however, the wartime experience brought major disillusionment. World War I broke out in the year after Wilson took office, and a bitter debate regarding the merits of American involvement poisoned the world of Progressivism. The bitterness of this controversy eventually killed the Progressive movement and helped usher in a backlash against reform in the 1920s. Whatever the merits of American participation in the war, and whatever the merits of Wilson's vision of a postwar international league, even Wilson's admirers admitted that in matters of war and peace he assumed an air of messianic certitude. At his worst, he was utterly lacking in Lincolnesque skills of political strategy. He turned himself in the end almost willfully into a martyr and refused to entertain compromise on any significant features of the treaty he brought back from Versailles. The Senate would not submit to his dictation. With the collapse of Wilson's campaign for the League of Nations came a widespread feeling that America's participation in the war had been pointless and that Americans should never again allow themselves to be "suckered" into minding other people's business. And the success of the Bolsheviks in Russia did much to arouse public fear regarding the potentially radical results of any concern about America's industrial order.

Consequently, in the 1920s a revival of conservative laissez-faire swept away the Progressive spirit to a great extent. As it was in the decades following the Civil War, an age of moral crusading yielded to an interlude of drift. Harding's "Back to Normalcy" administration was a weird re-enactment of the scandal-ridden Grant era. By the same token, the do-nothing mood that followed during Calvin Coolidge's administration was almost a throwback to Gilded Age politics. Republican Progressives such as Hiram Johnson, George Norris, and Robert LaFollette were shunted to the sidelines by Harding and Coolidge, and proposals for governmental stewardship were generally laughed away as crankish rot, or as the dangerous and alien claptrap of revolutionary Russia.

As it was in the Gilded Age, however, there were special exceptions to laissez-faire: exceptions in the form of higher tariffs, a federal road-building program, and a pro-active Commerce Department. Indeed, under Herbert Hoover's leadership — both as secretary of commerce and as president — the public works efforts of the federal government increased substantially. Much of the activity was grounded in earlier Progressive Era legislation. The Boulder Canyon project resulting in Hoover Dam, for example, was constructed by the Bureau of Reclamation, an agency created by the Newlands Act of 1902.[46]

Hoover had served in the Wilson administration as wartime food administrator, and he was regarded in the twenties as a combination whiz-kid engineer and moderate progressive. So he was — notwithstanding his bitter attacks of later years against the New Deal's "socialism." Hoover responded to the plight of farmers by supporting — well before the Wall Street crash — the Agricultural Marketing Act of 1929, an act that created a Federal Farm Board endowed with $500 million for loans to agricultural cooperatives. Historian David Burner has observed that Hoover urged the creation of a federal Department of Public Works, a federal Home Loan Bank, and a federal Employment Bureau as early as 1919, that he "worked for the expansion of water-power facilities" by the federal government throughout the 1920s, and that "both as Commerce Secretary and as President he put particular effort into getting a St. Lawrence Seaway."[47] He played a key role in expanding the federal government's flood control efforts after the devastating Mississippi River flood of 1927. A significant degree of continuity linked the Hoover Dam project and the TVA project of Franklin D. Roosevelt, much as the Reconstruction Finance Corporation (RFC), Hoover's "pump-priming" agency for economic recovery, was retained in the Roosevelt years. Among the major public works projects commenced with RFC loans in the final days of the Hoover administration were the Mississippi River bridge at New Orleans, Jones Beach on Long Island, and electric power lines from Hoover Dam to Los Angeles.[48] It is fair to say that Hoover did more than any previous president had done to counteract an economic depression and to stimulate recovery. But his actions were always hampered by a reluctance to "go too far" by unbalancing the budget. The tragedy for Hoover — and the predicament for FDR before the Second World War — was the fact that the Great Depression of the 1930s was an economic calamity exceeding anything Americans had ever experienced, a calamity demanding intervention by government on a scale that many Americans regarded as unthinkable in peacetime. The principal difference between Hoover and FDR was this: as the crisis deepened, Hoover became more remote and isolated, whereas Roosevelt was willing to experiment with new and ever more daring forms of governmental stewardship.

The prosperity of the 1920s contained weaknesses that market forces worsened. By the end of the decade a number of economists ex-

pressed concern that paychecks were not keeping pace with productivity. In their 1927 book *Business Without a Buyer*, William Trufant Foster
(the former president of Reed College) and Waddill Catchings (an iron
manufacturer) warned that Americans had reached the point where
"we cannot sell the goods . . . because the people who would like to buy
them do not have sufficient incomes."[49] Amid signs that consumer purchasing power was indeed falling short of industrial production, corporations began to divert capital to short-term speculation. People followed the tipsters and drove up the prices of stocks whose value often
bore little relation to the economic health of the companies that issued
them. A huge amount of money (much of it borrowed) was channeled
by corporations into the bull market.

When the market broke — when the selling frenzy began and the
value of the stocks plummeted — everyone who had borrowed significant sums to invest in the get-rich-quick speculation had to pay the
money back or face ruin. What followed was the usual chain reaction
that results from financial panics: investors cannibalized available resources to raise the cash that they needed to keep their creditors ap-
peased. They closed the doors to their factories, they laid off workers,
they diverted payroll to stave off foreclosure. Life-savings were lost as
depositors stampeded to withdraw whatever funds might be left in the
uninsured banks that had loaned out money to be gambled on Wall
Street. Banks failed across the continent, and factory closings increased.
Within a few years between a fourth and a third of America's work
force was unemployed, and America's industrial output was cut in half.

This was economic devastation on a scale that was absolutely staggering, and when Franklin D. Roosevelt took the oath of office in 1933,
Congress was prepared to give him virtually anything he asked for in
the first "hundred days" of his administration. Certain key legislation
— such as measures to save the banking system — rushed through
Congress in a matter of hours, with Republican leaders in full support.[50]

"Even the iron hand of a national dictator," said Alfred M. Landon, "is in preference to a paralytic stroke."[51]

To understand FDR's most important policies, one has to comprehend the links between the New Deal and the Square Deal of FDR's fifth-cousin Theodore: the links, for instance, between the dam-building programs resulting from the Newlands Act of 1902 and the conception of the Tennessee Valley Authority; between Theodore Roosevelt's creation of the U.S. Forest Service and FDR's creation of the Civilian Conservation Corps; between the New Nationalist vision — the vision of industrial society's interdependence and "mutualism" — and FDR's venture in industrial coordination via the National Recovery Administration (NRA). Much of the New Deal record in programs such as social security and unemployment compensation could be traced to the "Bull Moose" platform of 1912. It was no coincidence that New Deal planners such as Rexford Guy Tugwell were joined by erstwhile "Bull Moose" Republicans like Harold Ickes who accepted positions in federal agencies as well as in the cabinet itself.

FDR was a Democrat, and he inherited the party's Jefferson-Jackson traditions along with the historic identification of the Democratic Party with the "liberal" side of American politics. Accordingly, it was Franklin D. Roosevelt's New Deal that completed the reconciliation in America of liberal ideology and governmental stewardship. "New Deal liberalism" has long since come to embody the association of liberal values and "the welfare state." This association has proved so fateful that even Republicans who adhere to the idea of governmental stewardship are generally known to this day as "liberal Republicans."

But it would be a serious mistake to dissociate Franklin D. Roosevelt from the intellectual lineage of interventionist conservatism. James MacGregor Burns has said that while FDR's mind was "open to almost any idea" and "welcomed liberal and radical notions," he was on balance "far closer to the conservative tradition than any other." Burns has affirmed that the Hamiltonian elements in Roosevelt's policies bespoke "a conservative acting in the great British conservative tradition."[52]

Franklin D. Roosevelt was fully aware of this association when he proclaimed in 1936 that "liberalism becomes the protection of the far-sighted conservative. . . . I am that kind of conservative because I am that kind of liberal."[53] He told a campaign audience in the same year that his aim was to preserve the essence of American traditions by adapting and strengthening them: "It was this administration which saved the system of private profit and free enterprise after it had been dragged to the brink of ruin."[54] In a 1938 "Fireside Chat" he explained that he wanted to restore the vitality of the market; specifically, he believed that "we suffer primarily from a failure of consumer demand because of lack of buying power. Therefore it is up to us to create an economic upturn. . . . Lost working time is lost money. Every day that a workman is unemployed, or a machine is unused, or a business organization is marking time, it is a loss to the nation."[55] Historian Carl Degler has said that Roosevelt was definitely "a conservative at heart," and that "in his pragmatic and common-sense reactions to the exigencies of the depression, Roosevelt, the easy-going conservative, ironically enough became the embodiment of a new era."[56]

FDR's conservative side was apparent throughout the New Deal. One could see it embodied in the work of the Civilian Conservation Corps, which enhanced through reforestation the nation's patrimony of parks and historic sites. One could see it in FDR's support for the war against crime led by J. Edgar Hoover — the war against criminals like John Dillinger, "Pretty Boy" Floyd, "Baby Face" Nelson, and "Machine Gun" Kelly that inspired a memorable series of Hollywood "G-Man" movies. One could see it in Roosevelt's continued enthusiasm for the turn-of-the-century "City Beautiful" precepts in architecture and planning. So many of the buildings that the public reveres in monumental Washington, D.C. — the National Gallery of Art, for example, and the Jefferson Memorial — were built under the interested supervision of that devoted patron of classicism, Franklin Roosevelt. Burns has spoken of FDR's Burkean "belief in the unity of the past, the present, and the future," his "solicitous concern for the national heritage . . . that was passing through one generation of Americans after another." The list of conservative traits could go on, says Burns, but probably

> the most persistent interest he had in public policy involved conserva-
> tion of natural and human resources. . . . Roosevelt defended change
> as essential to holding on to values of lasting importance. For over a
> century conservatives in Britain had been demonstrating, through
> such reforms as factory acts and social welfare services, that minor
> changes in institutions and laws were necessary to conserve enduring
> ends. And in this sense, too, Roosevelt was a conservative.[57]

Essentially all of these qualities had been present in *Theodore* Roosevelt's policies. But while laissez-faire conservatives had been doomed in Theodore Roosevelt's time to the status of obstructionist fuddy-duddies who could do little more than hold back the Rough Rider's "radicalism" as best they could, in the 1930s — at least after the honeymoon year of 1933 when FDR could do no wrong — the laissez-faire element unleashed a ferocious attack upon "that man in the White House." The instrumentality of this attack was a group called the American Liberty League, and it was heavily funded by a few wealthy families, notably the du Ponts. At first the campaign attacked the New Deal as misguided; the League issued pamphlets with titles like *Government by Busybodies.* But by 1936, the Liberty League began to assault the New Deal as a spearhead of communist collectivism.

Even this was just the beginning of the vilification: obscene and vicious allegations began to make the rounds of patrician clubs, and a hate-Roosevelt mania assumed extravagant proportions in upper-class circles. Some of the stories were so extraordinarily obscene as to elicit astonishment from the worldly-wise press corps.[58]

Comparisons of the two presidential Roosevelts are instructive in

this regard. Think what you would about Theodore Roosevelt, his status as a military hero — the Rough Rider — imparted an aura to his
leadership that surely made his enemies think twice about assaulting
his character. In 1912 a madman shot Theodore Roosevelt on his way to
make a speech — and the Rough Rider actually proceeded to his desti-
nation and made the speech, histrionically proclaiming to his audience
that he spoke to them with a bullet in his chest. However heroic were
Franklin D. Roosevelt's struggles against polio, he remained a man in a
wheelchair, and George Wolfskill's study of the Liberty League has documented the extent to which the "Roosevelt stories" made reference to
him as a "cripple."[59] A resentful sadism was present in the vitriol directed at FDR, the sadism of the schoolyard bully. And Franklin, unlike
Theodore, had not produced elaborate demonstrations of his power to
ward off bullies. Franklin was a *nice* man, a warm and easy-going gentleman, and this quality was quickly written off by some as the weakness
of a dilettante who was the dupe of communists and Reds. But the
vilification was not consistent, for FDR was also accused of harboring
dictatorial ambitions. His ill-advised "Court-packing" scheme of 1937
was immediately cited as evidence supporting this assertion.

But Roosevelt only turned to this scheme when it seemed as
though the Supreme Court was on the verge of gutting the New Deal.
Far from revealing truly radical or revolutionary instincts, Roosevelt
passed up chance after chance to change American capitalism in radical ways. He renounced the opportunity to nationalize the banks in
1933.[60] He warily swung his support to the Wagner Act — the act sanc-
tioning the right of organized labor to strike and engage in collective
bargaining — only at the last moment, and he earned the resentment
of labor leaders like John L. Lewis when he kept a cool distance from
the struggles of organized labor in the "sit-down strikes." Perhaps most
significantly, the Keynesian economists are quite convincing when they
attribute the long delay in recovery to Roosevelt's repeated unwillingness to spend the sums on public works that both Keynes himself and

Roosevelt's more radical rivals — such as the messianic power artist Huey Long — were demanding.[61]

As early as 1928, the economic writers Foster and Catchings argued in their book *The Road to Plenty* that "the Government should adopt long-range planning of public works for the purpose of stabilizing employment," adding that if public works projects to stimulate purchasing power were not built, "the country might lose more than they cost, through the idleness of men and of capital savings."[62] This is exactly what happened in the 1930s, though in far more disastrous terms than Foster and Catchings had envisioned. It was John Maynard Keynes who predicted how great an economic stimulus was needed to reverse the economic contraction that began in 1929. "There will be no . . . escape from prolonged and perhaps interminable depression," warned Keynes in 1932, "except by direct state intervention to promote and subsidize new investment" through deficit spending on a scale commensurate with war:

> Formerly there was no expenditure out of the proceeds of borrowing that it was thought proper for the State to incur except for war. In the past, therefore, we have not infrequently had to wait for a war to terminate a major depression. I hope that in the future we shall not adhere to this purist financial attitude, and that we shall be ready to spend on the enterprises of peace what the financial maxims of the past would only allow us to spend on the devastations of war. At any rate, I predict with an assured confidence that the only way out is for us to discover *some* object which is admitted even by the deadheads to be a legitimate excuse for largely increasing the expenditure of someone on something![63]

Keynes said that a powerful economic stimulus could never be provided through a balanced budget. "The voices which . . . tell us that the path of escape is to be found in strict economy . . . are the voices of fools and madmen." But "unluckily the traditional and ingrained beliefs" of American policymakers "grew out of experiences which contained no parallel to the present."[64]

Keynes's worst predictions came true. It took the unprecedented spending of World War II to end the Great Depression in America. Even though Roosevelt's public works programs surpassed the efforts of Hoover many times over, it was still not enough to restore the purchasing power obliterated by the Depression. Unemployment continued to hover at the level of eight to ten million throughout the decade. It was only the colossal military spending of the 1940s (spending made possible through massive deficit finance) that brought health to the American economy. Compared to the wartime spending — which escalated from $13.3 billion in 1941 to $98.4 billion in 1945 — New Deal relief and public works spending never exceeded $3–5 billion per year. New Dealer Thurman Arnold, looking back upon the Depression from the vantage point of the 1950s, confessed that "we did not learn the real nature of our economic difficulties until the tremendous spending of the Second World War pulled us out of our static economy and made us the richest nation the world had ever known."[65]

Why was FDR cautious? His caution resulted from the fact that like his older fifth-cousin Theodore, he "believed in change, but gradual change; change within established institutions . . . change 'on suspicion,'" as John Morton Blum expressed it. What he sought was the moderate balance that the careful and benevolent guiding hand of an enlightened country squire could furnish.

This was anything but communist collectivism. To be sure, the Soviet Union possessed allure for certain liberals during the 1930s, much as the French Revolution was alluring at first to contemporaneous liberals like Jefferson and Paine. Conservative critics undoubtedly provided an important service by exposing the horrors of the Soviet system, just as left-wing critics like George Orwell deserved accolades for their own contributions to exposing Stalinist evil. But the association of Franklin D. Roosevelt's domestic policies with communist totalitarianism was (and is) preposterous. At its worst, the New Deal was a grab-bag of experimental and sometimes contradictory programs. At its best it was an attempt to revive the intermittent American synthesis of Hamiltonian and Jeffersonian values.

But since FDR was a Democrat, he found it less easy than Theodore Roosevelt to cite the tradition of Lincoln — less easy to rebuke the laissez-faire theorists with Lincoln's belief that "the legitimate object of government is to do for the people what needs to be done, but which they can not, by individual effort, do at all, or do so well, for themselves."[66] Party politics aside, however, a quotation from Lincoln's 1864 speech about liberty figured in an FDR speech that was aimed at the Liberty League in 1936.[67] The FDR-Lincoln connection would continue to develop during World War II.

If there was "socialism" in the New Deal, it was not the coercive kind; it was a public enterprise in which the common man was empowered as an owner-shareholder in cooperative ventures. When the Roosevelt administration built the model planned community of Greenbelt, Maryland, the planners created a substantially self-governing town possessing every normal attribute of local self-government with one exception: preliminary land-use restrictions to prevent despoliation of the land and over-development.[68] The town's commercial center was run by a citizen cooperative owned through shares by the residents themselves. In later years the housing blocks were sold to another citizen cooperative.[69] This organization (which still exists) is about as communistic as a condominium apartment house.

What historian William Leuchtenburg has called the "Heavenly City" of the New Dealers was distinguished from totalitarian schemes by insistently democratic values. The Heavenly City of the New Dealers was a vision of industrial power democratically *tamed* by the great republic. It included

> the greenbelt town, clean, green, and white, with children playing in light, airy, spacious schools; the government project at Longview,

Washington, with small houses, each of different design, colored roofs, and gardens of flowers and vegetables. . . . most of all, the Tennessee Valley, with its model town of Norris, the tall transmission towers, the white dams, the glistening wire strands, the valley where a "vision of villages and clean small factories has been growing into the minds of thoughtful men." Scandinavia was their model abroad, not only because it summoned up images of the countryside of Denmark, the beauties of Stockholm, not only for its experience with labor relations and social insurance and currency reform, but because it represented the "middle way" of happy accommodation of public and private institutions the New Deal sought to achieve.[70]

To produce this "middle way," scores of wealthy philanthropists repudiated laissez-faire to join Roosevelt in his work of noblesse oblige. Aristocrats like Gerard Swope, Francis Biddle, John Gilbert Winant, Herbert Claiborne Pell, and Averell Harriman served the New Deal. Francis Biddle described the "satisfaction derived from sinking individual effort into the community itself, the common goal and the common end. This is no escape from self; it is the realization of self."[71] It was also the realization of the Social Gospel. Angered at last by the vilifications of the Liberty League and determined to turn the other cheek no longer, Franklin D. Roosevelt struck back at his laissez-faire critics in the following oft-quoted terms as the election of 1936 approached its crescendo:

> Governments can err, Presidents do make mistakes, but the immortal Dante tells us that divine justice weighs the sins of the cold-blooded and the warm-hearted in different scales. Better the occasional faults of a Government that lives in a spirit of charity than the consistent omissions of a Government frozen in the ice of its own indifference.[72]

If Roosevelt's critics wished to look for the ideological sources of what they viewed as his "betrayal," those sources were not to be found in the works of Marx and of Lenin. They had probably come from the sermons of the Rector Endicott Peabody — those sermons delivered so long ago in the chapel at Groton where he impressed upon the minds of his pupils the duty of a Christian gentleman.[73]

Chapter Four

☆ ☆ ☆

Americans Torn Between Conservative and Liberal Follies

I

T WAS FITTING THAT WHEN FRANKLIN D. ROOSEVELT confronted the issues of World War II his path intersected that of Winston Churchill, a twentieth-century exemplar of Tory reform. Historian and critic Peter Viereck observed the way in which Churchill's early domestic politics harmonized lingering Tory stewardship values and liberal post-laissez-faire governance:

> Following the Disraeli tradition of his father Randolph, young Winston . . . sought to revive the alliance between nobles and the common people against the alleged plutocrats of big business. Because his party abandoned that alliance, Churchill temporarily joined the Liberal party. There he worked closely with the Liberal orator, David Lloyd George (1863–1945). Together they achieved social reforms, lower tariffs, workers' pensions, improved factory conditions, and other social security measures long before the American New Deal. Churchill's motive was . . . to root the workers in the traditional framework by showing them they could satisfy their needs within that framework instead of with Marxist class war.[1]

In 1909, Churchill advocated social security measures to protect working-class families in case "any exceptional disaster or accident, like recurring sickness, like the death or incapacity of the breadwinner, or prolonged or protracted unemployment, [should] fall upon them. . . . You do not make a man self-reliant by crushing him under a steam roller."[2]

It was therefore an alliance of profoundly kindred spirits that characterized the FDR-Churchill partnership when domestic priorities yielded to war. In confronting Axis predation Roosevelt and Churchill summoned up the finest themes of the struggle that every generation must face, though at different levels of intensity: the struggle against the malignant side of human nature, the potential in the human spirit that can warp and transfigure merely fallible human beings and convert them — as it did the Nazis — into fiends.

In a fundamental manner, this challenge relates to the legacy of Lincoln, and historian Merrill D. Peterson has shown the way in which the Lincoln legacy helped American interventionists like FDR to face the Axis menace. According to Peterson, Robert E. Sherwood's 1938 play *Abe Lincoln in Illinois* was "a big hit . . . because it struck a political nerve." The play's context was "more allusive to the imminent threat of totalitarianism than to the southern slavocracy. . . . Raymond Massey, for whom Sherwood had written [the role] and whose portrayal of Lincoln contributed much to its success, remarked in an interview, 'If you substitute the word dictatorship for the word slavery . . . it becomes electric for our time.'"[3]

Peterson has said that "as the Second World War came on, Roosevelt saw the challenge in global terms and grew increasingly conscious of treading in Lincoln's footsteps."[4] This consciousness was heightened by FDR's deepening friendship with Lincoln biographer Carl Sandburg. The growing FDR-Lincoln connection was substantive: Lincoln's warnings before the Civil War regarding the expansive power of slavery — his insistence that Americans confront the supposedly "impossible" scenario of slavery in the northern states — were comparable to the warnings delivered by FDR before Pearl Harbor regarding the supposedly "impossible" scenario of Axis power in the western hemisphere.

Roosevelt warned the Congress on May 16, 1940, that if Great Britain were overrun, the North Atlantic would soon be infested with Nazi Luftwaffe bases — and then

> from the fjords of Greenland it is four hours by air to Newfoundland; five hours to Nova Scotia . . . and only six hours to New England. . . . If Bermuda fell into hostile hands it would be a matter of less than three hours for modern bombers to reach our shores.[5]

A year later Roosevelt told the American people in a "Fireside Chat" that the Nazis "have the armed power at any moment to occupy Spain and Portugal" and then to threaten "the island outposts of the New World — the Azores and Cape Verde Islands," which were "only seven hours' distance from Brazil by bomber or troop-carrying planes."[6] Roosevelt was especially alarmed by Nazi contingency plans for South America. On October 27, 1941, he announced that American intelligence agents had acquired

> a map of South America and a part of Central America as Hitler proposes to reorganize it. Today in this area there are fourteen separate countries. The geographical experts of Berlin . . . have divided South America into five vassal states, bringing the whole continent under their domination.[7]

FDR's fear of an Axis-encircled America was made particularly nightmarish by his (and Churchill's) suspicion that the Nazis were developing nuclear weapons. Much as Churchill dreaded "a new dark age, made more sinister, and perhaps more protracted, by the lights of perverted science," Roosevelt spoke of "an unholy alliance of pelf and power to dominate and enslave the human race," asserting that "today the whole world is divided, divided between human slavery and human freedom — between the pagan brutality and the Christian ideal. We choose human freedom — which is the Christian ideal."[8] It was not surprising that FDR, having spoken of a "world divided" into slavery and freedom, closed his nomination speech in the 1944 election by quoting the final passage of Lincoln's second inaugural address.

But the Allies' triumph was marred by accumulating revelations of Stalinist butchery: the horror of the Nazi death camps was compounded by the growing acknowledgement that the Soviet partner in the Allies' victory was all the while a totalitarian regime only slightly less reprehensible than Hitler's Germany.

There are times, of course, when a tragic choice must be made between lesser and greater evils, and the Axis seemed appallingly close to victory when Roosevelt and Churchill assisted the Soviet Union in repelling Hitler's invasion. With the "Big Three" alliance in place, a number of Americans — Republicans like Wendell Willkie and Democrats like Roosevelt — were hopeful regarding postwar Soviet-American cooperation. Willkie, for instance, declared in 1943 that "Russia is an effective society. It works . . . The record of Soviet resistance to Hitler has been proof enough of this to most of us . . . [and] we must work with Russia after the war. . . . There can be no continued peace unless we learn to do so."[9]

But as the Cold War began, revulsion against Stalinism became a significant feature of postwar intellectual culture, both left and right. And insofar as opposition to Stalinism carried over into libertarian insurgency against "the state," the postwar mood was hardly auspicious for the politics of Hamiltonian-Jeffersonian synthesis in the United States, either in Republican or Democratic terms.

To be sure, some of the New Deal legacy was extended in the postwar years. The Employment Act of 1946 vested the federal government with permanent responsibility for guaranteeing economic prosperity. The benefits of the GI Bill were delivered, with handsome results. In the Truman years the National Science Foundation was created, the Marshall Plan was established, and a major federal housing program was launched in 1949. On the other hand, Truman's attempt to extend the federal stewardship mission through new legislation in the areas of civil rights and health care came to nothing. By 1950, the emergent McCarthy era put almost every form of governmental stewardship except the maintenance of national security under the ideological cloud of "statist collectivism."

The right-wing reaction against the New Deal had been triggered already by the agitation of the Liberty League and by the activities of anti-communist conservatives like Representative Martin Dies, who had investigated communist influence in New Deal programs during the 1930s. But in the postwar period conservatives began to cite the hegemony of Soviet power in eastern Europe — supposedly resulting from FDR's alleged "sellout" at Yalta — as fresh and decisive proof that the New Deal had been a communist-tending affair from start to finish.

The war years had been fateful years in the emergence of the Cold War. Defeat of the Axis powers — by no means a foregone conclusion — was of course the paramount international issue, yet strategic decisions by the allies were laden with postwar ramifications. Massive attention has rightly been focused on the nature of the wartime alliance of Roosevelt, Churchill, and Stalin to determine what mistakes (if any) were committed by FDR in his relations with the Soviets. Roosevelt was hoping for a postwar international peacekeeping organization, and he hoped to underwrite its strength by committing the "big powers" to police the world scene. This idea was in many ways derived from Theodore Roosevelt. The Soviet Union was of course a superpower, and there is evidence to suggest that Roosevelt was naively hopeful regarding the prospects for turning the Soviet Union of Stalin into a cooperative conservator of peace.

But there is something else to be remembered before any fair consideration of the issue of "Roosevelt and Yalta" can begin. Roosevelt was hardly the only player in the give-and-take with Stalin. Churchill had a great deal to say about issues of strategy and diplomacy; and while Churchill's anti-communist credentials were impeccable, his wartime decisions contributed as much to the postwar power balance with the Soviet Union as decisions of FDR's may have done.

Specifically, Churchill's military instincts were "peripheralist." While Stalin's armies bore the brunt of the fighting against the Nazis, Churchill believed that the British and American forces should engage the Germans in peripheral theatres like North Africa or Norway. Roosevelt, together with most of the American high command, favored opening up the "second front" by putting a major British-American expeditionary force into western Europe at an early date. But Churchill and the British high command — fearful that a premature invasion might fail — vetoed the idea. The second front was delayed from 1942 to 1944. British concerns about a premature invasion were probably justified: even in 1944, the Normandy invasion was in many ways a close call.

The point is that the Americans and British invaded the European continent long after Stalin had turned back the Nazi invasion and was pushing in hot pursuit into eastern Europe. Stalin *occupied* the areas in question — so how could his troops have been removed without the sort of massive Russo-American war that no sane politician would have started? (In the aftermath of D-Day, Churchill suggested that British and American troops who were poised for the invasion of southern France should be diverted into central Europe. But this recommendation was opposed by Roosevelt, upon advice from General Eisenhower).[10] Consequently, the discussions at Yalta were conducted in the knowledge that Soviet troops unfortunately controlled a great deal of eastern Europe already because of the complicated military choices that the Allies had confronted from 1942 through 1944. The Soviet sphere of influence in the Balkans was largely settled in a meeting of Churchill and Stalin in October 1944.[11]

But none of this mattered by the early 1950s to Senator Joseph McCarthy or other anti-communist conservatives who revived the accusation that Roosevelt and his New Deal associates had been dupes of the communists. The issue became particularly ugly in 1948 when Whittaker Chambers, an editor at *Time* magazine, proclaimed himself an ex-communist and alleged that he and his fellow travelers had infiltrated several New Deal agencies. The Chambers allegations went far beyond the issue of Soviet espionage; Chambers alleged that the New Deal as a whole was communist-related. "All of the New Dealers I had known were Communists or near-Communists," Chambers declared in 1952. "None of them took the New Deal seriously as an end in itself. They regarded it as an instrument for gaining their own revolutionary ends." Chambers had no doubt that "the New Deal was only superficially a reform movement."[12]

Meanwhile, McCarthy proclaimed that the Truman administration was infested with communists, and his war cry — "twenty years of treason" — became a right-wing obsession. From the 1940s hearings of the House Un-American Activities Committee to the rise of the John Birch Society in the 1950s, the association of New Deal liberalism and "creeping socialism" became a major issue in American politics. "The Democratic label is now the property of men and women who have . . . bent to the whispered pleas from the lips of traitors . . . men and women who wear the political label stitched with the idiocy of a Truman, rotted by the deceit of an Acheson, corrupted by the red slime of a [Harry Dexter] White," McCarthy proclaimed.[13] It made no difference that Truman had embarked upon Cold War "containment" of Soviet power and had commited American troops in Korea. As Richard Rovere has pointed out, McCarthy suggested that Truman's deployment of military force was in fact a "diversion from the struggle against the domestic conspiracy," a ploy to conceal through military grandstanding the extent of communist subversion in the federal government.[14] In any case, right-wing polemicists insisted, the liberals had once again demonstrated their "softness" by failing to prevent the triumph of the Chinese Communists in 1949.

McCarthyism was part of a postwar political catharsis that was comparable in some respects to the anti-reform backlashes of the 1870s and early 1920s. Once again, Republican as well as Democratic social reformers were on the defensive. In the era of FDR, Republicans had wavered between the ideological agenda of the Liberty League and the moderate-equivocal policies of presidential nominees like Alfred Landon, Wendell Willkie, and Thomas Dewey. Willkie and FDR — who actually agreed on most major policy issues by 1942 — discussed in the wartime interlude the possibility of a postwar party realignment that would pull both Republican and Democratic supporters of governmental stewardship into a unified party.[15] But Willkie and Roosevelt were both in their graves by the end of the war.

Concurrent with the onset of McCarthyism, conservative laissez-faire enjoyed another significant revival. The work of the Liberty League was taken up by a new cadre of conservative theorists and activists. If anything, the theorists of laissez-faire displayed a new audacity. Willmoore Kendall, a conservative scholar at Yale, was willing to delve into the Republican legacy of governmental activism preceding the New Deal and to condemn the activist governance of Lincoln as a form of "Caesarism."[16] One of Kendall's pupils, William F. Buckley, Jr., spoke for the new generation of laissez-faire conservatives by insisting that "the statist solution" to American social problems was "inadmissible." Only an implacable refusal to submit to any form of "collectivism" would "keep conservatives busy . . . and the nation free." Call it a No-Program, Buckley proclaimed, but

> I will not cede more power to the state. I will not willingly cede more power to anyone, not to the state, not to General Motors, not to the CIO. I will hoard my power like a miser, resisting every effort to drain it from me. I will then use *my* power as *I* see fit.[17]

In economics, Friederich von Hayek — later joined by Milton Friedman and a host of other laissez-faire economists — touched off a revival of classical èconomics that excoriated public-sector intervention. Hayek and Friedman insisted (for what it was worth) that they were latter-day classical liberals. Nonetheless, their writings were received as canonical texts by postwar "movement conservatives." Hayek's book — *The Road to Serfdom,* published in 1944 — argued that the nineteenth-century free-market creed was the most dependable antidote to fascist as well as to communist totalitarianism. The same message was presented in even more insistent terms by Ludwig von Mises, whose book *Bureaucracy* was also published in 1944. "The main issue in present-day political struggles," he said,

> is whether society should be organized on the basis of private ownership of the means of production (capitalism, the market system) or on the basis of public control of the means of production (socialism, communism, planned economy). . . . There is no compromise possible between these two systems. Contrary to a popular fallacy there is no middle way, no third system possible as a pattern of a permanent social order. The citizens must choose between capitalism and socialism or, as many Americans say, between the American and the Russian way of life.[18]

These crusaders for a purified free market dismissed what had happened between 1929 and 1933 with various rationalizations. But by the early 1950s it was no longer the record of Coolidge or Hoover that was on the firing line. It was the issue of whether liberals were "pink" and "soft on communism" that was forced to the center of American politics.

Notwithstanding the resurgence of laissez-faire, the Eisenhower administration proved to be moderate. Moreover, the economic boom of the 1950s was compatible with continued public works — many of them rationalized as a matter of "keeping up with the Russians" — and also with expanding national debt. The federal budget was in deficit most of the time in the 1950s.[19] Between 1945 and 1959 the national debt rose from $258.7 billion to $287.5 billion. But the gross national product soared from $213.4 billion in 1945 to $494.2 billion in 1959.[20] Much of this economic growth could be linked to the "multiplier effect" of federal spending — spending for defense, for research and development, for ongoing programs like the GI Bill, and for the Interstate Highway System, one of the greatest public works efforts in American history, created in the Eisenhower years. The highway program was funded through a package of deficit finance — bonds — and gasoline taxes.[21] Historian Stephen E. Ambrose has explained the program's motivation:

> The American people . . . had never seen so many cars; the problem
> was that the road system was woefully inadequate. . . . Except for the
> Pennsylvania Turnpike and a few other toll roads in the East, the
> country had no four-lane highways connecting the cities. . . . Ever
> since his cross-country trip by Army convoy in 1919, Eisenhower had
> been concerned about America's highways. . . . To him, it was an ideal
> program for the federal government to undertake. First, the need was
> clear and inescapable. Second, a unified system could only be erected
> by the federal government. Third, it was a public-works program on a
> massive scale, indeed the largest public-works program in history,
> which meant that the government could put millions of men to work
> without subjecting itself to the criticism that this was "make-work.". . .
> By tailoring expenditures for highways to the state of the economy,
> Eisenhower could use the program to flatten out the peaks and valleys
> in unemployment. . . . [B]y advocating a highway program on a gigan-
> tic scale, Eisenhower was putting himself and his Administration
> within the best and strongest tradition of nineteenth-century Ameri-
> can Whigs. John Quincy Adams, Henry Clay, and other great Whigs
> had all been advocates of internal improvements paid for by the fed-
> eral government. Eisenhower's highway program brought that tradi-
> tion up to date.[22]

Yet Eisenhower expressed mixed feelings with regard to other forms of public works. He fought the expansion of the TVA and he allegedly referred to the project (off-the-record) as "creeping socialism."[23] He

privately disparaged the motives of FDR's domestic policies and vilified the New Deal.[24] Republicans were deeply ambivalent regarding the
relationship of public works to "conservatism."

In 1964, Senator Jacob Javits tried to convince his fellow Republicans that governmental stewardship was far more characteristic of Republican Party traditions than laissez-faire. In his book *Order of Battle,*
he declared that

> history shows . . . that the clearest and most vital line of evolution in
> the Republican Party was the line whose great human links were
> Alexander Hamilton, a Federalist; Henry Clay, who revitalized the
> Federalist strain . . . and made it the basis of the newly formed Whig
> Party; Abraham Lincoln, a former Whig who . . . became a founder of
> the new Republican Party; and Theodore Roosevelt. . . . This is the
> spirit which has represented the most dominant strain in Republican
> history.[25]

Javits said that he acknowledged his own reputation as a "liberal Republican" with reluctance. He deplored the "web of confusion which
has entrapped many thoughtful Republicans and Democrats about the
meaning of the words 'liberalism' and 'conservatism,'" adding that a
"gain in the conduct of our political debates" would occur "if we dealt,
rather than by such designations, with concrete proposals on a case-
by-case basis," in light of three pragmatic tests:

> Will the specific terms of this concrete proposal enlarge the area of
> freedom and opportunity for the individual while serving the com-
> mon good? Given the aim of this concrete proposal, is it beyond the
> reach of private resources, and, therefore, must it be made a govern-
> mental matter? If a governmental matter, is it beyond the reach of
> local and state resources, and must it, therefore, be entrusted to the
> central government?[26]

While Javits accepted the "liberal" label with fatalistic misgivings,
a few attempts were made in the postwar period to save the idea of

governmental stewardship as an explicitly conservative proposition. Peter Viereck eloquently pleaded the cause of "the great conservative social reformers, from the 7th Earl of Shaftesbury through Disraeli, as well as the necessary New Deal reforms of our own great Squire of Hyde Park."[27] He pleaded for "the *conservation* not of economic greed and privilege but of the value-heritage for which America rightly entered World War II." He tried to convince conservatives that New Deal policies were grounded to a far more significant extent in Churchillian noblesse oblige than in "creeping socialism." But Viereck reluctantly concluded by the 1960s that a "smug reactionary misuse of conservatism" had triumphed to an "appalling extent" in the United States.[28]

It is safe to generalize that most American conservatives did not regard Viereck as their intellectual hero in the fifties and sixties. Their hero was Russell Kirk, who argued in his book *The Conservative Mind* that Hamiltonian political principles were "almost naive." In his search for a "true conservatism," Kirk condemned the "unitary state" and looked wistfully back upon the "nullification" politics of John C. Calhoun. In the course of praising John Adams, Kirk declared that progress can only result from "the snail-slow influence of historical example and just constitutions rather than from deliberate legislation."[29]

The fight between laissez-faire conservatives, moderates, and progressives or "liberals" for control of the Republican Party extended into a decades-long contention. "Liberal Republicans" like Javits and John Lindsay were important figures in the party throughout the 1960s, but the ideological direction in which Republican politics relentlessly flowed from the 1950s through the 1980s was symbolized by the catcalls hurled at Nelson Rockefeller in San Francisco when Barry Goldwater captured the Republican nomination in 1964. Rockefeller in many ways epitomized the spirit of noblesse oblige in the early sixties. As such, he served as a perfect target for the laissez-faire right to jeer at, a target symbolizing everything Joe McCarthy had scorned when he spoke of patricians born with silver spoons in their mouths, patricians who would willingly deliver their country into the shackles of Soviet commissars by drugging the American people with "collectivization."

Goldwater's defeat in 1964 was just a temporary setback to laissez-faire conservative hegemony in Republican politics. From the ashes of the Goldwater movement arose the phoenix of what some commentators have called the conservative "Counter-Establishment" — the movement that established conservative libertarian "think tanks" in the 1970s, that captured the White House in 1980, and that remains a tremendously potent force in American politics. With a few significant exceptions relating to defense, to criminal justice, and to the goals of the religious right, it is a movement that defines conservatism as a "pure free market" creed. This is the movement that came to power with Reagan in 1980, the movement to "de-regulate" American life, to entrust the conservation of public lands to a character like James Watt, to entrust the fight against pollution to a person like Anne Burford, and to justify minimal governance through legal theories like the doctrines of Edwin Meese, who cited the "original intent" of the Founding Fathers as the basis for eviscerating government — the Founding Fathers who had argued so bitterly among themselves in the 1790s regarding the choice between "strict" versus "broad" interpretation of the newly-ratified Constitution.

· I I ·

EVEN THOUGH SCOUNDRELS LIKE MCCARTHY eventually exploited and distorted the situation, the fact remains that certain New Deal liberals *did* display an indulgent attitude toward the Soviet Union. By the same token, liberals in Jefferson's day were inclined to view revolutionary France with optimistic indulgence. This did not mean that every New Dealer was a latent or secret "fellow traveler," as McCarthy alleged with such malice. FDR and his cabinet denounced the communist system repeatedly. Roosevelt proclaimed in

1936 that "I have not sought, I do not seek, and I repudiate the support of any advocate of Communism."[30] His secretary of the interior, Harold Ickes, stated that "Fascism and Communism are equally abhorrent to us. Both are tyrannies. Both should be resisted with all our strength."[31] His secretary of labor, Frances Perkins, averred that "Communism, in my opinion, has no place in American life."[32]

And yet a definite susceptibility in liberal culture prompted scores of American liberals to "go easy" on the issue of Stalinist oppression in the 1930s. And this susceptibility has proven to be a perennial problem. When liberals are forced to react to aggressive or even totalitarian behavior by people who claim to represent the downtrodden, their instincts are often undependable. Many people who call themselves liberals seem temperamentally inclined to look for the best in revolutionary-radical movements and avoid (as long as they can) acknowledging the worst. Why should this be so? Has it something to do with a liberal blind spot regarding the ugly side of human nature?

It is not quite so simple. Liberals seldom deny the obvious presence of evil in human affairs. Even Jefferson, while serenely optimistic in some respects, preached a doctrine of eternal vigilance against resurgent tyranny. Every liberal who has ever wished Godspeed to revolutionary freedom-fighters was surely urging them on to do battle *against* something — against tyranny of one sort or another. But liberalism will not easily embrace the traditional conservative belief that the ugly side of human nature can assert itself in virtually anyone. The persistent unwillingness of many liberals to accept this principle has a great deal to do with the current widespread rejection of liberal values in American politics.

It is human nature to invest a certain amount of faith in particular heroes. But those who have absorbed the more wary conservative beliefs about human nature are less inclined to be stunned or confused if their heroes go wrong. Consider the following examples. John Adams was deeply conservative when he explained his skepticism regarding human nature by citing the *universal* proclivity for self-deceit in the human mind, the tendency of people to talk themselves into doing whatever is most expedient, all the while viewing their acts as unimpeachable deeds of valor. "Power always thinks it has a great Soul," Adams once wrote to Jefferson in their old age,

> and vast Views, beyond the Comprehension of the Weak; and that it is doing God Service, when it is violating all his Laws. Our Passions, Ambition, Avarice, Love, Resentment etc. possess so much metaphysical Subtilty and so much overpowering Eloquence, that they insinuate themselves into the Understanding and the Conscience and convert both to their Party.[33]

It was quintessentially conservative of Edmund Burke to regard the presence of evil as a free-flowing potentiality that could insinuate itself into any political or social relations, and usually in the most surprising way:

> Seldom have two ages the same fashion in their pretexts and the same modes of mischief. Wickedness is a little more inventive. Whilst you are discussing fashion, the fashion is gone by. The very same vice assumes a new body. The spirit transmigrates; and, far from losing its principle of life by the change of its appearance, it is renovated in its new organs with the fresh vigour of a juvenile activity. It walks abroad; it continues its ravages; whilst you are gibbeting the carcass, or demolishing the tomb. You are terrifying yourself with ghosts and apparitions, whilst your house is the haunt of robbers. It is thus with all those, who attending only to the shell and husk of history, think they are waging war with intolerance, pride, and cruelty, whilst, under colour of abhorring the ill principles of antiquated parties, they are authorizing and feeding the same odious vices in different factions, and perhaps in worse.[34]

Conservatism in this sense — in contrast to so many of the shallow dogmas that pass for "conservatism" today — is willing to adapt its methods of governance to respond to any new and unpredictable chal-

lenges to civilization. For this reason Burke proclaimed that "I repro-
bate no form of government merely upon abstract principles."[35]

Whereas this older brand of conservatism — even with its upper-
class biases — was inclined at its best to stand guard against tyranny
from *any* direction, liberalism has regarded the problem of evil in a
different way. Liberals have tended to hope that the sources of evil can
be localized and then progressively diminished through time. Millenial
dreams remain alive within the liberal tradition. On the liberals' hori-
zon is a long-abiding vision of humanity and history redeemed: a fated
alliance of liberal theorists and democratic masses that will usher in a
great epoch of decency. Not content with mere *progress* in liberty — for
progress is fragile and can be reversed — the liberal mind has repeatedly dallied with the notion of sweeping the historical process around
an irreversible corner beyond which the forces of tyranny will permanently recede. Liberal theorists have faithfully striven to provide the
oppressed peoples of the world with a dependable formula (or formu-
lae) to achieve this transformation.

The millennial side of the liberal spirit was apparent in 1776 when
Thomas Paine stated that "we have it in our power to begin the world
over again" through social reforms.[36] It was apparent in the aftermath
of World War I as Woodrow Wilson crusaded for his League of Nations
by envisioning a permanent redemption of history through a global
act of reform:

> The stage is set, the destiny disclosed. It has come about by no plan of
> our conceiving, but by the hand of God who led us into this way. We
> cannot turn back. We can only go forward, with lifted eyes and fresh-
> ened spirit, to follow the vision. . . . America shall in truth show the
> way. The light streams upon the path ahead, and nowhere else.

And then:

> Nothing less depends upon us, nothing less than the liberation and

salvation of the world. . . . We have accepted that truth and. . . it is going to lead us, and through us, the world, out into pastures of quietness and peace such as the world never dreamed of before.[37]

Compare this vision to the world-view of Theodore Roosevelt, who had argued that reform is always a temporary business of adaptation since "every new social relation begets a new type of wrong-doing." Compare it to the world-view of Lincoln, whose liberal affinities — so apparent when he called America "the last best hope of earth" — were balanced by his tough and conservative admonitions that the ugly side of human nature will eternally challenge civilization. No such caveats as these encumbered the vision of Woodrow Wilson: the light shone upon the pastures of quietness and peace that were promised if humanity reformed.

In World War II, millennial wishes again characterized the spirit with which many liberals went to war. A moving example may be found in the words of an American soldier named Clarence Weinstock, who wrote from a military hospital the following message to his countrymen:

> Today we fight a great just war of liberation. We do not idealize conquest like the Nazi historians and Prussian officer-landowners. We do not cry, "War is beautiful," like the Fascist poet, Marinetti. . . . No, we did not pant for war like our enemies; but now we thirst for victory. The destroyers must be destroyed. The killers of Guernica, Lidice, Nanking, Pearl Harbor, the torturers of Russian farmers have to be erased from our human world. Our hate will only burn out when it has dealt with them all, the "Leaders," the "Dukes," the Gauleiters, and the Squadristi, the Iron Guards and the Samurai.[38]

The destroyers have to be erased from our human world. How interesting to toy with this vision: the vision of sweeping every torturer, rapist, and assassin in the world to some gloriously rectifying purgatory — sweeping them off the face of the earth with such finality that no others would ever take their places. Wise conservatives know that there will *always* be others to take their places. Liberals tend — not always, but often enough — to indulge the hope that somehow the children of light will get the upper hand in a way that is permanent and guaranteed. This is perhaps the most important reason why liberals seem to be instinctively inclined to "emphasize the positive" in dealing with self-proclaimed liberation movements on behalf of the downtrodden. It was so in the age of Jefferson and Paine with regard to the French Revolution. It was so in the first few decades of the Russian Revolution as well.

Significant numbers of American liberals were naively optimistic regarding the potential of the Soviet Union between the world wars. An exemplar of this trend was the "muckraker" Lincoln Steffens, whose *Autobiography* (1931) suggested that his fellow liberals acknowledge the sincerity and vision of the Communists, whom Steffens viewed as the egalitarian vanguard of social justice. By 1934 his views were more extreme; he told a correspondent that

> As a liberal bourgeois I have come to see not only that the Communist
> Party is the only organisation in existence that really wants to deal
> with our situation in *all* its phases, but I see also, as few liberals do,
> that the workers and peasants, the dispossessed . . . must lead, control,
> and carry through this program. . . . We liberals must not have power,
> not ever. . . . The liberals, all privileged persons, and all the associates
> of the privileged, belong in the second line, — when their eyes are
> opened. . . . [W]e, who have fitted successfully into the old culture, are
> to the very degree of our education and adjustment, — we are cor-
> rupted and unfit for, — the kingdom of heaven.[39]

With regard to the totalitarian price of admission to this alleged kingdom of heaven, Steffens informed the *New Republic*'s editor that he was "not interested in muckraking Russia," since mistakes were "inevitable in the early stages of a planned evolution."[40] Wishful thinking such as this was even more seductive after Stalin's creation in 1935 of the "Popular Front" — a supposed cooperative alliance of all "progressive" forces in the world against the threat of fascism. As late as the "Progressive" presidential candidacy of Henry Wallace in 1948, certain liberals remained susceptible to this kind of naiveté regarding Stalinist evil.

But increasingly by the late 1930s and early 1940s, American liberals started reacting to the ugly news of the Moscow purge trials, the joint Nazi-Soviet invasion of Poland, and the Soviet invasion of Finland. After World War II the Soviets' totalitarian repression in Poland, Hungary, and Czechoslovakia made it clear that American liberal hopes about Russia had been misplaced to a spectacular extent. The "morning after" in the 1940s and 1950s was a miserable affair. An authentic contrition infused many postwar liberal denunciations of the Soviet system. The cries of postwar liberal anti-communism were more than just defensive maneuvers to ward off McCarthy. They were cries of outraged idealism from people who were genuinely sickened by the revelations of Stalinist mass-murder and forced labor and police-state terror. They were the cries of people who received the message of Orwell's *Animal Farm* and Koestler's *Darkness at Noon*.

Out of the McCarthy era came the reinvigorated figure of the Cold War liberal, purged of any earlier illusions about the Soviet Union and eager for redemption by *competing* with the communist left for the hearts and minds of the downtrodden. Out of the 1940s emerged the Americans for Democratic Action, the foremost organization to offer Americans a vigorously liberal version of anti-communism. Representative of this movement was Arthur Schlesinger, Jr.'s *The Vital Center*, published in 1949 with the following subtitle: *Our Purposes and Perils on the Tightrope of American Liberalism.* "Today, finally and tardily, the skeptical insights are in process of restoration to the liberal mind," Schlesinger said.[41] He declared that liberals should learn from their errors and return to the fight for social decency: "Can we win the fight? We must commit ourselves to it with all our vigor in all its dimensions: the struggle within the world against Communism and fascism; the struggle within our country against oppression and stagnation."[42]

Schlesinger called upon liberals to toughen themselves in innumerable ways. He endorsed the "neo-orthodox" teachings of theologian Reinhold Niebuhr, who was urging reformers to restrain utopian
expectations and reform society in a "realistic" spirit cognizant of the
tragic and ironic limitations of the human condition. Niebuhr warned
of the dangerous results that can occur when our idealism leads us to
"try to play the role of God to history."[43] Accordingly, much of the Cold
War liberal movement adopted a self-consciously pragmatic and managerial tone that seemed to preclude millennial expectations. Walt W.
Rostow's *The Stages of Economic Growth, A Non-Communist Manifesto*,
presented a Cold War agenda in 1960 that was striking in its tone of
steady matter-of-factness:

> The fact is that Communism as a technique of power is a formidable
> force. Although it was an un-Marxist insight, it was a correct insight of
> Lenin's that power could, under certain circumstances, be seized and
> held by a purposeful minority prepared to use a secret police. Al-
> though it was an un-Marxist insight, it was a correct insight that soci-
> eties in the transition from traditional to modern status are peculiarly
> vulnerable to such a seizure of power. . . . For those who would prefer
> to see the aspiring societies of the world not follow this particular road
> to modernization . . . the Communist technique for mobilizing power
> and resources poses a formidable problem, almost certainly what
> historians will judge the central challenge of our time; that is, the
> challenge of creating, in association with the non-communist politi-
> cians and peoples of . . . a partnership which will see them through
> into sustained growth on a political and social basis which keeps open
> the possibilities of progressive, democratic development.[44]

But for all of the attempts to keep the Cold War liberal ethos dispas-
sionate, skeptical, and "cool," certain liberals were discontented with
this Cold War reform agenda and yearned for an openly compassionate, emotive politics. Such liberals in the 1950s viewed rising politicians
like John F. Kennedy as self-absorbed and opportunistic "centrists."

Regardless, nothing could suppress the thrill of many liberal Americans when Kennedy delivered his inaugural address and let the word go forth about the gallantry of this new generation of Americans. Moreover, as Kennedy's term began, the twentieth-century civil rights movement was approaching its years of triumph. The synergism established in the early 1960s between this non-violent grassroots movement for social justice — for the liberation of the downtrodden — and the renaissance of interventionist governance in Washington, D.C., recalled the Lincoln era, which was just falling due for a lavish commemoration in the Civil War Centennial. Step by step, John and Robert Kennedy responded to the civil rights activists with Justice Department protection, with draft civil rights legislation, and with preliminary plans for a war on poverty. To the Lincoln Memorial came Martin Luther King, Jr. and the civil rights marchers in 1963. And in 1963 the young president was suddenly taken away.

Lyndon Baines Johnson pledged himself to complete the Kennedy agenda — and the New Deal agenda as well. He promised to commence the war on poverty and spoke in Rooseveltian terms on behalf of the ill-clad, the ill-housed, the ill-nourished. He buried the laissez-faire conservatives in 1964 beneath what was then the greatest electoral landslide in presidential politics. He continued the practice of dispatching federal marshals and troops to protect civil rights workers from the Klan and the lynch mob element. Like Kennedy, he promised to deter all predatory aggression from totalitarian sources. He invoked the lessons of World War II: aggression would never again be allowed to get out of control. By the same token that he sent the troops to Mississippi and Alabama to safeguard freedom, Johnson sent the troops to Asia. In 1965 he escalated the war in Vietnam, and while non-interventionist liberals — the "doves," as they were soon to be called — had very different views in this matter, their hour had not yet arrived. The moment belonged to liberals like Hubert H. Humphrey, who proclaimed in 1964 that liberalism becomes a mockery when it is spineless and cowardly. No slogans, no long-range policies offering economic and social progress can defeat the threat of immediate, naked force. . . . We should have learned from our internal struggles against Communist penetration (and we had a sharp and severe political battle with the Communist Party during my own early years in Minnesota politics) that Communist determination is strong. We should have learned from our efforts to stem Communist subversion in Latin America, the Middle East, Africa, and Southeast Asia that the enemy is ingenious . . . and that he will utilize every political, economic, and military weapon at his command.[45]

Humphrey hastened to add that interventionist foreign policies did not preclude liberal ideals for social justice. To the contrary,

military force *alone* is relatively helpless against a determined and intelligent exploitation of a people's despair and hopelessness. The shield of military defense — while it may stave off disaster for a time — must be used to support a program of genuine progress and re-form. . . . The whole concept of U.S. military aid to prevent a nation from "going Communist" founders when not accompanied by at least an equal effort in the political, economic, and social areas.[46]

By 1965 interventionist Cold War liberalism stood redeemed in the minds of its leaders. The lessons of FDR were once again applied, both at home and abroad. Continuity was re-established. The years of McCarthyism and right-wing persecution — the years in the wilderness that perhaps amounted to a time of penance for a dalliance with false gods — were definitely over. Liberalism would prove itself clean of any Marxist associations by challenging communism directly for the loyalty of the oppressed peoples of the world. America had promises to keep to the memories of Kennedy and Roosevelt. The Hamiltonian state was now fully at the service of triumphant democratic America.

·III·

I T ALL FELL APART FOR THE LIBERALS, of course, and except for the brief interregnum of Jimmy Carter they found themselves effectively barred from the White House until the problematical era of Bill Clinton. Vietnam was the cause of the disaster, and everyone has come to the obvious conclusion that the war involved grievous mistakes. Historians will doubtless revise their interpretations of Vietnam for a long time. Regardless of what we may think about that particular episode in American intervention overseas, it is the *effects* of the Vietnam War, and the protest movement against it, that twisted the American liberal outlook into its current — and perverse — configuration.

The unexpected duration of the war short-circuited Johnson's attempt to fight a war on poverty. But this was hardly the only damage that liberalism sustained. The worst effect of the war was to place American liberals again on the moral firing line: not as targets for right-wing inquisitors (though a right-wing backlash would start soon enough) but as targets for a left-of-center coalition speaking the liberals' own language, a coalition that accused the Cold War liberals of betraying humane ideals.

Some of the accusations came from the Marxist left — and these accusations, to a certain extent, could be taken in stride. After all, the Cold War liberals had gone to great lengths to dissociate themselves from the radical left in the 1950s and 1960s. The Vietnam War was very clearly an anti-communist war. Indeed, Cold War liberals had frequently challenged and even taunted left-of-center radicals to wash the blood of Stalinism from their hands. The emergent "New Left" in the fifties and sixties had been trying to do that by renouncing "elitist statism" in favor of decentralized or even neo-anarchistic forms of radical politics. The Vietnam War gave the radical left a delicious opportunity to get even with the liberals — to claim that they had now caught the liberals with blood on *their* hands.

If the protest movement had encompassed nothing more than the voices of Marxists, its effect upon the liberal mind would not have been very consequential. But the chorus of protest arising from the Marxist left was swelled by the wounded voices of a truly liberal constituency: the young idealists who had joined with the Kennedy and Johnson administrations in direct nonviolent action on behalf of the oppressed. They had risked their lives in Mississippi, Alabama, and Georgia to defy the Klan, they had marched to the choruses of "We Shall Overcome," and they now turned out to bear witness against the Cold War liberals' "aggression" in Vietnam. College students who a few years earlier might have done a stint in Kennedy's Peace Corps were now drifting off to Haight-Ashbury to "drop out," to repudiate the bureaucratic and death-dealing ways of "the system": the *liberals'* system. Others remained politicized: they became anti-war "doves." To the Pentagon they came in 1967 — some placed flowers in the guns of the Pentagon's military police — and Robert S. McNamara looked desolately out at them. To Chicago they came in 1968, to replace Johnson's designated heir, Vice President Hubert Humphrey, with Senator Eugene McCarthy, a *noninterventionist* liberal who questioned the Vietnam War. As Chicago police beat the protesters savagely, Humphrey, though appalled by the violence, was denounced as a cynical, immoral accomplice. All the while the televised news coverage from Vietnam portrayed the war as a nearly unintelligible struggle that was devastating the population without making real inroads against the enemy.

The intermittent riots in America's black inner cities, together with the rise of inner-city militants such as the Black Panthers, dealt a final demoralizing blow to the liberals' dreams of a "Great Society." And the assassinations in 1968 of Robert Kennedy and Martin Luther King, Jr. deepened the sense of despair and chaos among the alienated.

More and more the New Left began to take over the "peace movement." Converts were told that the movement would not succeed unless it produced a revolutionary struggle to overturn capitalism. The most extreme New Left polemicists accused the liberals of "genocide" and "imperialism." New Left historians explained that the liberal tradition was nothing more than a front for an aggressively managerial elite. Gabriel Kolko, for instance, concluded in 1969 that "a coercive elite, quite willing to undermine democracy at home as well as abroad, will rule the society, even in the name of 'liberalism.'"[47] There was nothing left to do, said many campus radicals, but take to the streets and confront the liberal "establishment" — confront "the pigs" — with the massed revolutionary violence of "the people."

But the people who comprised the American electorate were not amused, and in 1968 they put the Republicans back in power with a general mandate for "law and order." The administration of Richard Nixon toned down the conservative laissez-faire agenda in favor of the genuinely primal — indeed the primeval — conservative mission: the counter-revolutionary mission. For this reason the Republican ascendancy in Nixon's administration was inclined to flaunt the power of the state and to gird itself in all the institutional panoply of national security.

It does bear noting that while Nixon at times chose to verbalize the right wing's resentment of "bureaucratic Washington" — he condemned "the patronizing idea that government in Washington, D.C. is inevitably more wise, more honest, and more efficient than government at the local or State level" — he nonetheless displayed a penchant for regulatory governance.[48] He experimented with wage-price controls, for example, and proclaimed himself a Keynesian. He endorsed the overall aims of the environmental protection movement and established an exemplary record that included the creation of the Environmental Protection Agency. In 1971 he told journalist Nancy Dickerson that after the Vietnam War he hoped to "get this country thinking of clean air, clean water, open spaces."[49] The year before he had told Congress that "clean air is not free," that Americans' "carelessness" had "incurred a debt to nature," and that the "program I shall propose . . . will be the most comprehensive and costly program in this field in America's history."[50] In the same message he declared that government should care for the built environment as well as for the natural landscape. "The Federal government must be in a position to assist in the building of new cities and the rebuilding of old ones."[51] He spoke of reforming America's health-care system, recommending "a program to insure that no American family will be prevented from obtaining basic medical care by inability to pay." He asked Congress for $100 million "to launch an intensive campaign to find a cure for cancer," adding that "the time has come . . . when the same kind of concentrated effort that split the atom and took man to the moon should be turned toward conquering this dread disease."[52]

On the other hand, he qualified these proposals for federal stewardship with plans to transfer some federal power to the states through revenue-sharing.[53] In any event, conservative revision of "the welfare state" could be resumed in due time. The immediate concern of the right in the Nixon years was to get the unpatriotic "bums," as Nixon described them, under control. And so the wrath of Nixon, of Spiro Agnew, of John Mitchell and the others was duly unleashed against the radical left.

Within the Democratic Party, and in liberal America generally, the world appeared like one of those demented fifteenth-century depictions of hell by the painter Hieronymous Bosch. Everything had gone wrong, horridly wrong. The liberals had been chased once again from power, and perhaps, the anti-war Democrats concluded, the liberals *deserved* to be kept from power until they could put their moral house back in order. In the aftermath of the 1968 Democratic convention, Senator Eugene McCarthy consoled his youthful supporters by telling them they were "the government of the people in exile."[54] Allard Lowenstein, the anti-war activist who had started the "dump Johnson" movement in 1967, urged the "doves" to continue their efforts to wrest control of the Democratic Party from liberal "hawks."[55] The Vietnam

War had supposedly revealed an "arrogance of power" in the Cold War liberals, an arrogance that tainted the pretensions of the liberal cause, and the Cold War liberals would therefore have to step aside — the outrages of the Chicago convention in 1968 would have to be atoned for — before Nixon and the Republicans could be taken on.

There were lessons to be learned from grass-roots protest, declared the liberal "doves" — lessons to be learned from more radical spokesmen for the downtrodden. Perhaps the words of the prophets were written on the subway walls, as the rock musicians said. If so, a more "sensitive" and non-interventionist liberalism was the only sort of liberalism worthy of taking on Nixon in 1972.

So it was that George McGovern was sent to his political doom in that year, after he had thanked the Democratic convention for its "people's nomination" and proclaimed that "American politics will never be the same again."[56] And so it was that Nixon met his own political doom as his police-and-security theme crossed the border into paranoia and triggered the Watergate crimes.

The Democrats were back (briefly) in power by 1976, and the gospel of George McGovern ("Come Home, America") seemed to resonate in the sweet-natured promises of Jimmy Carter: the promises that America would now have a government "as good as its people." America was chastened, but America was also rescued, Carter declared. The arrogance of foreign intervention in Vietnam and the arrogance of Nixon's "imperial presidency" at home were now to be cleansed by the healing waters of a neo-Jeffersonian sincerity and non-interventionism. In dozens of ways that are now generally forgotten, Carter initiated policies of de-regulation — in this case a 1970s throwback to the culture of classical liberal laissez-faire — well before the Reagan Revolution of 1980. "Government cannot solve our problems," said Carter in 1978. "Government cannot . . . provide a bountiful economy, or reduce inflation or save our cities."[57] There was little rededication to the dream of a new frontier or a great society in the Carter years. The Carter message was an ersatz ecological message, a deferential attempt to respond to the peace movement's old slogan: "Power to the People." It was an admonition to live simply, to love goodness, to serve as a mediatory influence for good in the world, and to recognize one's limitations. "Your strength can compensate for my weakness," Carter told the American people in his inaugural address, "and your wisdom can help to minimize my mistakes."[58]

The Carter appeal was short-lived, to put it mildly. All too rapidly his leadership appeared to be vacillating and incompetent. His message grew stale and almost befuddled. Meanwhile, all the pent-up anger the American people had experienced in over a decade's worth of bitterness, turmoil, and disillusionment continued to seethe in the popular culture. A trendy nihilism, a taste for grotesquerie and sleaze, infected the American mind in the 1970s — and continues to infect it today. Liberal culture was at loose ends. Its social conscience was spellbound by the memory of Vietnam and the protest riots of the 1960s. Its political message was confused. It was plagued by radical hangers-on like defense attorney William Kunstler who never tired of excusing the anti-social acts that his clients committed by blaming society as a whole for its "repression." If the "post-Vietnam syndrome" created a crisis of national confidence for many Americans, it created a crisis of neurotic guilt for American liberals. The wise and sophisticated humor of observers like Jules Feiffer would acknowledge this crisis through the medium of friendly satire. Even so, the problem of liberal guilt was no longer a laughing matter by the late 1970s.

In countless ways — anxious and humorless ways — liberals were striving for absolution, striving to prove that American liberal culture was *clean* of any guilt for Vietnam: *clean* of any "complicity" with "repression." The moral compass of the liberal world had swung a hundred and eighty degrees. In the 1950s chastened Cold War liberals had fended off right-wing attacks by repudiating communists and radicals. By the 1970s chastened post-Vietnam liberals — concluding that anti-communism had gone too far — reversed course, and proceeded to stave off *left*-wing attacks by indulging radical demands. In foreign policy, they projected an attitude of temperamental non-interventionism. On the issue of race, they responded to the demagoguery of radicals by abandoning the unifying civil rights ethic of the Kennedy-Johnson era — the ethic of "color-blind" nondiscrimination and de-emphasis regarding the physical appearance of our fellow Americans — in favor of well-intentioned but deeply divisive policies emphasizing race at every opportunity.

In matters pertaining to civil liberties, many liberals supported — actively or tacitly — a new libertarian "anti-elitist" extremism. Some of them condoned the round-the-clock presence of gigantic and hideous protest billboards on the sidewalk in front of the White House during the late 1970s. Some of them protected the "right" of the mentally ill to resist attempts to remove them for their own safety from sidewalks on icy winter evenings. And some of them defended the "right" of avant-garde artists to receive federal funding for projects resulting in images like "Piss Christ," a depiction of a crucifix floating in a jar of urine.

And on issues pertaining to crime, the liberals' growing reputation for knee-jerk leniency hovered between the lines of countless newspaper stories of murders and rapes committed by criminals released on parole or by violent psychotics released from psychiatric prisons after being declared "rehabilitated."

It finally became too much for the American electorate. It was only a matter of time before the liberals' post-Vietnam guilt would be exploited by foreign aggressors. It was only a matter of time before the Iranian hostage episode, the sad (never angry) and muted response by Carter, the failed rescue attempt, and finally the groveling entreaties by Ramsey Clark — with his praise of Khomeini's revolution as a "miracle" of Third World self-liberation — caused the patience of America to snap, and to snap decisively. Ronald Reagan and the laissez-faire "movement conservatives" romped their way to power in 1980. And to the camp of the laissez-faire conservatives poured a steady stream of "neo-conservatives," embittered defectors from left-of-center politics unable to stomach all the liberal self-flagellation any longer.

The liberals were back in exile. Some of them attempted to revive the spirit of conservative-liberal synthesis. Charles Peters, for example, in his 1982 "Neo-Liberal Manifesto," admitted the validity of certain conservative opinions while suggesting that conservatives return the favor by admitting the genuine work-ethic value of work-creation programs like the WPA. And yet in order to accommodate the moods of the Reagan era, Peters also cautioned his readers that he and his fellow "Neo-Liberals" — people such as Gary Hart and Paul Tsongas — "no longer automatically favor . . . big government"; indeed, "our hero is the risk-taking enterpreneur."[59] Whatever the merits of this manifesto, it did very little to counteract the sweeping assertion of Ronald Reagan that "government is the problem" in American life.

Reagan's soothing personality brought a country club nonchalance — a posh veneer of charm and self-satisfaction — to the surface of American culture while just below that surface all manner of social and economic sicknesses continued to fester. Bank de-regulation (a process initiated by Carter) led directly to the savings-and-loan debacle. The deterioration of America's public infrastructure proceeded apace. The purchasing power of middle-class families declined with each passing year, while the wealthy got extraordinary tax breaks. Republican "supply-side economics" presumed that the Keynesian emphasis on consumer purchasing power (the "demand side") became unnecessary if policies of tax-relief for the wealthy unleashed a new wave of capital investment and production (the "supply side"). Presumably, the market system would ensure that the decisions of investors would benefit everyone.

A study making use of Congressional Budget Office data contends that the top one percent of America's families increased their annual income (after taxes) during the 1980s by 122 percent — from an average of $203,000 per year in 1977 to $451,000 per year in 1988. The top 5 percent of America's richest families increased their income by 60 per cent in the same period.[60] But according to the 1991 *Green Book* published by the House Ways and Means Committee, the median net worth of all other American families, as measured in monthly household income, *fell* in the 1980s. This was true of every income-group except the families in the uppermost 20 percent of American society.[61] Moreover, as Kevin Phillips has shown, "the uncertainty and unreliability of employment" itself became a major middle-class issue in the Reagan years; "a 1988 poll found 'job security' reemerging as employees' number one concern. . . . Corporate chairmen and presidents as a class feasted in the 1980s, but the number of mid-level management jobs lost during those years was estimated to be as high as 1.5 million."[62] In part due to corporate downsizing, with a shift to part-time employees, the percentage of American workers covered by unemployment compensation fell from 76 percent in 1975 to 37 percent by 1990.[63] By the end of the 1980s thousands — perhaps millions — of middle-class families were barely hanging on as the wealth was redistributed upward. As Phillips has elaborated,

> the 1983–89 boom itself was far from uniform. . . . As the Dow-Jones industrial average soared between 1980 and 1986, the value of U.S. farmland simultaneously dropped from $712 billion to $392 billion as collapsing commodity prices put more farmers out of business. Corporate chief executives' compensation set new records as workers' real hourly wages declined. Young workers watched their inflation-adjusted wages and net worth fall behind what their fathers had at a similar age. And while financial assets like stocks and bonds were surging, the value of family homes in roughly half of the nation's metropolitan areas shrank. . . . The new conservatism . . . began as a move to limit big government, but by the late 1980s had revealed a less popular aspect: a developing inattentiveness to public-sector func-

tions, economic fairness and jobs. . . . [W]hile speculators and corporate raiders took home huge sums, the average American family
wound up fearing for the safety of its bank accounts, insurance coverage, home values and pension coverage.[64]

Voters put up with these results in part because there appeared to
be no alternative; the foibles of contemporary liberal culture had become unbearable. The world remained a dangerous place — and as
Republicans took credit for creating conditions that allegedly "forced"
Mikhail Gorbachev to de-escalate the Cold War, they asked Americans
to consider how Jimmy Carter would have played his cards with the
Soviet Union (notwithstanding his efforts to put the Soviets on the
defensive for their invasion of Afghanistan) in a second term. Republican leaders provided the voters with confident rhetoric, the illusion of
middle-class tax relief, a major military build-up, and a few successful
applications of military force abroad. And Republican leaders provided
them with one thing more: in part to rub salt in the liberals' wounds,
and in part to make amends — perverse amends — for the moral abdication of their economic dogmas, they indulged the religious right in
its abrasive fundamentalist agenda for moral uplift.

What did the Democrats offer in response to all this? They offered the foredoomed presidential candidacies of Walter Mondale and
Michael Dukakis.

As America lurched into the 1990s, both the post-Vietnam liberals and the laissez-faire conservatives were incapable of dealing with
the rot that was eating away at our strength as a nation. A brief attempt
had been made by the columnist George F. Will to balance his critique
of liberal culture by reviving the stewardship tradition of conservative
noblesse oblige. "If conservatism is to engage itself with the way we live
now," Will stated in the New Republic of May 9, 1983, "it must address
government's graver purposes with an affirmative doctrine of the welfare state," and with "a wholesome ethic of common provision" to promote "social cohesion."[65] The effect of this article was nil — and subse-

quent attempts by Will to write constructive essays on the benefits of public works were effectively ruined by his constant denigrations of "liberal statism" and the "nanny state."

Conservatives proceeded to regale themselves with the naiveté of the liberals. But at the same time they reveled in their own Pollyanna rhetoric — "It's morning in America" — with regard to the blessings of deregulated enterprise.

Among the pundits, in academia, and in all of the leading right-of-center public policy circles, the tenets of conservative laissez-faire doctrine were guarded by an interlocking network of laissez-faire foundations, laissez-faire institutes, and laissez-faire journals that stamped out heresy before it could spread. And the liberals? They remained in the wilderness talking to themselves — locked in their search for a formula, some kind of moral formula, some kind of soothing and politically correct position that would finally take all the guilt away and make sense of the past quarter century.

Chapter Five

☆ ☆ ☆

The Ambiguous Age of Clinton

THE LINCOLN-AND-ROOSEVELT ACHIEVEMENT was nearly in ruins by the 1980s. After Vietnam, Watergate, and the blunderings of Jimmy Carter, American confidence in government plummeted. A trendy libertarianism spread over the political spectrum. By the middle of the 1970s it became the mode to prove one's "neo-populist" credentials by decrying the evils of "bureaucracy." The only president to capture and retain a high level of popularity after Watergate — Reagan — used all of his charisma to weaken the reputation of government even further. As often as not, the constituencies that continued to seek governmental activism sought to use government to promulgate divisive agendas — agendas like affirmative action on the left and the crusade against abortion on the right — that increased the general public's aversion to governmental action.

Reagan seized every opportunity to praise deregulation. Concurrently, conservative laissez-faire think tanks such as the Heritage Foundation and the Cato Institute emerged by the 1980s. The Cato Institute sought to rally libertarians of all persuasions, and its efforts paid off: officials of the American Civil Liberties Union expressed admiration for the minimal-government doctrines of the institute before long.[1] Free marketeers and crusaders for carte blanche property rights gained greater hegemony than ever within the Republican Party and in right-

of-center intellectual circles. Even the traditional conservative emphasis on public safety was gradually redirected from support for the FBI
(and support for the police on gun control measures) to the anarchist-
tending vigilantism of the National Rifle Association and the paranoid
"survivalism" of private militias.

Meanwhile, a number of Democrats smarting from the beatings
they had taken in 1980 and 1984 became convinced that they had to
"get right" with the moods of anti-Washington "populism." Under the
aegis of "centrist" politics, such "New Democrats" established the Democratic Leadership Council and its spin-off Progressive Policy Institute,
founded in 1989. The writers of the PPI Prospectus tried to strike a "centrist" balance on the issue of "big government." While their policy recommendations made provision for a residue of governmental stewardship, they expressed a very clear preference for market-driven solutions and deregulation. They condemned both the "adverse consequences of conservative theory and practice" and the "interest group
liberalism" that has "sought to shift the traditional progressive emphasis on . . . civic responsibility to statism."

What manner of "progressivism" were these New Democrats offering? Implicitly, their philosophy rejected the progressive "New Nationalism" that Theodore Roosevelt had offered in 1912. Though the
PPI founders acknowledged their support for "government intervention to correct distortions and promote economic justice," they included
"decentralization" in their list of policy principles, and they showcased
the writings of theorists like David Osborne who advocated a program
of "reinventing government" through localization.[2] Moreover, as these
Democrats marketed their "new public philosophy that transcends the
limits of the conventional, left-right debate," Republicans like James P.
Pinkerton promoted a parallel effort to construct a "New Paradigm"
that would dissipate left-versus-right dialectics through a new consensus on the virtues of "breaking down centralized structures."[3]

Such was the extent to which national stewardship had fallen into disrepute by the early 1990s. Concurrently, however, a counter-movement was developing — a movement focused on the need for reinvestment in public works and on the opportunities for civic renewal through provision of public works jobs. This counter-movement had been slowly building strength in the 1980s. It began with exposés of America's worsening infrastructure problems — exposés that were typically dismissed in the Reagan era. The smugness of Reaganite politics precluded any fundamental doubts about the sunny new "morning in America." During the Bush administration, however, some conservatives desisted from attacks on the "nanny state" just long enough to recognize the national interest of maintaining the public's bricks and mortar. In 1990, for example, Bush's secretary of transportation, Samuel K. Skinner, issued a report entitled *Moving America* that called for major reinvestments in the field of transportation. Responding to this report, George F. Will avowed that "transportation and other infrastructure issues should bring out a strong Hamiltonian streak in American conservatives, who too often talk the anachronistic language of Jeffersonian small-government sentimentality." In praising the "kind of conservative who understands the need to spend in order to conserve and enlarge the nation's sinews," Will contended that "the first Republican President" was such a conservative: a "crimson thread of consistency connects Lincoln's passion for internal improvements with his later mission of binding the nation together as a land of opportunity."[4] In the following year, Congress passed the "Intermodal Surface Transportation Efficiency Act" (ISTEA), which authorized $151 billion for transportation improvements over six years. President Bush signed the bill near Fort Worth, Texas, and press accounts speculated that the site was chosen "to smooth the political waters" in an area "where 14,000 people have been put out of work by cutbacks in the defense industry's A-12 aircraft and F-16 programs."[5]

Will's conservative defense of infrastructure spending was paralleled by left-of-center calls for revival of public works jobs programs in preference to welfare. Several versions of this idea were proposed in early

1992. Oklahoma's Senator David Boren, for example, introduced legislation to revive the New Deal's WPA: he called his program the "Community Works Progress Administration."[6] Concurrently, the *New Republic*'s Mickey Kaus suggested "replacing AFDC and all other cashlike welfare programs that assist the able-bodied poor . . . with a single, simple offer from the government — an offer of employment for every American citizen over eighteen who wants it, in a useful public job." Kaus dismissed the hypothetical objection "that there aren't enough worthwhile jobs to be done" with the reminder that the "crumbling infrastructure that so recently preoccupied Washington hasn't been patched up overnight." Moreover, he argued, the cultivation of a new "civic liberalism" to create an American "Work Ethic State" would bring another important benefit: it would mean that "criminals could be treated as criminals without residual guilt about the availability of employment."[7]

As Americans prepared to elect a president in 1992, a faint glimmering of agreement on the merits of federal reinvestment in the nation's fundamentals — highways, bridges, training, jobs — had thus appeared among conservatives and liberals. But this agreement was evanescent compared to the power of the rival formulation for "centrist" politics: the "New Paradigm" of privatized, decentralized, and slickly "reinvented" government. The Civic Deal was not yet a possibility. At hand was the ambiguous, conflicted age of Clinton.

· I I ·

I T'S THE ECONOMY, STUPID," proclaimed the in-house dictum of the 1992 Clinton campaign. Both Clinton and Perot sensed the vulnerability of Bush because of the stagnation — or the outright decline — of middle-class earning power. Clinton said in his 1992 acceptance speech that he proposed to make the federal government a catalyst for economic renewal. "We have got to go beyond the brain-

dead politics in Washington, and give our people the kind of government they deserve," Clinton stated, "a government that works for them."
He compared his activist campaign against Bush to the impatience of
Lincoln with generals too timid to use the magnificent gathering of
power that was at their disposal:

> A president ought to be a powerful force for progress. But right now I
> know how President Lincoln felt when General McClellan wouldn't
> attack in the Civil War. He asked him, "If you're not going to use your
> army, may I borrow it?" George Bush, if you won't use your power to
> help people, step aside, I will.[8]

Clinton offered a "New Covenant" that would heal America's left-versus-right divisions. The Covenant would harmonize social compassion
with a "get-tough" attitude on crime. It would stress governmental activism where appropriate — in areas such as environmental protection, education, health care, and public safety — while reducing "bureaucracy." Clinton accused Bush of failing to "streamline the federal
government, and change the way it works." Bush would not "cut 100,000
bureaucrats and put 100,000 more police on the streets. I will."[9] Echo-
ing the theories of the Progressive Policy Institute he helped to found,
Clinton strove to delineate a "middle way" between the chaos of laissez-
faire and the much-maligned ways of bureaucracy:

> I don't have all the answers. But I do know that the old ways won't
> work. Trickle down economics have failed. And big bureaucracies,
> public and private, have failed.[10]

Above all, he would work toward a balanced budget. George Bush "promised
to balance the budget," Clinton charged, "but he didn't even try."[11]

This was all very well in the campaign, but as the victorious Clinton
prepared his legislative agenda for 1993 he was forced to determine what
balance to strike between spending for necessary public works and cuts
to reduce "the deficit." All through the previous decade Democrats had

sought consolation for the triumphs of Reaganism by linking Republican "supply-side" economic theories with increasing federal deficits. Before long, the "deficit crisis" was more than just a subject for partisan "blame games": it was a national obsession used by free-wheeling "populists" like Ross Perot to rail against both of the major parties. And now the moment had arrived for Clinton to reconcile spending for public-interest projects and the goal of a balanced budget.

At the Clinton-Gore Economic Conference of December 14–15, 1992, Alicia Haycock Munnell, senior vice president of the Federal Reserve Bank of Boston, made the case for increased public-works spending. She observed that "investment in the nation's infrastructure has moved to the forefront of the policy agenda" because "airports, roads, bridges have not kept pace with the growth in economic activity." She noted that investment in infrastructure had gradually dropped by half in the course of the previous four decades (from 3 percent of GDP in 1950 to 1.5 percent in 1991). Noting that "congestion in our transportation system is already slowing our economy," that public-works "investment in the United States falls far below that of other developed countries," and that "recent research shows that public infrastructure helps increase private sector output," Munnell concluded that

> people are willing to pay for more government investment. Whenever they are asked to vote on spending more money for bridges, water and sewer systems, roads, or environmental projects, they generally approve the proposals, and by very large margins.[12]

Charles A. Bowsher, the comptroller-general of the United States, told Congress a few weeks later that "maintaining, renewing, and enhancing the surface transportation infrastructure will require on the order of a half trillion dollars as we approach the next century. The Department of Transportation estimates that about $280 billion would be needed just to maintain the nation's roads and bridges at 1989 conditions." Referring to the ISTEA legislation of 1991, Bowsher observed that "while Congress enacted landmark legislation to help pay for and guide this work, a major challenge will be to invest wisely because the needs far outweigh the resources."[13]

Spurred by these public works advocates, Clinton proposed within his $16.3 billion economic stimulus package for 1993 an increase of approximately $3 billion in highway spending, $736 million for improvements in mass transit systems, $250 million in airport grants, $188 million for Amtrak maintenance and modernization, $235 million for repairs to veterans' hospitals, and $94 million for flood control, hydropower, waterway, harbor, and environmental protection projects.[14]

No sooner had the stimulus package arrived in Congress than partisan opposition, featuring a filibuster led by Senator Bob Dole, slashed it to shreds. To be sure, there were causes of this outcome that went beyond partisan revenge. For one thing, the public works agenda got lost in a welter of news-making crises, some minor and some major — from the trivial but newsworthy Zoe Baird fiasco to the Branch Davidians' *Götterdämmerung* in Waco — that distracted the public's attention and weakened the administration's credibility. Moreover, Clinton's foibles and miscalculations, not least of all his penchant for indulging egotistical subordinates who broadcast administration policy disputes to reporters, helped to do him in. So did the derisive attack-dog culture of the print and television media. Furthermore, the bungled mission in Somalia eroded public confidence and so did the obvious bluffing on the issue of Bosnia. There was no "honeymoon" for the Clinton administration.

Above all, the public's aversion to "big government" was whipped up with consummate skill by commentators of the right. One of these was George F. Will — who with nary a word of explanation abandoned his earlier praise for "the kind of conservative who understands the need to spend in order to conserve and enlarge the nation's sinews" of infrastructure. Instead, Will enlisted for the season in the moonshine laissez-faire rebellion of the Cato Institute. Week after week, he hammered away at the "omnipresent, officious, intrusive, bullying and expensive government" that Clinton was allegedly foisting on the nation. Will assailed the "banality" of Clinton's "pork-laden stimulus package" and its place in a (supposedly) leftist agenda of "metastasizing government." Admitting that "perhaps new infrastructure technologies" might "fuel economic growth," he stressed that "analysis must begin by establishing what, if anything, needs to be done that the private sector . . . cannot do." He scorned the "further melding of America's public and private sectors, in the name of industrial policy," pouring disdain upon those "business leaders who, having no principled opposition to collectivism . . . seek profits and security in the genteel socialism of a 'cooperative' relationship with government." The author who ten years earlier had written a conservative "Defense of the Welfare State" knew nothing of Tory reform in the early months of 1993: "Conservatives are predisposed to protect the market's allocation of resources and opportunities," he preached, while "liberals are predisposed to expand government's scope."[15]

The same message was sent to a larger audience by newly ascendant radio talk-show "personalities." "More and more Americans are discovering how incompetent government is," Rush Limbaugh told his self-styled "Dittohead" listeners, "so doesn't it stand to reason that we should try to have less of it?"[16]

As early as April 1993, Clinton's public works package was in grave trouble. It made little difference that Republicans like William J. Althaus, Mayor of York, Pennsylvania, and president of the U.S. Conference of Mayors, declared themselves "bitterly disappointed" that the "president initiates what . . . the people of this country wanted, and Congress kills it."[17] The anti-government ethos was far too strong in the Republican Party for such views to make themselves heard. Whereupon, Clinton made deficit reduction his top economic priority, commencing a long-term austerity contest with Republicans that left the economic premises of balanced-budget politics completely unchallenged. To save face, he pretended that the economic stimulus defeat was not at all significant compared to the "victory" of his deficit-reducing budget package.[18]

Concurrently, Clinton asked Vice President Gore to launch a major initiative to "reinvent government" — a project that seemed to be designed, in part, to steal the right wing's "anti-bureaucracy" thunder. Yet for all of his subsequent promotion of the concept of governmental decentralization, Clinton still remained devoted to appropriate forms of "big government." He won a modest victory when Congress approved his "Americorps" youth service program. And to Hillary Clinton he entrusted the task of preparing an enormous health care reform proposal that would finally achieve a goal that FDR, Harry Truman, and Richard Nixon had found elusive.

Gore's "National Performance Review" to cut governmental red tape was completed in September 1993, and in the very same month Clinton went before Congress to advocate sweeping reforms in health care. The strategy was obvious: using deficit-reduction and "reinventing government" to prove his credentials as a foe of bureaucracy, Clinton hoped to neutralize the left-versus-right dialectic and clear the way for centrist health care reform. He secured the impressive support of Ronald Reagan's surgeon-general. Former presidents Jimmy Carter and Gerald Ford joined forces to urge bipartisan action.[19] Clinton's fatal problem was timing: while the "reinventing government" report was ready, the details of the health care plan were uncompleted when he made his big speech to Congress. Consequently, he lost irreplaceable momentum as the months rolled by and his enemies sniped at the never-quite-completed plan.

Medical insurers launched an opulently funded and cynical campaign against intrusive and interfering government. The Health Insurance Association of America ran a series of thirty-second television "sound-bite" ads in which characters named "Harry and Louise" alleged that Clinton's plan "forces us to buy our insurance through these new mandatory government health alliances . . . run by tens of thou-

sands of new bureaucrats."[20] Clinton had explicitly stated in his speech
to Congress that "Americans believe they ought to be able to choose
their own health care plan, keep their own doctors, and I think all of us
agree. Under any plan we pass, they ought to have that right."[21] But this
promise proved hard to reiterate as "Harry and Louise" did their sleazy
work. The health care initiative slowly sank amid arcane revisions, fili-
bustering obstruction, and congressional posturing.

At the end of his first year in office, Clinton's substantive accom-
plishments consisted of deficit-reduction (for what it was worth), the
passage of the Brady gun-control law, and the small "Americorps" program. Otherwise, his domestic agenda had been botched. A cogent critique of Clinton's failures as a "centrist" was provided in the commen-
taries of journalist E. J. Dionne, Jr., whose 1991 book *Why Americans
Hate Politics* argued that conservative-liberal enmities were poisoning
public debates about the functions of government. Early in 1993 Dionne
warned that "if Democrats can't make the case for government, they'll
not only lose, they'll deserve to." The activist proposals in the Clinton
program and his emphasis on deficit-reduction were potentially on a
collision course, said Dionne, especially since "the anti-government
mood makes deficit reduction the one and only test of his seriousness
for a lot of voters." Ironically, the "anti-government constituency has
swelled because of people who would like government to do good things,
but have lost faith in its capacity to do so." Such people tend to "fall
back on calls for cutting government down to size."[22]

In the middle of 1994, with Clinton's public works efforts reduced
to triviality, his health care plan disappearing in congressional "gridlock,"
his crime bill to help put 100,000 more police on the streets only nar-
rowly escaping conversion to amorphous "block grants," and with deficit reduction on the way to becoming America's national *idée fixe*,
Dionne recalled that in 1992

Clinton spoke incessantly about economic pressures on the "forgotten middle class" and government's need to respond to fears of middle class collapse. Clinton talked about programs to retrain the work force, to educate kids for a more competitive new environment, to ease the transition from old jobs to new jobs. Clinton still loves this rhetoric, and a variety of programs have been launched. But mostly they are not very big or very visible, having been ground into small pieces by budget pressures. . . . The central threads of his presidency have disappeared.[23]

Not all of the blame was Clinton's; laissez-faire conservatives and trash-talk artists had thwarted him at every turn. In October 1994, Ann Devroy of the *Washington Post* reported that "one GOP strategist, unwilling to allow his name to be used, said: 'I tell you, I wake up every morning happy. . . . And every time I think we are going too far, I think, hell, no, hit 'em again."[24] The next month the Republicans gained control of both houses of Congress with their anti-government "Contract With America."

· I I I ·

T HE MARKET IS RATIONAL AND THE GOVERNMENT IS DUMB." This dumbest of axioms composed by Rep. Dick Armey was one of the more memorable slogans of the legislative "revolution" of 1995.[25] Among its various provisions, the Republican "Contract With America" called for a balanced budget amendment to the Constitution and a seven-year balanced budget plan. It called for the slashing or complete elimination of scores of public works and transportation programs. It demanded a loosening of food and drug regulation. It proposed the evisceration of certain environmental laws by requiring the government to compensate owners of land subjected to development controls or corporations subjected to pollution controls — it would have forced Uncle Sam to pay polluters not to pollute. And it called for the "devolution" of as many governmental functions to the states and localities as possible.

The balanced budget amendment to the Constitution came very close to passage. As drafted, the amendment would have required a congressional super-majority of 60 percent to permit the federal government to incur new debt. A number of commentators suggested the ludicrous and even frightening results that might occur if the amendment were engrafted into the Constitution: the outcome might be a paralyzed federal government unable to assist disaster victims or reverse an out-of-control financial panic or recession.

Sociologist and journalist Paul Starr observed that the amendment's provisions could cripple conservative as well as liberal agendas: "These measures . . . severely weaken the government's capacity to achieve any purpose." A "minority in either house would be able to impede preparations for national defense as well as spending on the poor. . . . It would be all the harder to find money for purposes that conservatives prefer, whether 'Star Wars' defense systems, more prisons or intensified border patrols." America's enemies, too, would understand and take advantage of our "weakened fiscal powers." Above all, the amendment could leave the United States helpless in the face of a recession:

> The dangers would be likely to be greatest in a recession. If revenue fell along with economic activity and if three-fifths of Congress could not agree to run a deficit, the Government would be forced to aggravate the downturn by cutting public expenditures as well — a recipe for turning recessions into depressions.[26]

Richard Kogen, a Fellow at the Center for Budget and Policy Priorities, showed that federal insurance of bank deposits would be jeopardized:

> Doesn't the FDIC charge annual fees to banks, building up large balances, which would automatically be available in a banking crisis?

Not after the amendment. It prohibits spending borrowed funds [and] incredibly, it also prohibits using accumulated savings; it requires that all federal spending in any fiscal year be covered by that year's revenues. This requirement is like telling a family to finance a new house or a child's college tuition out of that year's wages, no matter how much money the family has in the bank. In this case, the amendment precludes a sudden increase in deposit insurance payments if that increase would cause federal spending to exceed federal revenues in that year.

Kogen spelled out the real possibility of re-enacting what happened to the banks between 1929 and 1933: "By the time Congress fully understands the scope of a developing banking crisis and gathers the three-fifths vote (if it can), the problem would have grown, perhaps to a dangerous degree."[27]

Bowing to the clamor for this primitive amendment, politicians rushed to support it. The amendment failed in the Senate by the margin of only one vote. Within a few months House Republicans proposed to abolish the Council of Economic Advisors.[28]

Critics of other provisions in the "Contract With America" strove to call attention to its dangers in the early months of 1995. Both consumer advocates and some business leaders were troubled. Food safety experts, for example, were alarmed that some of the "Contract" legislation would cripple or halt improvement of federal inspections of bacteria-contaminated hamburger, chicken, and other meats that cause approximately four thousand deaths and five million illnesses every year.[29] Businesspeople like Alfred Zeien, the CEO of Gillette, complained that the "devolution" of product labeling requirements and employment regulations to the fifty states could cause chaos for companies doing business on a national scale.[30]

While talk-show hosts and the flamboyant new Speaker of the House, Newt Gingrich, regaled their followers with quips about the weirdness of bureaucrats, the momentum of the anti-government rebellion started to diminish. As early as March 1995, polls began to reflect a broad national concern that the Republicans were going too far, and Clinton cautiously suggested that Americans "read the fine print" in their "Contract." And then came the Oklahoma bombing: it was suddenly clear that all the ridicule — and in some cases, outright demonization — of government had been inciting a demented and violent fringe in the body politic.

Through the summer and fall of 1995, the slow backlash against the Republican "Contract" continued. Officials at the federal Center for Disease Control warned that cutbacks were hampering the search for new antibiotics to fight mutant strains of bacteria. "If we continue to let this get out of hand," said the center's Ruth Berkelman, "we're setting ourselves up for a major catastrophe. . . . I'm talking about going in for a routine operation and dying from an infection."[31] The American Association for the Advancement of Science predicted that scientific research in the civilian sector would decrease by as much as a third because of the "Contract's" seven-year balanced budget plan.[32] Conservationist groups condemned Republican proposals to close two hundred of the nation's 360 national parks, to privatize the management of some and sell off parts of others. Clinton joined the conservationists in fighting these proposals, declaring that plans "to just sell some of our natural treasures to the highest bidder" were "wrong."[33]

Perhaps the most amusing backlash against the "Contract" came from sportsmen and hunters. In reaction against a bill to take 270 million acres of land from the federal Bureau of Land Management and turn it over to the states, hunters launched an angry radio campaign to "Keep Public Lands in Public Hands" that caused one of the bill's co-sponsors to repudiate it.[34]

In general, Clinton tried to roll with the punches after losing control of both houses of Congress, while counter-punching on issues where Republican budget cuts were unpopular. In May, cabinet secretaries and senior administration staff began attacking Republicans' proposed reductions in Medicare, Medicaid, environmental protection laws, and education.[35]

But Clinton resisted the advice of Laura D'Andrea Tyson — formerly chair of the Council of Economic Advisors and subsequently director of the White House's National Economic Council — who argued that the Republicans' balanced budget plan "exposes the macroeconomy to considerable . . . risk."[36] A month after Tyson had issued that warning, Clinton joined the Republicans in calling for a multiyear balanced-budget plan, while arguing over some of the details. The consequences of this choice were articulated once again by E. J. Dionne, Jr., who ruefully observed that "if your message is that government can work, you'd better make it work. The Democrats' problem, in 1994 and now, is that they didn't do that."[37]

Clinton should realize, said Dionne, that "people not obsessed with the federal budget (i.e., most people)" normally talk about things like "their living standards, the children's schools, the pressures on families." The Democrats, he suggested,

> can probably convince the country that what the Republicans propose *won't* solve such problems. But they also need to persuade people that despite past foul-ups, Democrats really *can* do something about them. That's hard to pull off when you have already put government in the strait-jacket of a seven-year balanced budget.[38]

Regardless, Clinton had decided to embrace the balanced budget as essential to his centrist politics. At the same time he battled it out with Republicans — through excruciating governmental shut-down confrontations in the holiday season of 1995 — regarding cuts in popular programs. All the while, Democrats were deeply divided over strategy, tactics, and philosophy. "For congressional Democrats, these are confusing times," reported *Washington Post* writers Paul Taylor and Thomas B. Edsall in mid-1995: "No matter what their stripe, all Democrats are having trouble articulating a coherent message about the role of government — not only because of their internal fissures, but because many say they have no idea where the head of their ticket will finally come down on the issue."[39]

The "internal fissures" were significant: New Democrat centrist decentralizers continued to be influential in Democratic politics. Clinton's secretary of housing and urban development, Henry Cisneros, and his National Park Service director, Roger Kennedy, sent Clinton a policy essay in 1995 urging him to "decentralize with a vengeance."[40] Meanwhile, Democrats Paul Tsongas and Tim Penny had joined with Republicans such as Lowell Weicker and John Anderson to form a new centrist group called the "Concord Coalition" to reconcile concerns about civil rights and environmental protection with deficit reduction and balanced-budget frugality.[41] In his 1996 State of the Union message, Clinton kept on struggling to somehow articulate the essence of his New Covenant: "The era of big government is over. But we cannot go back to the time when our citizens were left to fend for themselves."[42]

The Civic Deal was not yet a possibility: the ambivalence and drift of Clinton's politics made public works and public safety linkages nearly impossible. The hegemony of laissez-faire doctrine in Republican political culture was brutally apparent. The domination of American politics by partisan games prevented grass-roots support for governmental stewardship from finding many satisfying outlets.

But on the eve of the 1996 election, peculiar portents appeared in Republican circles and even in explicitly right-of-center politics. Item: James P. Pinkerton, the Republican centrist who touted a "New Paradigm" for "breaking down centralized structures," published his *magnum opus* in 1995: a book entitled *What Comes Next: The End of Big Government and the New Paradigm Ahead*. Amid the usual arguments for liberating enterprise, the author advocated one colossal exception to the "end of big government" — he proposed the revival and ambitious expansion of FDR's Civilian Conservation Corps.[43]

Item: When Speaker Newt Gingrich called for the rebirth of

America's space program, the ever-mercurial George F. Will applauded in a column date-lined Hoover Dam, musing that "many people will be surprised, and certain kinds of conservatives scandalized, by the speaker's belief that government is competent for, and has a duty to attempt, the peacetime mobilization of people for projects explicitly designed to elicit nobility through collective action. . . . But he has much modern American history on his side."[44] A few months later, Will announced that the nation's transportation needs were "alarming, as the conditions of highways and airports demonstrates." Consequently, he said, Republicans should remember that "Eisenhower's championing of more than 40,000 miles of new highways reflected thinking with a long, strong Republican pedigree."[45]

· I V ·

YET THE POWER OF LAISSEZ-FAIRE DOCTRINE was still too strong for these ideas to make a difference. The 1996 Dole campaign went out of its way to make Clinton the candidate of "government." In the first presidential debate, Dole explained that the "basic difference" between himself and Clinton was that "I trust the people. The President trusts the government." "Where possible," Dole continued, "I want to give power back to the states and back to the people."[46] Time and again Dole repeated on the stump that Clinton "talks like a Republican, but he's a liberal" — a liberal nurturing "a million little plans to spend your money and rob the future of all the young people."[47] By proposing a huge across-the-board tax cut, Dole said that he wanted to create even greater fiscal austerity so that "government has to pinch pennies."

Clinton's response was to stay "on theme" with the strategy of "reinventing government." He told reporters in a late summer interview that while he had "never been an advocate of a weak federal government," he had definitely advocated "a smaller one, where people got more for less. . . . That's why, even though I never expected it to have any traction, I guess, politically — and I don't think it has — this reinventing government effort has been very important to me."[48]

Notwithstanding his admission that a politics based on retrenchment could not achieve political "traction," Clinton used such tactics in staving off Republican attacks. And within the constraints of defensively reinvented government — through initiatives designed to "give people the tools to make the most of their own lives" — Clinton showed his commitment to peripheral forms of public action.

The election of 1996 took place at a time when the moods of the public were subsiding into testy ambivalence. The results of the election were conflicted: the Democrats retained the White House, but Republicans retained control of Congress. No mandate emerged. For the most part, no one was proposing any drastic rearrangement of the governmental *status quo*. Dole's rhetorical assault upon "government" — except for his tax-cut proposal — was mostly hot air. Though he ran against "Washington," he followed his party in retreating from its 1994 "Contract."

Moderate Republicans began to rebel against the right-wing's imperative to privatize. "Government is the enemy until you need a friend," proclaimed Republican William Cohen as he prepared to retire from the Senate. "Is the public ready to say: 'Let the private sector handle everything?' Clearly not."[49] Even right-wing Republicans continued to support certain forms of statist intervention. The Buchanan boom in the Republican primaries showed resurgent right-wing support for protectionist tariffs over free trade, and a congressional push to raise the minimum wage put Republican free-marketeers in a very tough position. Their position became no easier after the May 11 crash of Valujet Flight 592 sent 110 people to a blazing death and put deregulators on the defensive. A subsequent probe revealed the cut-rate airline had given short-shrift to safety by carrying explosive cargo along with its passengers.

Concurrently, some carefully targeted Clinton initiatives expanded

governmental regulation in crowd-pleasing ways. Federal meat inspection standards were overhauled and tightened for the first time since
Theodore Roosevelt's era. Clinton set up a national database to track
convicted child-molesters, thus getting the jump on a similar bipartisan measure that was moving through Congress. Clinton simultaneously joined the supporters of a victims' rights amendment to the
Constitution. The administration accepted the recommendations of a
White House Commission on Aviation Safety and Security that the
federal government assume far more of the cost of anti-terrorist security measures in airports — security measures hitherto provided
through the limited funds of private airlines.[50]

Congressional Republicans rushed to share the credit for such
cautious governmental stewardship. Congress passed legislation to
tighten drinking water standards and to loan $1 billion annually to the
states to enable them to upgrade drinking water quality. The bipartisan Kennedy-Kassebaum bill made health insurance more portable; it
also limited the power of insurers to deny coverage to people with pre-
existing conditions. Republicans hastened to go on record in support
of funding for popular programs. "We are shortchanging investments,"
warned Republican Senator Pete V. Domenici. "We've got to find some
way to increase appropriations" for necessary programs.[51]

Most importantly, congressional Republicans and Clinton found
common if controversial ground in legislation to revamp America's
welfare system in order to move the underclass from welfare-depen-
dency to jobs — private-sector jobs.

When Clinton and Dole squared off in their debates, their positions were not far apart. Though he did his very best to paint Clinton as
a liberal addicted to outlandish forms of governmentalism, Dole heat-
edly emphasized his full-fledged support for Medicare and Social Security. Retreating from an earlier pledge to the National Rifle Association
to repeal the 1994 crime bill's ban on selected assault weapons, he embraced the Brady Law's provision for computerized background checks

for the purchasers of guns. After hit-and-run quips about the liberals'
ill-starred plans for a government "take over" of the health care industry, he went on record in support of the Kennedy-Kassebaum bill. And
on several occasions when he spoke about his service in World War II,
he reminisced about the GI Bill and what it meant to America.

Dole's mordant and laconic delivery — "I'm a plain-spoken man
(or whatever)" — came off rather badly in comparison to Clinton's
virtuosity in speaking the electorate's language. Yet for all of his charisma, Clinton's vision for the country seemed hollow: it almost seemed
timid. His talk about a "bridge to the twenty-first century" was boring,
a rhetorical let-down. He had plenty of proposals, but most of them
appeared to be embroidery. "He has followed brilliant tactics," said one
political scientist, "that have left him with no strategy."[52] He survived
— to grapple with another Republican Congress and to grope for a
special niche in history.

Would he find it through balancing the budget? Would he find it
in the wonders of the Internet? Would he find it in the worst-case long-
term scenario for phasing out the welfare system? "We have a responsibility," he had lectured the 1996 Democratic convention, "we have a
moral obligation to make sure the people who are being required to
work have the opportunity to work. We must make sure the jobs are
there."[53] As usual, Clinton was depending on indirect and reinvented
governance — in this case some improvised promptings and incentives
that were aimed at the private sector — to ensure that "the jobs will be
there."[54] What will happen if the jobs are not there? Will the Civic Deal
become a possibility?

Chapter Six

☆ ☆ ☆

Coming to Our Senses

IT IS OBVIOUS ENOUGH THAT AN ACTIVIST GOVERNMENT should never be regarded as a panacea, but we have little patience with the civic implications of the doctrine "fend for yourself." Americans are thinking very hard these days about the nature of their social compact. Rival formulations have competed: "Reinventing Government," Clinton's "New Covenant," the laissez-faire "Contract With America." None of them has given satisfaction. Some of them are crude, and most of them are weak.

The primitivism of the right-wing "Contract" has fortunately run its course. But the Clinton formulation of "reinvented" governance remains a problematical affair. Surely Clinton-style governance in some ways reflects the electorate's own ambivalence. In other ways, however, the public was impatient with the mushiness of Clinton's "New Covenant." Clinton admitted that a centrism based upon fiscal austerity combined with dispersal of governmental efforts has been lacking in political "traction." Naturally: it is nebulous. Decentralization may have seemed like a shortcut to centrist reconciliation when Clinton decided to embrace it. But the shortcut is now a dead-end.

While Clinton succeeded (at least temporarily) in rescuing his party from the worst of "political correctness" — except for a die-hard insistence on affirmative action — he did not succeed in achieving a strong combination of conservative and liberal ideas. To the contrary, both right-wing and left-wing polemicists dismissed him (unfairly) as an opportunist — or as a liberal who pilfered some expedient conservative themes. The sincere side of Clinton eluded such people for a sad and fundamental reason: his program was inconsequential.

To be sure, some resistance from the left and the right will be triggered by *anything* "centrist." The most battle-hardened veterans of ideological warfare are hopelessly stubborn. Such people have invested the most precious years of their lives in developing their one-sided outlooks. Anything that threatens this investment of intellect and ego will be resisted.

But conservatives and liberals have also been suffering frustrations, divisions, and setbacks. Struggle as they will to maintain a united front, the ideologists of both persuasions cannot escape an untidy political reality: conservative and liberal traditions amount to unstable clusters of ideas. Fissures are increasingly apparent at both extremes of the ideological spectrum.

While laissez-faire dogma maintains an overpowering hold on conservative thought, the principles of free-marketeering and government-bashing can never paper over some embarrassing conservative divisions. In the first place, the old pro-government traditions of noblesse oblige are not dead. From time to time, a dissident conservative will manage to defy the Republican guardians of minimal-government orthodoxy. In September 1997, for example, authors William Kristol and David Brooks proclaimed in the *Wall Street Journal* that a "National Greatness" conservatism that "does not despise government" should revive the statecraft of Theodore Roosevelt and build upon the pro-active governance of leaders like New York City's Republican Mayor Rudolph Giuliani.[1] Republican responses to the op-ed essay were bitterly divided. So were the Republican responses to the maverick Republicans who joined in the 1998 campaign to boost federal infrastructure spending. Such people had to face down derisive resistance from the anti-government zealots of their own party.[2]

Conservative culture cannot be contained within the rubric of trusting free enterprise. Moreover, the internal divisions of conservatism extend across a very wide range of issues. Fundamentalist Christians are furious because Republican moderates will not submit to their religious decrees. But fundamentalists are also attacking "permissiveness" in ways that covertly challenge the defiant individualism of right-wing libertarian politics.[3] Conservatives seeking to maximize their wealth are now targets for conservative populists like Kevin Phillips who decry the short-sightedness of corporate and individual greed. "Supply-side" enthusiasts (while paying lip service to the fetish of balancing the budget) are contending with "balanced budget hawks." In foreign policy, the old animosity between isolationists and interventionists has re-emerged.

Notwithstanding the tribalistic unity that flows from attacking common enemies — in this case liberals and "government" — the fragmentation of right-wing politics increases. Divided themselves, conservatives divide the American people, especially on lines of class and religion. Tax-cuts that favor the wealthy more than anyone else are rather difficult to swallow, and tax-cuts of any sort are useless to the unemployed victims of corporate down-sizing and workforce globalization. And the mischief of religious fundamentalism splits the electorate in ways that are even more self-defeating for conservatives. Instead of contenting themselves with a politics based upon spiritual themes that are near-universal, the Christian right keeps provoking a people brought up to prize freedom of conscience, to practice religious toleration, and to pride themselves upon America's role as a haven for the victims of persecution.

So much for the divisions and follies of the right. But there are elements in conservative thought that are worthy of salvage: specifically, traditional conservative themes regarding national power and public safety. The most valuable themes in conservatism — the themes that quite properly possess enduring mass-appeal — derive from the old Tory instinct to thwart the obnoxious side of human nature. True, conservatives will sometimes forget themselves in this regard when they slip into silly forms of right-wing utopian rhetoric ("It's morning in America"). But the essence of traditional conservatism endures. It was distilled in a memorable joke that made the rounds in the late 1960s. A neoconservative (the aphorism ran) was a liberal who just got mugged.

This returns us to the weaknesses of liberalism. While the Democrats under Clinton have adopted a tough position on public safety issues, liberals — at least those who have never been the victims of a mugging — remain grotesquely lenient in reacting to violent crime. Consider a selection at random from the "slow news" of the last presidential election year. In May 1996, a three-judge panel handed down a criminal sentence in Maryland. The defendant, who had pleaded guilty to assault and battery, was a forty-eight-year-old mental patient who killed a little girl some thirty years earlier and then went on to perpetrate a series of violent assaults. In this case, according to press accounts, the defendant "stalked and beat" a woman "because she refused to talk to him." The three-judge panel voted 2-to-1 to imprison this menace for ten years, but the dissenting judge "said that he would have liked to decrease the sentence to five years." The public defender asserted that this killer and batterer "posed little danger to the community."[4]

What manner of warped values — what manner of misplaced empathy — would lead a judge to say that he would have "liked" to *reduce* the time in which innocent citizens remain beyond the reach of this maniac? On a certain level it is probably true that the criminal "couldn't help himself" when he stalked and beat the woman. But on a level that is far more compelling for society and civilization, this is *exactly why he needs to be locked up*: society's rights are more legitimate in cases such as this. Psychopaths should not be allowed to run loose in the aftermath of murder. When it comes to the lives of our innocent loved ones, we should not be taking chances with psychotics.

It goes without saying that the criminally insane should have decent facilities and non-abusive treatment in psychiatric prisons. But the liberal urge to show lenient compassion to literally *anyone* — no matter how menacing — with a claim to the status of victimhood is now a clear and present danger to us all. Bob Dole was triumphantly right when he contended in his 1996 acceptance speech that "a nation that cannot defend itself from outrage does not deserve to survive."[5] A society that cannot provide its citizens with reasonable protection from the violence of predators does not deserve to be regarded as a decent civilization.

Most of us accept this principle — from the residents of bedroom suburbs to the residents of inner-city ghettoes. And this point deserves very strong emphasis: the residents of impoverished neighborhoods are every bit as vehement in their demands for safe city streets as the residents of middle-class America — *except* when such issues get clouded by racial resentment. And here again, the influence of liberalism in recent years has been perverse. By abandoning the civil rights ethos from the glory days of Martin Luther King, Jr. in favor of relentlessly race-emphasizing politics, liberals have been as guilty as right-wing fundamentalists in dividing American civic culture.

This brings us to the issue of "affirmative action" and of racially-cognizant "diversity." The civil rights movement through the early 1960s was based overwhelmingly upon the view that opportunity in a free society should be available *regardless* of physical characteristics. Affirmative action, of course, takes *special cognizance* of physical characteristics, especially race and gender. Most of the supporters of affirmative action appear to be altruistic. But the case can be made that the civil rights movement had it right the first time — that Martin Luther King was profoundly right when he implored us simply to *end* this obsession with the looks and physical characteristics of our fellow citizens.

Proponents of affirmative action justify themselves by claiming that racially-conscious justice is socially imperative: it overcomes furtive and hard-to-prove forms of discrimination. Such people have a point, for it is obvious that vulnerable groups can be excluded through a wink and a leer among people who connive to discriminate. But the *price* that we pay for maintaining — for prolonging and perhaps for perpetuating — America's hang-up on race must be weighed against the goals of affirmative action, especially if race-neutral strategies (through public works jobs, both blue- and white-collar) could be used to expand opportunities.

It is undeniable that some forms of group solidarity and group identity — including racial, gender, and ethnic identity — can play constructive roles in people's lives. On the other hand, there are reasons to worry about the ways in which our race obsessions have been blighting American life. It is one thing to take special cognizance of race as a secondary aspect of individual identity: as an aspect of one's existence that one should be free to emphasize, ignore, or take in stride, just as one pleases. It is altogether different when race becomes viewed as a primary aspect of one's identity. However valuable our cultural diversity can be, should we not seek the highest meaning of America in the great common culture through which no physical characteristics can prevent any person from living as unique a life as he or she wishes to do — within the social limits of ethics and the law?

One of the most sublime achievements of this (or any) society is the achievement of voluntary racial intermarriage — the achievement of an open society in which individuals from vastly different racial backgrounds feel free to fall in love and have children. But if more and more people of differing backgrounds succeed in attaining this goal, does it not become a weird, insulting, and dehumanizing thing to have to figure out the "correct classification" for the children of "mixed" marriages according to the fixed categories that affirmative action tabulations seem to require? Should it not be the basic right of each one of us to decide *for ourselves* to what extent — if at all — we wish to have our physical characteristics in any way define the "self" that we wish the world to judge?

That was the view of Ward Connerly, who chaired the California initiative to end racial preferences in 1996. "I'm a black man," he told the press. "I have Indian in me, I have French, some Irish. The choice of what I am should be mine. Yet I've had reporters call me African American. What does that mean?" It meant, among other things, that Connerly was vilified from one end of California to the other. "He's married to a white woman," a state senator complained; "He wants to be white. He wants a colorless society. He has no ethnic pride."[6]

Is this the kind of civic culture that we want — the kind that our nation can afford?

Certain older liberals such as Arthur Schlesinger, Jr. have protested race-conscious politics. But the same sorts of ideological foibles that have led them astray in so many other situations have seduced conscientious liberals into worsening our racial divisions.

So much for the follies of the left. But there are elements of liberal thought that should be salvaged, specifically the impulse to broaden opportunity and widen the scope of prosperity for all Americans. Richard D. Kahlenberg of the Center for National Policy has argued that while "conservatives are right to say that basing preferences on immutable factors like race and gender is unfair and promotes racial division and hostility," the liberals "are right to say that we need to address our history of discrimination and provide greater opportunity for those left behind." Kahlenberg has argued that the "hard work of finding constructive alternatives for thirty years of race- and gender-based preferences" must hinge upon a compromise between conservatives and liberals that acknowledges that "large numbers of Americans are uneasy about dismantling affirmative action without placing a positive program in its stead." Kahlenberg has argued for a class-based affirmative action that is targeted on economic need.[7]

Is it not high time for a program that unifies *some* of our conservative and liberal values — the strongest and the wisest values — through well-grounded forms of public action? Is it not high time for us to rescue our conservatives and liberals from some of the dogmas that ensnare them? How excellent a change it would be — how bracing for our civic culture — to create the kind of politics that takes the half-

truths of our conservatives and liberals and makes them more congru-
ent in a manner that benefits us all.

Public works in exchange for safe streets: opportunity and national
security delivered through a worthy new form of social compact. A new
reciprocity transcending our racial, economic, and ideological divisions
— a program of necessities delivered through the government ordained
by ourselves. Such a program would not be utopian. It would not solve
all of our problems. But it would build our society's power, prosperity,
and safety while grounding that safety in a fair and righteous formulation of community will — of civic coherence.

Maybe civic coherence is beyond our society's reach in this furious age. But we deserve to see a politician try it. We deserve to see a
leader tell conservatives to stop their attacks on Uncle Sam, to remind
them that business cannot do it all, and that public works can benefit
everyone. We deserve to see a leader tell the liberals to concentrate on
what we have in common, a leader to convince them that violent criminals deserve to be kept far away from our communities if every effort
has been made to have society's safety coincide with their self-fulfill-
ment. Every effort — with the necessary caveat that public works jobs
must depend upon competent performance.

There remains a vexing issue: *money*. The legacy of national stewardship can never be revived if our economic thinking is dogmatic. We
must re-enlarge our national "CAPACITY," as Hamilton conceived it, in
the century ahead.

· I I ·

FOR A GENERATION AFTER THE SECOND WORLD WAR, the principle of deficit spending by the federal government was generally accepted by Americans. In 1965, the economic writer Edwin
L. Dale, Jr., reported in the *New York Times Magazine* that "it is safe to
say that the big majority of economists, and a growing number of busi-

nessmen, bankers, and labor leaders, believe that the recent deficits in the Federal budget have been good, not bad, for America." The deficits were viewed as a way to channel federal investments into the economy — investments creating a beneficial stimulus that brought prosperity.[8]

Deficit spending was increasingly the norm after World War II. Notwithstanding its three budget surpluses, the Truman administration ran four budget deficits. In the Eisenhower years the federal government had three budget surpluses and *five* deficits.[9] The national debt climbed, but so did the gross national product. There was no need to "pay off" the debt. All that mattered was the issuance of new bonds as old ones matured. The federal government built the St. Lawrence Seaway, commenced the Interstate Highway System, created unprecedented military power to ward off danger in the nuclear age, and began a visionary program to explore outer space. The economy boomed, tax revenues increased, and Americans experienced the highest standard of living they had ever known.

Today thousands of Americans complain that it takes two incomes to approximate — let alone equal — the standard of living their families enjoyed in the 1950s with a single income.[10] Regardless of interminable end-of-the-decade ballyhoo about an economic boom that is supposedly reflected in stock market surges (a note reminiscent of the 1920s) and low inflation, our economic growth has been intermittently sluggish, the retail market is intermittently "soft," and the contractions of downsizing and organizational understaffing continue. Balanced-budget dogmatism has instilled the idea that only long-term patterns of budgetary surplus can justify major new initiatives by Uncle Sam.

Meanwhile, on the foreign policy front, we are rapidly losing the chance to purchase Russia's bomb-grade plutonium before it falls into the hands of terrorists. We have probably lost the chance to pre-empt the eventual resurgence of autocracy in Russia through a Marshall Plan program of assistance. Generations of Americans may curse us down the years for this short-sightedness.[11]

Economists are quite divided these days on the subject of fiscal policy. Some, like Charles L. Schultze, believe that federal deficits and interest on the national debt take dollars out of private investment that would otherwise stimulate economic growth. Others, like Robert Solow and James Tobin, believe that short-term additional deficit spending is justified so long as the money is invested in things that generate prosperity. Still others, like Robert Eisner, believe that national debt should grow steadily as a stimulant of GNP.[12]

Federal deficit spending has been virtually continuous since the 1950s. Indeed, with only one exception (1969), the federal budget was in deficit *every single year* from the Eisenhower presidency to the second Clinton term. Kennedy, Johnson, Nixon, Ford, Carter, Reagan, and Bush "unbalanced the budget." It is only since the 1980s, when the *size* of deficits increased so dramatically under Reagan, that the widespread presumption of a "deficit crisis" began to appear in American politics. Certain liberal observers like Arthur Schlesinger, Jr., have charged that the Reaganites contrived their big deficits deliberately to cripple the welfare state.[13] Whatever the truth of this accusation, conservative behavior on the issue has been erratic. Whereas supply-side theorists discounted the importance of deficits during the Reagan years — or else casually foisted the blame onto Congress — balancing the budget is a sacred mantra today in conservative politics.

Financier Felix Rohatyn supports the premises of budget-balancing, but with a crucial proviso: that the federal government adopt the practice of corporations and state governments of splitting its budget into two calculations, one for operating expenses and the other for long-term capital investments, some of which are best financed through bonds. His recent comments on the issue merit quoting at length:

> The federal budget is a grotesque document that reflects neither accounting nor economic reality. As opposed to state and local budgets, and corporate financial statements, it does not differentiate

between capital investment and ordinary expenses. So far as the federal budget accounts are concerned, a welfare payment is treated in exactly the same way as a payment to build a school or a bridge. The budget also does not take account of future liabilities or of expenditures whose repayment is guaranteed, such as student loans and certain foreign loans, among other obligations. The budget simply measures cash in and cash out over a twelve-month period.

Lowering the cost of capital as a result of lowering the deficit will certainly stimulate private capital investment; it will do nothing, however, for much-needed public investment. The administration and Congress should provide for a capital budget that will be quite separate from the expense budget. Borrowing for capital investment by issuing bonds is the traditional way to finance such investment, but it should be subject to two conditions: that the capital project create new assets with a useful life over a defined period, and that it provide for paying back the interest and principal on the bonds. Such repayment can be assured either by designating a particular source of revenue, such as a gasoline tax, to pay off the borrowing, or by limiting total government borrowing to a fixed percentage of GNP. Appropriations for public infrastructure, including schools, roads, airports, and water supplies, need not be seen as filling the "pork barrel." They can be a vital part of a twenty-first century advanced economy.[14]

Rohatyn is right about the need to sever capital investments from operating costs in the federal budget. It is ludicrous to talk about balancing a budget that is misconceived in its economic premises. State and local governments — the very governments to whom the enthusiastic decentralizers propose to "devolve" federal programs — routinely separate capital budgets from operating budgets, as do most normal corporations. An alternative proposed in recent years by a number of officials and policy analysts would be to take our infrastructure spending entirely "off budget." In any case, we are long overdue for a reality check in our national accounting.

Regarding Rohatyn's contention that reductions in deficit spending inevitably free up private investment, however, the issue is less clear. Eisner and other economists working in the Keynesian tradition dispute this assumption and their logic is convincing. How can anyone reasonably doubt that public borrowing for the purpose of investing in public works — regardless of whether we create a capital budget for the purpose — can strengthen and stimulate the market? It can transform laid-off workers into customers with money in their pockets — customers to stimulate our industries across the board. Economist David Alan Aschauer suggested in a macroeconomic study released in 1990 that "more than half of the decline in our productivity growth over the past two decades can be explained by lower public infrastructure spending." Conversely, "a one percent increase" in such spending "will increase GNP by as much as 0.24 percent. . . . After four years or so, each additional dollar of public investment in infrastructure will raise private investment by 45 cents." The Aschauer study concluded that in overall terms the likely "pay-off in GNP growth from an extra dollar of public capital is estimated to exceed that of private investment by a factor of between two and five."[15]

In 1997 the Clinton administration proposed to spend $175 billion over the course of the next six years on transportation infrastructure.[16] This was not much more than the feeble, inadequate ISTEA authorization of 1991. Under the prodding of an outspoken Republican Congressman, Bud Shuster of Pennsylvania, bipartisan support developed in 1998 to exceed this level. But Republican budget-balancers vilified Shuster while Clinton fretted over the loss of "fiscal discipline."[17] He also warned that such high levels of highway spending might threaten priorities such as education. Clinton's budgetary theology pre-empted his program. His strictures on budget-balancing made him wholly oblivious to the possibility of linking public works projects to a massive expansion of Job Corps training and public-service jobs.

"The age of big government is over," Bill Clinton has claimed — but what if a successor disagrees? What will happen if a Democratic president dissociates himself from the proposition in the near future? Alternatively, what will happen if a "National Greatness" conservative should manage to capture the Republican nomination and then get elected? The Civic Deal could become a reality in several distinct and bipartisan scenarios. When Kristol and Brooks took aim in their *Wall Street Journal* column at the anti-government dogmas in conservative culture, columnist Robert Novak retorted that they had thrown down the gauntlet in a "debate among conservatives that will shape the future of American politics."[18] Indeed it may — for by striking at the wellsprings of anti-government doctrine among conservatives, National Greatness Republicanism, as practiced by successful politicians such as Giuliani and Shuster, could affect liberals and Democrats as well as conservatives and Republicans. After all, it was Reagan-era government-bashing that drove many Clinton-style Democrats into the "can't beat 'em/ join 'em" posture of "Reinventing Government" and balancing the budget. By disavowing some ideological premises of Republican government-bashing, National Greatness conservatives could cause a great political realignment if they become part of a bipartisan governing coalition.

Some of our greatest presidents, and especially those who championed a vigorous federal presence, used bipartisanism as a strategy. Lincoln-era Republicanism emerged as a coalition of pro-government Whigs such as Lincoln himself and former Free-Soil Democrats such as Lincoln's cabinet members Edwin Stanton and Salmon Chase. Theodore Roosevelt's heroic agenda for Uncle Sam depended on support from Democrats like Francis Newlands — the author of the act that led to projects like Hoover Dam later on — against "stand-pat" Republicans like "Uncle Joe" Cannon who fought tooth-and-nail against the Republican Roosevelt's agenda. Likewise, Franklin D. Roosevelt worked in partnership with Republicans like George Norris in creating the Tennessee Valley Authority.

When our public infrastructure funding is due for re-authorization, a linkage of public works and safe streets could in all probability be achieved, regardless of whether a Democratic or Republican president is orchestrating the deal. The result could transform our civic culture.

Rohatyn has spoken of the "different social climate" that a program of public works linked to "safe streets and safe public transport" would bring to America.[19] Renewed opportunity provided through national rebuilding would strengthen us in many of our family and civic commitments: as Robert Kuttner has observed, "an employee fearful of his job security or working several jobs has less time or inclination to volunteer for the Little League. There is barely enough time to juggle work and family, let alone participate in civic and political activities."[20] The offer of a public works job for everyone who wants one with provision for safe streets in every community could also diminish our disastrous obsession with race. It would give us a unifying national culture in which our shared self-interests and community bonds could make our racial differences secondary, as they should be. Gerald F. Seib of the *Wall Street Journal* has observed that the "rampant cynicism" regarding the federal government has come at a time when America "needs unifying forces more than ever before."[21]

It does indeed: and with something like the Civic Deal to inspire us, perhaps some of the nihilism and the coarseness afflicting our culture might shrink from the center of our public life to its periphery, where such things belong.

It is especially urgent for conservatives to understand this time-tested — but long-lost — ethic of social cohesion. As David Brooks has argued in the conservative *Weekly Standard*, "democracy has a tendency to slide into nihilistic mediocrity if its citizens are not inspired by some larger national goal." And since "the best conservative thought knows that without a sense of national community, we balkanize," civilized Tories should be striving right now for a politics of "effort, cultivation, and mastery," knowing that "ultimately, the American purpose can find its voice only in Washington."[22]

It is vital for the Civic Deal to be viewed as a conservative-liberal reconciliation. Its unifying power emerges not only from provision of civic fundamentals but also in its genuine response to both conservative and liberal values. It will never be accepted if Americans regard it as nothing more than an updated version of the liberal welfare state.

The Civic Deal would represent a centrist politics like nothing we are offered today. Most of the self-styled centrists of the 1990s were in headlong retreat from the principle of national stewardship. Conversely, most supporters of activist government — people such as Robert Kuttner, Mickey Kaus, Michael Lind, Jacob Weisberg, and E. J. Dionne, Jr. — develop their proposals as explicit variations of liberal or left-of-center politics.

Kaus, for example, who proposed linking public works and full employment with a "get-tough" attitude on crime, has called for a new "civic *liberalism*" (my emphasis) to deliver this package. Lind recommends the creation of a "liberal nationalism" that would build upon this century's revisions of Hamiltonian politics.[23] Dionne — who expressed frustration in 1991 with conservative-versus-liberal politics — has more recently called for an affirmative-government "progressivism" that would balance and modify liberal principles while keeping them distinctly liberal. "Progressives — liberals . . . need to embrace a politics of liberty and community" through governmental policies that "strengthen civil society," he argued in his book *They Only Look Dead: Why Progressives Will Dominate the Next Political Era.*[24] It is questionable, however, whether advocates of governmental stewardship will achieve much of anything if they offer a "progressivism" that is widely perceived as a euphemism for the "L-word."

Dionne has called "contemporary liberals" the "heirs to the Progressive tradition" that began in the early twentieth century.[25] But reformers during the Progressive Era were by no means always in agreement, as Woodrow Wilson and Theodore Roosevelt revealed. As we have seen, the "progressivism" of Theodore Roosevelt was based upon the Lincolnesque Republican model: a synthesis of Hamiltonian and

Jeffersonian values. Since Hamilton and Jefferson partook (respectively) of some classical conservative and classical liberal principles, Roosevelt's progressivism had very old-fashioned conservative themes at its core.

So it is with the Civic Deal: its positive — "progressive," if you will — dimensions must be balanced with an unsentimental view of human nature, a world-view that used to be linked to old-style conservatism's impulse to regulate. Dionne has argued that "governments in democratic societies have the capacity to liberate," and so they do.[26] But the sort of liberation that democracies need can be profoundly two-sided. We need a positive kind of "liberation" through opportunity: opportunity enhanced through a government-stimulated abundance. But we also need liberation *from* certain things: from the breakdown of structures (water mains, bridges, and roads) that we depend on, from natural disasters whose effects are beyond our individual or regional power to overcome, and from the threat of malevolence from fellow human beings — from aggressors, terrorists, and thugs.

Lincoln showed us how to take from the liberal tradition the impulse to help and empower free men and women to achieve the very best of their potential. But he also showed us how to take from the conservative tradition a knowledge that the sinister side of human nature will menace society forever. This was the significance of his 1864 speech about the meaning of liberty. America was more than an experiment to see whether men and women could "govern themselves" through the forms of representative democracy. It was also an experiment to see whether people in a free society can govern the human instincts to tyrannize and dominate.

Statecraft for Lincoln was the challenge of using governmental power to do justice to the best and the worst of which our human nature is capable. Doing justice to the best of human nature, we have to liberate and empower, to protect and extend the egalitarian ideals — to underwrite human fulfillment. Doing justice to humanity's worst potential, we must curb the force of unfreedom, whether we see it asserted by means of an overseer's whip or the weapons of a rapist or mugger.

Since Lincoln's time the more degrading tendencies of human nature have been luridly on display. The twentieth-century experience has rubbed our noses in the side of human nature that feeds not only on tyranny but also on every obscene sensation that people can derive from sadistic mayhem. We have seen a malignity in some human beings that no sane person can ignore.

So to save our Jeffersonian freedoms — to preserve the ways of civilized society — we must use the methods of Hamilton, as some of our wisest leaders understood.

Does this appear to be too much to ask of our political leadership at this late date? The alternative is clear: continued drift, continued perversity, continued unraveling of national cohesion and morale. It is time for us to come to our senses. It is time to de-escalate the ideological wars that could poison our future. It makes an obvious difference if the Democratic Party, the Republican Party, or a catalyzing third-party venture turns out to be the instrumentality we choose for achieving this reconciliation. But somehow or other — unless we are so far gone in the ways of political folly that the legacy of Lincoln and the Roosevelts can teach us absolutely nothing — we will have to face up to the following fundamental choice. We can go on pelting one another with our cultural wreckage as it gradually piles up around us, or we can rediscover an achievement upon which much of our public life and our national greatness will prove to depend.

Notes

CHAPTER ONE

1. Theodore Roosevelt, "The New Nationalism," address in Osawatomie, Kansas, August 31, 1910, in *The Works of Theodore Roosevelt* (New York: Charles Scribner's Sons, 1925), XIX, 26–7.

2. Theodore Roosevelt, eighth annual message to Congress, December 8, 1908, in *Works*, XVII, 604, and *Autobiography*, in *Works*, XXII, 539.

3. Edward H. Crane, "Give Me Liberty, Not Utopia," *The Washington Post*, January 11, 1995, A-17.

4. Thomas Jefferson, first inaugural address, March 4, 1801, in *The Writings of Thomas Jefferson*, Andrew A. Lipscomb and Albert Ellery Bergh, eds. (Washington, D.C.: Thomas Jefferson Memorial Association of the United States, 1903), III, 320–1.

5. Thomas Jefferson, eighth annual message to Congress, November 8, 1808, in *Writings*, III, 484–5. It should be noted, however, that while Jefferson became reconciled to appropriations for public works at the end of his presidency, his reductions in federal spending nevertheless did substantial damage to America's infant navy — damage that became increasingly apparent in the years leading up to the War of 1812.

6. Theodore Roosevelt, "Limitation of Governmental Power," address in San Francisco, September 14, 1912, in *Works*, XIX, 420.

7. See Bruce R. Scott, "How Do Economies Grow?" *Harvard Business Review* (May–June, 1997), 156–64.

8. *Historical Statistics of the United States, Colonial Times to 1957*, Bureau of the Census, U.S. Department of Commerce (Washington, D.C.: U.S. Government Printing Office, 1960), 1961 edition, 73.

9. Ibid, 139.

10. *Economic Report of the President, Transmitted to the Congress, February 1988, together with the Annual Report of the Council of Economic Advisors* (Washington, D.C.: U.S. Government Printing Office, 1988), 248.

11. *Historical Statistics of the United States*, op. cit., 711.

12. Ibid, 713.

13. Ibid, 711.

14. Robert J. Donovan, *Eisenhower: The Inside Story* (New York: Harper & Brothers, 1956), 213–4.

15. *Economic Report of the President, Transmitted to the Congress, February 1993, together with the Annual Report of the Council of Economic Advisors* (Washington, D.C.: U.S. Government Printing Office, 1993), 348, 435.

16. Pat Choate and Susan Walter, *America in Ruins: The Decaying Infrastructure* (Durham, N.C.: Duke Press Paperbacks, 1983), 1.

17. Edward N. Luttwak, *The Endangered American Dream* (New York: Touchstone/Simon & Schuster, 1993), 261–2.

18. *Moving America: New Directions, New Opportunities* (Washington, D.C.: U.S. Department of Transportation, 1990), 23.

19. Felix G. Rohatyn, "Self-Defeating

Myths About America," *The Washington Post*, July 6, 1992, A-19.

20. Stuart Auerbach, "Clark Urges Iran to Release Hostages," *The Washington Post*, June 4, 1980, A-1, A-24, and Stuart Auerbach, "Iran's Anti-U.S. Conference Calls for Peaceful End to Crisis," *The Washington Post*, June 6, 1980, A-15.

21. Milton Friedman, *Capitalism and Freedom* (Chicago and London: University of Chicago Press, l962), 31.

22. E. J. Dionne, Jr., *Why Americans Hate Politics* (New York: Simon & Schuster, 1991), 14–5.

23. For an introduction to "communitarianism," see Amitai Etzioni, *The Spirit of Community: Rights, Responsibilities, and the Communitarian Agenda* (New York: Crown Publishers, 1993).

24. Thomas B. Edsall, "Conservatives Struggle to Find Strategy to Fight Clinton Health Plan," *The Washington Post*, February 12, 1994, A-5.

25. Anthony Lewis, "Where Power Lies," *The New York Times*, July 18, 1994, A-15.

26. David Osborne and Ted Gaebler, *Reinventing Government: How the Entrepreneurial Spirit is Transforming the Public Sector* (Reading, Mass.: Addison-Wesley Publishing Co., 1992), 252–3, 277.

27. David Osborne, "A New Compact: Sorting Out Washington's Proper Role," in Will Marshall and Martin Shram, eds. *Mandate For Change* (New York: Berkley Books/Progressive Policy Institute, 1993), 240–1.

28. Al Gore, "The Big Squeeze: Why This Time Reform Will Make Our Government Smaller and Smarter," *The Washington Post*, September 12, 1993, C-1, C-4.

29. Robert Reich, "Who is Them?" *Harvard Business Review* (March–April 1991), 85–6.

30. Louis Jacobson, "A Moderate Manifesto," *National Journal*, January 13, 1996, 93.

31. Robert A. Dahl, *After The Revolution? Authority in a Good Society* (New Haven and London: Yale University Press, 1970), 55, 93.

32. James P. Pinkerton, "Living With Fear," *The Baltimore Sun*, January 19, 1994, 13-A; and *What Comes Next: The End of Big Government and the New Paradigm Ahead* (New York: Hyperion, 1995), 313–7.

33. Herbert Croly, *The Promise of American Life* (New York: Macmillan & Co., 1909), 28–9, 168–70. While Croly admitted that his own "preferences are on the side of Hamilton rather than Jefferson," he also acknowledged that "neither the Jeffersonian nor the Hamiltonian doctrine was entirely adequate" in its original formulation. "A combination must be made of both Republicanism and Federalism," he said, but this combination had never before "been mixed in just the proper proportions." Theodore Roosevelt, in his opinion, came closer than anyone else in American history to getting the mixture right. The continuing relevance of the Hamilton-Jefferson dialectic was affirmed in an important recent symposium, "Alexander Hamilton and Thomas Jefferson: The Struggle to Define a New Republic," held at the University of Virginia on June 6–9, 1994. The importance of Croly's formulations has recently been re-emphasized by Jacob Weisberg, who argued in his book *In Defense of Government: The Fall and Rise of Public Trust* (New York: Scribner, 1996), 190–1, that Croly's "great contribution" was to "locate the affirmative use of government in a historical tradition." Attacks upon the legacy of Croly were assembled by the conservative

Hudson Institute in a 1995 volume; see
Lamar Alexander and Chester E. Finn, Jr.,
eds., *The New Promise of American Life*
(Indianapolis: Hudson Institute, 1995).

34. Thomas Jefferson to James Madison, December 20, 1787, in *The Writings
of Thomas Jefferson*, Paul Leicester Ford,
ed. (New York: G. P. Putnam's Sons,
1892–99), IV, 479.

35. Alexander Hamilton, *The Federalist* # 70, March 18, 1788, in *The Federalist* (New York: Modern Library/Random
House, 1937), 454.

36. See Leonard P. Curry, *Blueprint
for Modern America: Non-Military Legislation of the First Civil War Congress*
(Nashville: Vanderbilt University Press,
1968) and Heather Cox Richardson, *The
Greatest Nation on Earth: Republican
Economic Policies During the Civil War*
(Cambridge: Harvard University Press,
1997).

37. Abraham Lincoln, *Collected Works
of Abraham Lincoln*, Roy B. Basler, ed.
(New Brunswick, N.J.: Rutgers University Press, 1953), II, 221.

38. Abraham Lincoln to Henry Pierce
and others, April 6, 1859, in *Collected
Works*, op. cit., III, 375–6.

39. Abraham Lincoln, speech at
Springfield, Illinois, June 26, 1857, in
Collected Works, II, 406. Lincoln's understanding of Jefferson's outlook in this
matter was strikingly accurate. Compare
Lincoln's argument in the 1857 Springfield speech with the following statement by Jefferson in 1790: "The ground
of liberty is to be gained by inches. . . .
We must be contented to secure what
we can get from time to time, and eternally press forward for what is yet to
get." Thomas Jefferson to the Rev.
Charles Clay, January 27, 1790, in *The
Papers of Thomas Jefferson*, Julian P.
Boyd, et. al., eds. (Princeton: Princeton
University Press, 1961), XVI, 129.

40. Abraham Lincoln, speech at
Peoria, Illinois, October 16, 1854, in
Collected Works, II, 271.

41. Ibid, 271.

42. George Fitzhugh, *Sociology for the
South — Or, the Failure of Free Society*
(Richmond: A. Morris, Publisher, 1854),
Burt Franklin Research and Source
Book Series, # 102, 179.

43. Abraham Lincoln, Second Inaugural Address, March 4, 1865, in *Collected Works*, VIII, 333.

44. Abraham Lincoln, speech at
Baltimore, April 18, 1864, in *Collected
Works*, VII, 301–2.

45. Theodore Roosevelt, *Autobiography*, in *Works*, XXII, 481.

46. Theodore Roosevelt, "The Puritan Spirit and the Regulation of Corporations," address in Provincetown,
Mass., August 20, 1907, in *Works*, XVIII,
94.

47. Theodore Roosevelt, eighth
annual message to Congress, December
8, 1908, in *Works*, XVII, 604.

48. Franklin D. Roosevelt, address in
Syracuse, N.Y., September 29, 1936, in
*The Public Papers and Addresses of
Franklin D. Roosevelt*, Samuel I.
Rosenman, ed. (New York: Random
House, 1938), V, 389–90. The phrase
quoted by F.D.R. is an imprecise reproduction of the maxim — "Reform, that
you may preserve" — coined by Thomas
Babington Macaulay in the debate on
Britain's first Reform Bill, March 2,
1831.

49. Franklin D. Roosevelt, quoted in
Edmond D. Coblentz, ed., *William
Randolph Hearst: A Portrait in His Own
Words* (New York: Simon & Schuster,
1952), 178, and Arthur Schlesinger, Jr.,
The Politics of Upheaval (Boston:
Houghton Mifflin Co., 1960), 325.

50. Theodore Roosevelt, "The Purpose of the Progressive Party," address in

New York City, October 30, 1912, in *Works*, XIX, 459.

51. James MacGregor Burns, *Roosevelt: The Lion and the Fox* (New York: Harcourt, Brace & Co., 1956), 477, James MacGregor Burns, *Roosevelt: The Soldier of Freedom, 1940–1945* (New York: Harcourt Brace Jovanovich, Inc., 1970), 604, and Burns, *Roosevelt: The Lion and the Fox*, 476.

52. Felix G. Rohatyn, "Self-Defeating Myths About America," op. cit. See also David Alan Aschauer, *Public Investment and Private Growth: The Economic Benefits of Reducing America's "Third Deficit"* (Washington, D.C.: Economic Policy Institute, 1990).

53. Charles Mallar, Stuart Kerachsky, Craig Thornton, David Long, *Evaluation of the Economic Impact of the Job Corps Program, Third Follow-Up Report*, prepared for the Office of Research and Evaluation, Employment and Training Administration, U.S. Department of Labor (Princeton: Mathematica Policy Research, Inc., 1982), vi, 259, and Paul Taylor, "Job Corps Still Working," *The Washington Post*, September 2, 1991, A-1, A-6, A-7.

54. Rudiger Dornbusch, "Why America Needs Clinton's Economics," *The Wall Street Journal*, August 27, 1992, A-11.

55. Rick Weiss, "NIH Cancer Chief Vents Frustration," *The Washington Post*, December 24, 1994, A-7.

56. Ronald C. Moe, "Let's Rediscover Government, Not Reinvent It," *Government Executive*, June 1993, 48.

57. John Milton Cooper, Jr., *Pivotal Decades: The United States, 1900–1920* (New York and London: W. W. Norton & Co., 1990), 41.

58. Henry L. Stimson and McGeorge Bundy, *On Active Service in Peace and War* (New York: Harper, 1948), 17.

59. Donald Kagan, *Pericles of Athens and the Birth of Democracy* (New York: Touchstone/Simon & Schuster, 1991), 154–5. According to Plutarch, Pericles' purpose in the Acropolis building program went beyond creation of civic and religious monuments; it involved an almost proto-Keynesian attempt to create new wealth and prosperity for all social classes. In Plutarch's account, Pericles "boldly laid before the people proposals for immense public works and plans for buildings, which would involve many different arts and industries, . . . his object being that those who stayed at home, no less than those serving in the fleet or in the army . . . should be enabled to enjoy a share of the national wealth." Consequently, as the project advanced "the city's prosperity was extended far and wide and shared among every age and condition in Athens." Plutarch, "Life of Pericles," in *The Rise and Fall of Athens: Nine Greek Lives by Plutarch*, Ian Scott-Kilvert, trans. (New York: Penguin Classics, 1960), 178–9.

60. Alexander Hamilton, *The Federalist # 27*, December 25, 1787, op. cit., 168.

61. John M. Berry, "Economists Urge Investing Stimulus," *The Washington Post*, March 31, 1992, C-1, C-4, Hobart Rowen, "What We Need is More Debt," *The Washington Post*, March 26, 1992, A-21, Robert Kuttner, "More Important than the Deficit," *The Washington Post*, April 7, 1992, A-25.

62. Alexander Hamilton, *The Federalist # 34*, January 4, 1788, op. cit., 205.

63. William J. Baumol and Alan S. Blinder, *Economics: Principles and Policy* (Fort Worth: The Dryden Press/Harcourt Brace & Company, 1994), Sixth Edition, 727, 736, 730.

64. See Joel Kotkin and David Friedman, "As Wall Street Pats Itself on the

Back, Trouble Lurks Behind the Boom," *The Washington Post*, May 24, 1998, C-1, C-4.

65. See Lawrence Mishel, Jared Bernstein, John Schmitt, *The State of Working America, 1996–97* (Washington, D.C.: Economic Policy Institute, 1997), 97, passim.

66. Ibid, 243–4, passim.

67. Robert Eisner, "These Figures Spell Good Times, Not Bad," *The New York Times*, December 24, 1995, Section 3, 12. See also Max B. Sawicky, *Up From Deficit Reduction* (Washington, D.C.: Economic Policy Institute, 1994), and Richard Striner, "Debt Has Made Us Prosperous," *The Washington Post*, "Outlook," April 20, 1997, C-3.

68. Baumol and Blinder, op. cit., 811.

69. It is ironic at the close of the twentieth century to read this mid-nineteenth century account — by the great British historian Thomas Babington Macaulay — of the manner in which the development of the Bank of England (founded in 1694), and the associated development of a stupendous national debt in the centuries that followed, built the economic might of Great Britain in a way that defied conventional wisdom: "Such was the origin of that debt which has since become the greatest prodigy that ever perplexed the sagacity and confounded the pride of statesmen and philosophers. At every stage in the growth of that debt it has been seriously asserted by wise men that bankruptcy and ruin were at hand. Yet still the debt went on growing; and still bankruptcy and ruin were as remote as ever. When the great contest with Lewis the Fourteenth was finally terminated by the Peace of Utrecht, the nation owed about fifty millions; and that debt was considered, not merely by the rude multitude, not merely by foxhunting squires and coffeehouse orators, but by acute and profound thinkers, as an encumbrance which would permanently cripple the body politic. Nevertheless trade flourished: wealth increased: the nation became richer and richer. Then came the war of the Austrian Succession; and the debt rose to eighty millions. Pamphleteers, historians and orators pronounced that now, at all events, our case was desperate. Yet the signs of increasing prosperity, signs which could neither be counterfeited not concealed, ought to have satisfied observant and reflecting men that a debt of eighty millions was less to the England which was governed by Pelham than a debt of fifty millions had been to the England which was governed by Oxford. Soon war again broke forth: and, under the energetic and prodigal administration of the first William Pitt, the debt rapidly swelled to a hundred and forty millions. As soon as the first intoxication of victory was over, men of theory and men of business almost unanimously pronounced that the fatal day had now really arrived. The only statesman, indeed, active or speculative, who did not share in the general delusion was Edmund Burke. . . . Again England was given over; and again the strange patient persisted in becoming stronger and more blooming in spite of all the diagnostics and prognostics of State physicians. As she had been visibly more prosperous with a debt of a hundred and forty millions than with a debt of fifty millions, so she was visibly more prosperous with a debt of two hundred and forty millions than with a debt of one hundred and forty millions. . . . The beggared, the bankrupt society not only proved able to meet all its obligations, but, while meeting those obligations, grew richer and richer so fast that the

growth could almost be discerned by the eye. In every county, we saw wastes recently turned into gardens: in every city, we saw new streets, and squares, and markets, more brilliant lamps, more abundant supplies of water: in the suburbs of every great seat of industry, we saw villas multiplying fast. . . . While shallow politicians were repeating that the energies of the people were borne down by the weight of the public burdens, the first journey was performed by steam on a railway. Soon the island was intersected by railways. A sum exceeding the whole amount of the national debt at the end of the American war was, in a few years, voluntarily expended by this ruined people on viaducts, tunnels, embankments, bridges, stations, engines. Meanwhile taxation was almost constantly becoming lighter and lighter: yet still the Exchequer was full. It may be now affirmed without fear of contradiction that we find it as easy to pay the interest of eight hundred millions as our ancestors found it, a century ago, to pay the interest of eighty millions. It can hardly be doubted that there must have been some great fallacy in the notions of those who uttered and of those who believed that long succession of confident predictions, so signally falsified by a long succession of indisputable facts. . . They made no allowance for the effect produced by the incessant progress of every experimental science, and by the incessant efforts of every man to get on in life. *They saw that the debt grew; and they forgot that other things grew as well as the debt.*" (My emphasis) From Lord Macaulay, *The History of England* (1849–61), Penguin classics edition (London and New York: Penguin books, 1968, 1986), pp. 494–7.

CHAPTER TWO

1. Perry Miller, "Puritan State and Puritan Society," in *Errand into the Wilderness* (Cambridge, Mass.: Harvard University Press, 1956), 143. The link between State regulation and a harsh view of human nature is a venerable one. Citing the opinion of a number of Church Fathers to the effect that "political authority was a consequence of man's corrupted nature, a punishment and at the same time a remedy for his sins," historian John B. Morrall has argued that this view was influential throughout the Middle Ages, notwithstanding the presence of other countervailing doctrines. See John B. Morrall, *Political Thought in Medieval Times* (Toronto, Buffalo, London: University of Toronto Press, 1980, originally published 1958), 19. Furthermore, despite the centrifugal and decentralizing tendencies of feudalism, incipient statism may be seen in the governance of Charlemagne, followed by that of early German Emperors such as Frederick Barbarossa and the stronger English monarchs such as Henry II. Regulation was pervasive in Medieval guild restrictions that limited competition and controlled wages, prices, and production. Regulation of this sort was occasionally performed by the State, as in the case of England's Statutes of Labourers (1351, 1495) and Statute of Artificers (1563). Probably the most influential distillation of proto-conservative regulation was Thomas Hobbes's classic *Leviathan* (1651). A near-contemporary version of statist absolutism was Robert Filmer's *Patriarcha*, pub-

lished in 1680 though written earlier. The refutation of Filmer (through biblical commentary) was the purpose of Locke's *First Treatise of Government*. The seventeenth century witnessed an upsurge of divine-right monarchism, principally under Stuart and Bourbon auspices.

2. Roland N. Stromberg, *European Intellectual History Since 1789* (Englewood Cliffs, N.J.: Prentice-Hall, 1975), 54.

3. Ibid, 69. For a long time commentators have linked the emergence of liberalism and the philosophy of John Locke; Louis Hartz, for example, in his influential book *The Liberal Tradition in America* declared that "a liberal society" — such as he believed the United States to be — necessarily "begins with Locke." (Louis Hartz, *The Liberal Tradition in America* [New York: Harcourt, Brace & World, 1955], v, 5–6, passim). The contention that "Lockean liberalism" was the fountainhead of liberal culture has continued, along with the tendency of some academic writers to extend the argument of Hartz to the effect that liberalism has enjoyed a political hegemony in the United States; see Joyce Appleby's comment that "[l]iberalism entered the history of America as a set of powerful ideas; it remained to dominate as a loose association of unexamined assumptions." (Joyce Appleby, *Liberalism and Republicanism in the Historical Imagination* [Cambridge, Mass. and London: Harvard University Press, 1992], 1). Another influential idea in this tradition associates "Lockean liberalism" with aspirant individualism; this side of the "Lockean liberal" heritage has appealed to conservative adherents of laissez-faire. In my own view, while Locke's importance to the liberal tradition is beyond dispute,

his influence can be over-magnified. Further, the contention that "Lockean liberalism" has dominated American political culture to the point of overpowering significant conservative traditions is not convincing. Finally, excessive emphasis on the elements of individualism in Locke's thought obscures the presence of important cooperative themes in his theories of society. For analysis of such themes in Locke's *Second Treatise of Government*, see Forrest McDonald, *Novus Ordo Seclorum: The Intellectual Origins of the Constitution* (Lawrence, Kansas: University Press of Kansas, 1985), 60–6. For additional useful comments on the issue of Locke and his influence, see Garry Wills, *Inventing America: Jefferson's Declaration of Independence* (New York: Random House, 1978), 1979 Vintage edition, 169–71, passim.

4. Reinhold Niebuhr, *The Irony of American History* (New York: Charles Scribner's Sons, 1952), 72, Thomas Paine, "Common Sense" (1776), in *The Complete Writings of Thomas Paine*, Philip S. Foner, ed. (New York: The Citadel Press, 1945), I, 6.

5. Ibid, I, 4–5.

6. Thomas Paine, "The Rights of Man" (1791), in *Complete Writings*, I, 397.

7. Eric Foner, *Tom Paine and Revolutionary America* (London, Oxford, New York: Oxford University Press, 1976), 81.

8. R. K. Webb, *Modern England: From the 18th Century to the Present* (New York and Toronto: Dodd, Mead & Company, 1975), 287–8.

9. Roland Stromberg, *European Intellectual History*, op. cit., 54.

10. Forrest McDonald, *Novus Ordo Seclorum: The Intellectual Origins of the Constitution*, op. cit., 224. For the past several decades historians have engaged

in heated debate regarding American "political culture" in the age of the Founding Fathers. Following Bernard Bailyn, some have emphasized the influence of English Radical Whiggism on the Revolutionary generation. See Bernard Bailyn, *The Ideological Origins of the American Revolution* (Cambridge, Mass.: Harvard University Press, 1967). Others have joined in a dispute between scholars who emphasize "classical republicanism" (a political outlook idealizing certain aspects of classical antiquity and touting a program of civic virtue and responsibility) and those who argue that classical liberalism, with its emphasis on individual rights and opportunities, was the fundamental force in American politics. For key works exemplifying these schools of thought, see J.G.A. Pocock, *The Machiavellian Moment: Florentine Political Thought and the Atlantic Republican Tradition* (Princeton: Princeton University Press, 1976), and Joyce Appleby, *Liberalism and Republicanism in the Historical Imagination,* op. cit. In "The 'Great National Discussion:' The Discourse of Politics in 1787," *William & Mary Quarterly,* 3rd Series, 45 (1988), 3–32, Isaac Kramnick presented a pluralistic view of American political culture at the time of the Constitutional Convention, arguing that none of the "discernible idioms of politics" identified by scholars in recent years really "dominated the field." The best overall treatment of intellectual history relating to the politics of the Founding generation is Gordon S. Wood, *The Creation of the American Republic, 1776–1787* (Chapel Hill: University of North Carolina Press, 1969).

11. James Madison, *The Federalist #* 51, February 8, 1788, op. cit., 337. Madison was not a cynic. In *The Federalist #* 55 he observed that "[a]s there is a degree of depravity in mankind which requires a certain degree of circumspection and distrust, so there are other qualities in human nature which justify a certain portion of esteem and confidence." Nonetheless, he recognized and emphasized the ugly side of human nature throughout his career. "Wherever there is an interest and power to do wrong, wrong will generally be done," he told Jefferson in 1788, "and not less readily by a powerful & interested party than by a powerful and interested prince." (Madison to Jefferson, October 17, 1788, *Papers of James Madison,* Robert A. Rutland, et. al., eds., [Charlottesville: University Press of Virginia, 1977], XI, 297–300). Indeed, so mercurial was human mischief-making that "liberty may be endangered by the abuses of liberty as well as by the abuses of power." (*The Federalist #* 63).

12. James Madison to Thomas Jefferson, September 6, 1787, in *The Papers of James Madison,* Robert A. Rutland, et. al., eds. (Chicago and London: University of Chicago Press, 1977), X, 163–4.

13. George Washington to Bushrod Washington, November 10, 1787, in *The Writings of George Washington,* John C. Fitzpatrick, ed. (Washington, D.C.: Government Printing Office, 1939), XXIX, 311.

14. Max Farrand, ed., *The Records of the Federal Convention of 1787* (New Haven and London: Yale University Press, 1911, 1937), II, 645–6.

15. Thomas Jefferson to James Madison, September 6, 1789, *The Papers of Thomas Jefferson,* op. cit., XV, 395–6.

16. Winfred E. A. Bernhard, *Fisher Ames: Federalist and Statesman, 1758–1808* (Chapel Hill: University of North Carolina Press, 1965), 256.

17. Fisher Ames, Letter of October

26, 1803, name of recipient deleted, in *Works of Fisher Ames, Compiled by a Number of His Friends, to which are prefixed, Notices of His Life and Character* (Boston: T. B. Wait & Co., 1809), 483.

18. Fisher Ames, Letter of March 10, 1806, Ibid, 512.

19. Farrand, ed., *Records*, op. cit., Vol. I, 289.

20. Ibid, 288.

21. Alexander Hamilton, *Report on Manufactures,* December 5, 1791, in *The Papers of Alexander Hamilton*, Harold C. Syrett, ed. (New York and London: Columbia University Press, 1966), X, 296.

22. Alexander Hamilton, *The Continentalist* # 5, April 18, 1782, in Papers, op. cit., III, 76.

23. Forrest McDonald, *Alexander Hamilton: A Biography* (New York and London: W. W. Norton & Company, 1979, 1982), 55.

24. Alexander Hamilton, *Report on Manufactures*, in *Papers*, op. cit., X, 310.

25. Ibid, 303.

26. Thomas Jefferson to John Taylor, November 26, 1798, in *The Writings of Thomas Jefferson*, op. cit., X, 64–5.

27. Thomas Jefferson to Gideon Granger, August 13, 1800, Ibid, 168.

28. Thomas Jefferson to William Johnson, June 12, 1823, in *Writings*, op. cit., XV, 442.

29. Thomas Jefferson to James Madison, January 30, 1787, in *Papers*, op. cit., XI, 93.

30. James Madison, "Political Reflections," February 23, 1799, in *Papers*, op. cit., XVII, 237.

31. Alexander Hamilton, *Tully* # 3, August 28, 1794, in *Papers*, op. cit., XVII, 159. "Tully" was an English nickname for Marcus Tullius Cicero, much as "Livy" refers to the Roman historian Titus Livius. Hamilton was posing as a latter-day Cicero, saving the Republic from a modern Catiline conspiracy.

32. George Washington to Henry Lee, August 26, 1794, in *Writings*, op. cit., XXXIII, 475.

33. George Washington, Sixth Annual Message to Congress, November 19, 1794, in *Writings*, XXXIV, 29.

34. Thomas Jefferson to James Madison, December 28, 1794, in *Writings*, op. cit., IX, 294. Regarding the reality of crypto-monarchism among some Americans in the 1780s and 1790s, see Lance Banning, *The Sacred Fire of Liberty: James Madison and the Founding of the Federal Republic* (Ithaca, N.Y.: Cornell University Press, 1995), 122–3, 244–5, 339–41.

35. George Washington to Charles Carroll, of Carrollton, August 2, 1798, in *Writings*, op. cit., XXXVI, 384.

36. Thomas Jefferson to Thomas Lomax, March 12, 1799, in *Writings*, op. cit., X, 124.

37. Thomas Jefferson to Elbridge Gerry, January 26, 1799, Ibid, 77.

38. Albert Gallatin, *Report on Roads and Canals*, April 6, 1808, in *Selected Writings of Albert Gallatin*, E. James Ferguson, ed. (Indianapolis and New York: The Bobbs-Merrill Company, Inc., 1967), 229, 230, 232. For a comprehensive account of public works in the United States from the founding period through the mid-twentieth century, see Ellis L. Armstrong, Michael C. Robinson, and Suellen M. Hoy, eds., *History of Public Works in the United States, 1776–1976* (Chicago: American Public Works Association, 1976).

39. Thomas Jefferson to Samuel Kercheval, July 12, 1816, in *Writings*, op. cit., XV, 41.

40. James Madison, Second Annual Message to Congress, December 5, 1810, in *The Writings of James Madison,*

Gaillard Hunt, ed. (New York and London: G. P. Putnam's Sons, 1908), VIII, 127.

41. James Madison to William Eustis, May 22, 1823, in *Writings*, op. cit., IX, 135–6.

42. Henry Clay, Speech on Internal Improvements, January 14, 1824, in *The Papers of Henry Clay*, James F. Hopkins, ed. (Lexington: University of Kentucky Press, 1963), III, 587, 591.

43. John Quincy Adams, First Annual Message to Congress, November 25, 1825, in *The State of the Union Messages of the Presidents, 1790–1966*, Fred L. Israel, ed. (New York: Chelsea House/ Robert Hector, Publishers, 1966), I, 248.

44. George Dangerfield, *The Awakening of American Nationalism, 1815–1828* (New York: Harper & Row, 1965), 232– 3.

45. John Quincy Adams to Charles Upham, February 2, 1837, quoted in Henry Adams, *The Degradation of the Democratic Dogma* (New York: Macmillan Company, 1919), 25.

46. See "Remarks in Illinois Legislature, Concerning Resolutions Asking Information on Railroad and Fund Commissioners," December 8, 1838, in Basler, *Collected Works of Abraham Lincoln*, op. cit., I, 122–3. See also Lincoln's "Speech in United States House of Representatives on Internal Improvements," June 20, 1848, Ibid, I, 480–90. Lincoln biographer Benjamin P. Thomas pointed out that Lincoln "adhered to Alexander Hamilton's ideas of utilizing banks as fiscal agencies of government" and that he "favored direct government expenditures for public improvements, as well as grants in aid to states, and help to private enterprise." In all of this, "Lincoln's conception of the government's relation to the economic welfare of the people" rejected the "laissez-faire philosophy" of the "Jacksonian movement [which] aimed to divorce government from business." (Benjamin P. Thomas, *Abraham Lincoln: A Biography* [New York: Alfred A. Knopf, 1952], 79–80). Similarly, biographer Stephen B. Oates — basing his account to a large extent upon Illinois newspaper sources from the 1830s — described the proto-Keynesian response of Lincoln to the economic depression that followed the Panic of 1837: "In 1837 a terrible panic shook the U.S. economy with volcanic fury, toppling banks and businesses alike. . . . Unable to raise money, state governments in the South and Midwest repealed their internal improvement programs and defaulted on their loans. In Illinois . . . the legislature met in three successive sessions from 1837 to 1840 and debated what to do with the public works projects then under way. Lincoln, serving as Whig floor leader in the house, joined the majority in voting not merely to retain the internal improvements system, but to enact additional canal and railroad projects . . . since the programs would provide employment and stimulate the state's stricken economy." Lincoln "steadfastly refused to abandon the internal improvement system, which he was certain would benefit workers, farmers, and businessmen alike. He was pledged to public works, he declared, and would have his limbs ripped off before he would violate that pledge." (Stephen B. Oates, *With Malice Toward None: The Life of Abraham Lincoln* [New York: Harper & Row, 1977], 36–7, and especially 54).

47. Lawrence Frederick Kohl, *The Politics of Individualism: Parties and the American Character in the Jacksonian Era* (New York and Oxford: Oxford University Press, 1989), 113.

48. William W. Freehling, *Prelude to Civil War: The Nullification Controversy in South Carolina, 1816–1836* (New York and Evanston: Harper & Row, 1965), 127.

49. James Hamilton, Jr. to John Taylor, et. al., September 14, 1830, *Charleston Mercury*, cited in Freehling, *Prelude to Civil War*, op. cit., 256.

50. John C. Calhoun to Virgil Maxcy, September 11, 1830, Galloway-Maxcy-Markoe Papers, cited in Freehling, *Prelude to Civil War*, 257. As Calhoun abandoned his support for public works and assumed the leadership of the southern nullifiers, Jefferson followed a surprisingly similar course of action before his death in 1826. Slavery figured in both of these developments, even though Calhoun was an ardent defender of slavery while Jefferson remained committed to eventual emancipation. Some have accounted for this paradoxical inconsistency on Jefferson's part through a psychological theory. Historian Joseph J. Ellis has recently argued that Jefferson's relapse after 1820 into his older suspicion of governmental "consolidation" relates to the Missouri crisis and the manner in which it revealed something troubling that Jefferson was trying to evade: namely, the fact that he had failed to deliver on his vision regarding the long-term phase-out of slavery. The result, in Ellis's opinion, was a psychological game in which Jefferson mentally changed the subject — avoiding the unpleasant truth about slavery's expansion — by persuading himself that the Missouri agitation was less an expression of sincere anti-slavery views than a pretext for new and possibly menacing assertions of authority by the central government. See Joseph J. Ellis, *American Sphinx: The Character of Thomas Jefferson* (New York: Alfred A. Knopf, 1997), 270–3.

51. John Quincy Adams to Charles Upham, February 2, 1837, quoted in Henry Adams, *The Degradation of the Democratic Dogma*, op. cit., 25.

52. James M. McPherson, *Abraham Lincoln and the Second American Revolution* (New York and Oxford: Oxford University Press, 1991), 39–40.

53. The recent contention of historian David Herbert Donald in his book *Lincoln* (New York: Simon & Schuster, 1995) that Lincoln was a "passive" leader has been politely but effectively demolished by James M. McPherson in "A Passive President?" *The Atlantic Monthly*, November, 1995, 134–140.

54. See L. M. Ganaway, *New Mexico and the Sectional Controversy, 1846–1861* (Albuquerque: University of New Mexico Press, 1944). For analysis of southern contingency plans for the use of slave labor in western and Central American mining operations, see Eugene D. Genovese, *The Political Economy of Slavery* (New York: Random House/Vintage, 1965), 256–60.

55. See Robert E. May, *The Southern Dream of a Caribbean Empire, 1854–1861* (Baton Rouge: Louisiana State University Press, 1973), and John Hope Franklin, *The Militant South, 1800–1861* (Cambridge: Harvard University Press, 1956), 1964 Beacon Edition, 96–128.

56. See Kenneth Stampp, *The Peculiar Institution* (New York: Random House/Vintage Books, 1956), 65, and Robert S. Starobin, *Industrial Slavery in the Old South* (New York: Oxford University Press, 1970). For analysis of the use of slaves as rented strikebreakers in southern industry, see Eugene D. Genovese, *The Political Economy of Slavery*, op. cit., 199, 233.

57. See, for example, Harry V. Jaffa, *Crisis of the House Divided: An Interpretation of the Issues in the Lincoln-Douglas*

Debates (Chicago and London: University of Chicago Press, 1959, 1982), 395.

58. Abraham Lincoln, "A House Divided," speech at Springfield, Illinois, June 16, 1858, in *Collected Works,* op. cit., II, 461–2.

59. Abraham Lincoln to Joshua F. Speed, August 24, 1855, Ibid, II, 323.

60. Abraham Lincoln, "Fragment on Slavery," July 1, 1854 (?), Ibid, II, 222–3.

61. Abraham Lincoln, speech at Chicago, Illinois, July 10, 1858, Ibid, II, 501.

62. "South Carolina's Declaration of the Causes of Secession," in *The Causes of the Civil War,* Kenneth Stampp, ed. (New York: Simon & Schuster/Touchstone, 1959, 1974), 44–5.

63. Abraham Lincoln to William Kellogg, December 11, 1860, in *Collected Works,* op. cit., IV, 150.

64. Moncure Daniel Conway, *Autobiography, Memories and Experiences* (Boston and New York: Houghton, Mifflin and Company, 1904), 345–6. The William Ellery Channing who accompanied Conway at the Lincoln interview was a nephew of the famous Unitarian clergyman of the same name.

65. Abraham Lincoln, "Proclamation Revoking General Hunter's Order of Military Emancipation of May 9, 1862," May 19, 1862, and Abraham Lincoln, "Appeal to Border State Representatives in Favor of Compensated Emancipation," July 12, 1862, in *Collected Works,* V, 223, 319.

66. Abraham Lincoln to Horace Greeley, August 22, 1862, Ibid, V, 388.

67. Abraham Lincoln to James C. Conkling, August 26, 1863, Ibid, VI, 406–10.

68. John Hay, *Lincoln and the Civil War in the Diaries and Letters of John Hay,* Tyler Dennett, ed. (New York: Dodd, Mead & Company, 1939), 76.

69. *Freeman's Journal,* August 20,

1864, quoted in James M. McPherson, *Ordeal by Fire* (New York: Alfred A. Knopf, 1982), Vol. II, 449. See also Forrest G. Wood, *Black Scare: The Racist Response to Emancipation and Reconstruction* (Berkeley: University of California Press, 1968), 53–79.

70. Abraham Lincoln, Last Public Address, April 11, 1865, in *Collected Works,* VIII, 399–405. For a statement of the traditional but now outmoded view that Lincoln was averse to the Radical Republicans, see T. Harry Williams, *Lincoln and the Radicals* (Madison: University of Wisconsin Press, 1941). For a revisionist assessment of the commonalities that existed as early as 1860 between Lincoln's views and those of the Radical Republicans, see Eric Foner, *Free Soil, Free Labor, Free Men: The Ideology of the Republican Party before the Civil War* (London, Oxford, New York: Oxford University Press, 1970), 214–6. For exploration of the synergistic relationship between Lincoln and the Radical Republicans, see Hans L. Trefousse, *The Radical Republicans: Lincoln's Vanguard for Racial Justice* (New York: Alfred A. Knopf, 1969), and Lawanda Cox, *Lincoln and Black Freedom: A Study in Presidential Leadership* (Columbia, S. C.: University of South Carolina Press, 1981).

71. William Hanchett, *The Lincoln Murder Conspiracies* (Urbana: University of Illinois Press, 1983), 37.

72. Harry V. Jaffa, *Crisis of the House Divided,* op. cit., 395.

73. Abraham Lincoln, to Henry L. Pierce and Others, April 6, 1859, in *Collected Works,* op. cit., III, 375–6.

74. Harry V. Jaffa, *Crisis of the House Divided,* op. cit., 190.

75. Abraham Lincoln, speech at Peoria, Illinois, October 16, 1854, in *Collected Works,* II, 271.

76. Abraham Lincoln, speech at Baltimore, April 18, 1864, in *Collected Works*, VII, 301–2.

77. For analysis of the liberal side of Lincoln's political thought, see J. G. Randall, *Lincoln the Liberal Statesman* (New York: Dodd, Mead & Company, 1947). For presentation of some of the conservative aspects of Lincoln's statecraft, see Norman A. Graebner, "Abraham Lincoln, Conservative Statesman," in Norman A. Graebner, ed., *The Enduring Lincoln: Lincoln Sesquicentennial Lectures at the University of Illinois* (Urbana: University of Illinois Press, 1959). In *The Lincoln Persuasion: Remaking American Liberalism* (Princeton, N.J.: Princeton University Press, 1993), J.

David Greenstone has argued that Lincoln's thought synthesized variations of liberalism; Greenstone acknowledged, however, that Lincoln's "unionism and his Whiggish politics had a deeply conservative side" as well. Indeed, the overall significance of Lincoln must be understood as part of an intellectual continuum extending from seventeenth-century Puritanism to late nineteenth-century Social Gospel ethics (Ibid, 26, 276–85).

78. Phillip Shaw Paludan, *The Presidency of Abraham Lincoln* (Lawrence: University Press of Kansas, 1994), 316.

79. James M. McPherson, *Abraham Lincoln and the Second American Revolution*, op. cit., 62–3.

CHAPTER THREE

1. Walt Whitman, "Democratic Vistas" (1871), in Floyd Stovall, ed., *Walt Whitman, Prose Works 1892* (New York: New York University Press, 1964), II, 369.

2. See John Hay, *Lincoln and the Civil War in the Diaries and Letters of John Hay*, Tyler Dennett, ed., op. cit., 119, 135. For an optimistic assessment of the prospects for cooperation between Lincoln and the Radicals if Lincoln had lived, see Herman Belz, *Reconstructing the Union: Theory and Policy During the Civil War* (Ithaca, N.Y.: Cornell University Press, 1969), 311.

3. See Kenneth M. Stampp, *The Era of Reconstruction, 1865–1877* (New York: Random House, 1965), Vintage edition, 173–184, and Eric Foner, *A Short History of Reconstruction, 1863–1877* (New York: Harper & Row, 1990), 165–8.

4. Roscoe Conkling, address at Rochester, N.Y., Sept. 26, 1877, quoted in Matthew Josephson, *The Politicos, 1865–*

1896 (New York: Harcourt, Brace & Co., 1938), 246, 728, n. 32, and in Alfred R. Conkling, *The Life and Letters of Roscoe Conkling, Orator, Statesman, Advocate* (New York: Charles L. Webster, 1889), 540, 541.

5. John J. Ingalls, *Congressional Record*, Mar. 26, 1886, 2786.

6. Richard Hofstadter, *Social Darwinism in American Thought* (Philadelphia: University of Pennsylvania Press, 1944), Beacon edition, 1955, 7.

7. Herbert Spencer, *Social Statics* (1850) (New York: D. Appleton & Co., 1864), 414–5.

8. Andrew Carnegie, *Autobiography* (Boston and New York: Houghton Mifflin Co., 1920), 339.

9. See Alfred H. Kelly, Winfred A. Harbison, and Herman Belz, *The American Constitution: Its Origins and Development* (New York and London: W. W. Norton & Company, 1983), 400–404.

10. See Eric Foner, *A Short History of*

Reconstruction, 1863–1877, op. cit., 195.

11. Ignatius Donnelly, address in St. Louis, Feb. 24, 1892, Donnelly MSS, Minnesota Historical Society, St. Paul, Minn., cited in Martin Ridge, *Ignatius Donnelly, The Portrait of a Politician* (Chicago and London: University of Chicago Press, 1962), 295.

12. See Franklin Folsom, *Impatient Armies of the Poor: The Story of Collective Action of the Unemployed, 1808–1942* (Niwot, Colorado: University Press of Colorado, 1991), 180–6.

13. William Jennings Bryan, "The Cross of Gold Speech," in *William Jennings Bryan: Selections,* Ray Ginger, ed. (Indianapolis, New York, Kansas City: The Bobbs-Merrill Company, Inc., 1967), 41.

14. Walter Rauschenbusch, *Christianity and the Social Crisis* (New York: The Macmillan Company, 1907), 70, 339.

15. Mathew Carey, quoted in Richard T. Ely, *Ground Under Our Feet: An Autobiography* (New York: The Macmillan Company, 1938), 131.

16. Lester F. Ward, "The Psychologic Basis of Social Economics" (1892–93), in Lester F. Ward, *Glimpses of the Cosmos* (New York and London: G. P. Putnam's Sons, 1913), IV, 351, 355.

17. Ibid, 357–8.

18. Richard T. Ely, *Ground Under Our Feet,* op. cit., 136.

19. Ibid, 143.

20. See Thomas Beer, *Hanna* (New York: Alfred A. Knopf, 1929), 132–3.

21. See Herbert Croly, *Marcus Alonzo Hanna: His Life and Work* (New York: The Macmillan Company, 1912), 388–400, 444. Hanna exemplified the ethics of reform-to-conserve — noblesse oblige — among enlightened businessmen at the turn of the century. Eric F. Goldman perceived in Hanna and successors such as George W. Perkins — a Morgan partner and director of International Harvester and U.S. Steel — contributors to the legacy of American liberalism. See Eric F. Goldman, *Rendezvous with Destiny: A History of Modern American Reform* (New York: Alfred A. Knopf, 1952), 1977 Vintage edition, 160–1. From a New Left perspective, James Weinstein maintained that "the growing maturity and sophistication" of men such as Perkins bespoke an enlightened conservatism: Perkins and his peers had "come to understand, as Theodore Roosevelt often told them, that social reform was truly conservative." See James Weinstein, "Big Business and the Origins of Workmen's Compensation," *Labor History,* VIII, Spring 1967, 156–74. For a further study of the contributions of reform-to-conserve business leaders in the origins of the modern American welfare state, see Edward D. Berkowitz and Kim McQuaid, *Creating the Welfare State: the Political Economy of 20th-Century Reform* (Lawrence, Kansas: University Press of Kansas, 1988).

22. Walter Rauschenbusch, *Christianizing the Social Order* (New York: The Macmillan Company, 1913), 124.

23. Ibid, 5.

24. See George E. Mowry, *The Era of Theodore Roosevelt and the Birth of Modern America, 1900–1912* (New York: Harper & Row, 1958), 134–9.

25. See John Milton Cooper, Jr., *Pivotal Decades,* op. cit., 98–9.

26. Theodore Roosevelt to James Wolcott Wadsworth, May 26, 1906, in *The Letters of Theodore Roosevelt,* Elting E. Morison, ed. (Cambridge, Mass.: Harvard University Press, 1952), V, 282–3.

27. Theodore Roosevelt, "The Puritan Spirit and the Regulation of Corporations," address in Provincetown,

Mass., August 20, 1907, in *The Works of Theodore Roosevelt*, op. cit., XVIII, 94.

28. Theodore Roosevelt, eighth annual message to Congress, December 8, 1908, in *Works*, XVII, 604.

29. John Milton Cooper, Jr., *Pivotal Decades*, op. cit., 36.

30. Henry L. Stimson and McGeorge Bundy, *On Active Service in Peace and War*, op. cit., 4.

31. See *The Letters of Theodore Roosevelt*, op. cit., IV, 1131, n. 1.

32. See Edmund Morris, *The Rise of Theodore Roosevelt* (New York: Ballantine Books, 1979), 41.

33. Herbert Croly, *The Promise of American Life* (New York: Macmillan & Co., 1909), 168–9, 170.

34. Theodore Roosevelt, "The New Nationalism," address in Osawatomie, Kansas, August 31, 1910, in *Works*, XIX, 26–7.

35. Ibid, 18.

36. Theodore Roosevelt, *Autobiography*, in *Works*, XXII, 539.

37. Theodore Roosevelt, Address at the Union League Club, Philadelphia, January 30, 1905, *Presidential Addresses and State Papers by Theodore Roosevelt* (New York: Review of Reviews Company, 1910), III, 217–24. The element of regulation in Progressive Era reform — which included an important amount of lingering noblesse oblige conservatism — has been the subject of critiques from both the left and the right; critics have denounced Progressive "supervision" of America's new industrial order as both "liberal" and "conservative" in its character, depending on their own ideological orientation. From a New Left perspective, Gabriel Kolko argued that "the period . . . labeled the 'progressive' era by virtually all historians was really an era of conservatism" because "national political leaders during the

period 1900–1916 . . . in virtually every case . . . chose those solutions to problems advocated by the representatives of concerned business and financial interests." Consequently, it was "business control over politics" rather than "political regulation of the economy" that typified the "triumph of conservatism" by businessmen seeking stability and predictability through the subterfuge of regulatory reform. See Gabriel Kolko, *The Triumph of Conservatism: A Reinterpretation of American History, 1900–1916* (London: Collier-Macmillan Limited, 1963), 2–3. Though at first inclined to view Progressive reform in similar terms, James Weinstein later argued that it was elitist liberals — rather than conservatives — who used Progressive reforms to stabilize the capitalist system: "Corporate liberalism . . . appealed to leaders of different social groupings and classes by granting them status and influence . . . on the condition only that they defend the framework of the existing social order." See James Weinstein, *The Corporate Ideal in the Liberal State, 1900–1918* (Boston: Beacon Press, 1968), xiv. Not surprisingly, conservative (especially libertarian conservative) scholarship is also inclined to attack Progressive regulation as the work of liberalism — or socialism — but to argue that regulation undermined the strength of private enterprise instead of supporting it. See the Hudson Institute's compilation of attacks upon the legacy of Herbert Croly: Lamar Alexander and Chester E. Finn, Jr., eds., *The New Promise of American Life* (Indianapolis: Hudson Institute, 1995). See also Robert Higgs, *Crisis and Leviathan: Critical Episodes in the Growth of American Government* (New York and Oxford: Oxford University Press, 1987), 116, although Higgs acknowledges that regulatory ideas were widespread at the turn of the century.

38. John Morton Blum, *The Republican Roosevelt* (Cambridge, Mass: Harvard University Press, 1954), Atheneum edition, 1962, x–xi, 5. The conservative elements in Theodore Roosevelt's statecraft have elicited both criticism and praise from American historians. Writing from a moderately left-of-center perspective, Richard Hofstadter devoted a chapter to T.R. in his iconoclastic study *The American Political Tradition* (1948). In labeling Roosevelt "The Conservative as Progressive," Hofstadter tried to expose what he believed to be the shallowness (by liberal standards) of Roosevelt's "progressivism." John Morton Blum, writing in 1954, countered that Roosevelt's conservative qualities were far more admirable than liberal critics believed: "An institutionalist, a gradualist, a moralist, from the position he attained he ruled strongly and quite well. Learning the while, he developed large plans for the uses of power. These had one common, revealing objective: stability." (Blum, *Republican Roosevelt*, op. cit., 6). By the 1960s, such reasoning had brought Hofstadter around: in his preface to the 1967 edition of *The American Political Tradition*, Hofstadter acknowledged that if he were to rewrite the volume he would treat T.R. very differently: "[I]n writing of Theodore Roosevelt, I was, I think, unduly taken with my 'discovery' of the element of sham in his progressivism and was led to arrive at a conclusion which I would now take as my starting point if I were to write about him again. Instead of viewing T.R. as a bogus progressive, suppose one were to begin with the assumption that he was indeed distinctly a conservative at heart, but a most flexible and adroit conserva-

tive?" Richard Hofstadter, *The American Political Tradition and the Men Who Made It* (New York: Alfred A. Knopf, 1948), 1974 Vintage Edition, xxx–xxxi.

39. Theodore Roosevelt, "Limitation of Governmental Power," address in San Francisco, September 14, 1912, in *Works*, XIX, 420. For documentation of the statement by Wilson that Roosevelt was quoting, see Woodrow Wilson, "An Address to the New York Press Club," September 9, 1912, in Arthur S. Link, et. al, eds., *The Papers of Woodrow Wilson* (Princeton: Princeton University Press, 1978), XXV, 124.

40. Theodore Roosevelt, speech before Progressive National Convention, Chicago, August 6, 1912, in *Works*, XIX, 376.

41. Theodore Roosevelt, "The Purpose of the Progressive Party," address in New York City, October 30, 1912, in *Works*, XIX, 459.

42. John Stuart Mill, *Principles of Political Economy* (1848) (London, New York, Bombay, Calcutta: Longmans, Green, and Co., 1909), Book V, Chapter 1, Section 3, 800.

43. David Harris, "European Liberalism in the Nineteenth Century," *American Historical Review*, LX, 3, April 1955, 515–6. See also Roland Stromberg, *European Intellectual History Since 1789*, op. cit., 103–4, and 173, in which the 1880s are identified as "the critical decade for the turn away from laissez-faire liberalism" in Britain.

44. Winston Leonard Spencer Churchill, *Lord Randolph Churchill* (New York: The Macmillan Co., 1906), I, 269.

45. Omaha Platform of the People's Party, July 1892, in John D. Hicks, *The Populist Revolt: A History of the Farmers' Alliance and the People's Party* (Minneapolis: The University of Minnesota Press, 1931), Appendix F, 441.

46. Lois Craig, et. al, *The Federal Presence: Architecture, Politics, and Symbols in United States Government Buildings* (Cambridge, Mass. and London: MIT Press, 1978), 280. For a brief history of the agency in charge of constructing Hoover Dam, see William E. Warne, *The Bureau of Reclamation* (New York: Praeger, 1973). For accounts of the Hoover Dam project, see Joseph E. Stevens, *Hoover Dam: An American Adventure* (Norman and London: University of Oklahoma Press, 1988), Andrew J. Dunar and Dennis McBride, *Building Hoover Dam: An Oral History of the Great Depression* (New York: Twayne Publishers, 1993), and U. S. Department of the Interior, Water and Power Resources Service, *Project Data: Boulder Canyon Project, Hoover Dam* (Denver, U.S. Government Printing Office, 1981), 79–88.

47. David Burner, *Herbert Hoover: A Public Life* (New York: Alfred A. Knopf, 1979), 143, 229, 230. For coverage of Hoover's role in the flood disaster of 1927, see John M. Barry, *Rising Tide: The Great Mississippi Flood of 1927 and How It Changed America* (New York: Simon & Schuster, 1997).

48. Ibid, 277.

49. William Trufant Foster and Waddill Catchings, *Business Without a Buyer* (Boston and New York: Houghton Mifflin Company, 1927), second edition, 1928, 19.

50. See Frank Freidel, *Franklin D. Roosevelt: Launching the New Deal* (Boston and Toronto: Little, Brown and Company, 1973), 227.

51. Alfred M. Landon, quoted in Arthur Schlesinger, Jr., *The Age of Roosevelt: The Coming of the New Deal* (Boston: Houghton Mifflin Company, 1958), 3.

52. James MacGregor Burns, *Roosevelt: The Lion and the Fox* (New York: Harcourt, Brace & World, 1956), Harvest edition, 235, 238. For an assessment of the New Deal's conservative aspects presented with the disapproving slant of a New Left perspective, see Barton J. Bernstein, "The New Deal: The Conservative Achievements of Liberal Reform," in Barton J. Bernstein, ed., *Towards a New Past: Dissenting Essays in American History* (New York: Pantheon Books, 1968), 263–88.

53. Franklin D. Roosevelt, address in Syracuse, New York, September 29, 1936, in *The Public Papers and Addresses of Franklin D. Roosevelt*, op. cit., V, 389–90.

54. Franklin D. Roosevelt, address in Chicago, Oct. 14, 1936, in *Public Papers*, op. cit., V, 487.

55. Franklin D. Roosevelt, "Fireside Chat," April 14, 1938, in *FDR's Fireside Chats*, Russell D. Buhite and David W. Levy, eds. (Norman, Oklahoma: University of Oklahoma Press, 1992), Penguin Edition, 1993, 116, 119.

56. Carl Degler, *Out Of Our Past* (New York: Harper & Row, 1959), 1984 edition, 445. See also David Burner, *Herbert Hoover: A Public Life*, op. cit., 331, for a critique of Hoover as a reformist conservative who failed to appreciate the links between his own social vision and the programs of the New Deal: "WPA and its sister programs turned relievers into workers, sharing in grandly visionary projects for building the nation and regenerating its spirit. . . . [This] meant an American version of the Burkean taste for a concrete living social order. Hoover the conservative, truly conservative in his commitment to association and to a national heritage, should have been at home with it." For additional analysis of Hoover-F.D.R. continuities, see Carl Degler, "The Ordeal of Herbert Hoover," *The Yale Review*, LII, Summer 1963, 563–83.

57. James MacGregor Burns,

Roosevelt: The Lion and the Fox, op. cit., 235, 237, 238.

58. See, for example, Marquis Childs, "They Hate Roosevelt," *Harpers*, May 1936, 634–42.

59. George Wolfskill, *The Revolt of the Conservatives: A History of the American Liberty League, 1934–1940* (Boston: Houghton Mifflin Co., 1962), 107–8.

60. See Bronson Cutting, "Is Private Banking Doomed?" *Liberty*, March 31, 1934, 10, quoted in Schlesinger, *The Coming of the New Deal*, op. cit., 5. Cutting, a progressive Republican Senator, stated that "I think back to the events of March 4, 1933 with a sick heart. For then . . . the nationalization of the banks by President Roosevelt could have been accomplished without a word of protest. It was President Roosevelt's great mistake."

61. For hints of the massive public works programs that Long envisioned as an adjunct to his "Share Our Wealth" program, see Huey P. Long, "Every Man a King," March 1, 1934, in *Kingfish to America: Share Our Wealth — Selected Senatorial papers of Huey P. Long*, Henry M. Christman, ed. (New York: Schocken Books, 1985), 43, and Huey P. Long, *My First Days in the White House* (Harrisburg, Pa.: The Telegraph Press, 1935).

62. William Trufant Foster and Waddill Catchings, *The Road to Plenty* (Boston and New York: Houghton Mifflin Company, 1928), 158, 194.

63. John Maynard Keynes, "The World's Economic Outlook," *The Atlantic Monthly*, May 1932, 525.

64. Ibid, 525–6.

65. Thurman Arnold, *Fair Fights and Foul: A Dissenting Lawyer's Life* (New York: Harcourt, Brace & World, Inc., 1951), 1965 edition, 143.

66. Abraham Lincoln, *Collected Works*, op. cit., II, 221.

67. See Merrill D. Peterson, *Lincoln in American Memory* (New York and Oxford: Oxford University Press, 1994), 320.

68. Joseph L. Arnold, *New Deal in the Suburbs: A History of the Greenbelt Town Program, 1935–1954* (Columbus, Ohio: Ohio State University Press, 1971), 84–5, 91–3. See also Rexford Guy Tugwell, "The Meaning of the Greenbelt Towns," *The New Republic*, February 17, 1937, 42–3.

69. Joseph L. Arnold, *New Deal in the Suburbs*, op., cit., 173–4, 236–8. The Greenbelt consumer co-op was established in 1938–39. The housing co-op was established later (1947–48) because when the federal government attempted to establish a Greenbelt Housing Authority in the 1930s the Maryland General Assembly (which had to draft and approve the charter for such an authority) refused to include a sufficient amount of citizen representation on the governing board. Both the federal government and the Greenbelt citizens refused to proceed on this basis and the matter was deferred until after World War II.

70. William Leuchtenburg, *Franklin D. Roosevelt and the New Deal* (New York: Harper & Row, 1963), Harper Torchbooks edition, 345.

71. Francis Biddle, quoted in Arthur Schlesinger, Jr., *The Coming of the New Deal*, op. cit., 19.

72. Franklin D. Roosevelt, address in Philadelphia, June 27, 1936, in *Public Papers*, op. cit., V, 235.

73. See Frank Freidel, *Franklin D. Roosevelt: Launching the New Deal*, op. cit., 7, regarding the fact that "Roosevelt more than once reiterated in years that followed that he was trying not to forget his Groton ideals."

CHAPTER FOUR

1. Peter Viereck, *Conservatism, From John Adams to Churchill* (Princeton: D. Van Nostrand Co., 1956), 45–6.

2. Winston Churchill, "The Spirit of the Budget," address at Leicester, Sept. 5, 1909, in Winston Churchill, *Liberalism and the Social Problem* (1909) (New York: Haskell House, 1973), 376.

3. Merrill D. Peterson, *Lincoln in American Memory*, op. cit., 321–2.

4. Ibid, 321.

5. Franklin D. Roosevelt, "Message to Congress Asking for Additional Appropriations for National Defense," May 16, 1940, in *The Public Papers and Addresses of Franklin D. Roosevelt*, op. cit., IX, 199–200.

6. Franklin D. Roosevelt, "Fireside Chat," May 27, 1941, in *F.D.R.'s Fireside Chats*, Russell D. Buhite and David W. Levy, eds., op. cit., 179.

7. Franklin D. Roosevelt, "Navy Day Address on World Affairs," October 27, 1941, in *Nothing To Fear: The Selected Addresses of Franklin Delano Roosevelt, 1932–1945*, B. D. Zevin, ed. (Boston: Houghton Mifflin Co., 1946), 297.

8. Franklin D. Roosevelt, "Fireside Chat on National Security," December 29, 1940, in *Nothing To Fear*, op. cit., 253, and Franklin D. Roosevelt, "Fireside Chat," May 27, 1941, in *F.D.R.'s Fireside Chats*, op. cit., 186.

9. Wendell L. Willkie, *One World* (New York: Simon and Schuster, 1943), 53–4.

10. Winston Churchill, *The Second World War: Triumph and Tragedy* (Boston: Houghton Mifflin Company, 1953), 60–5, Dwight D. Eisenhower, *Crusade in Europe* (Garden City, N.Y.: Doubleday and Company, Inc., 1949), 231.

11. Winston Churchill, *The Second World War: Triumph and Tragedy*, op. cit., 226–8. For a contemporary example

of the "Yalta sell-out" canard, see Robert D. Novak, "Betrayal at Yalta," *The Washington Post*, August 18, 1997, A-19.

12. Whittaker Chambers, *Witness* (New York: Random House, Inc., 1952), 471, 472.

13. Joseph McCarthy, quoted in Richard Rovere, *Senator Joe McCarthy* (Cleveland and New York: The World Publishing Co., 1959), Meridian edition, 11.

14. Richard Rovere, *Senator Joe McCarthy*, op. cit., 41.

15. James MacGregor Burns, *Roosevelt: The Soldier of Freedom*, op. cit., 511–2.

16. Willmoore Kendall, "Source of American Caesarism," *National Review*, Nov. 7, 1959, 461–2.

17. William F. Buckley, Jr., *Up From Liberalism* (New Rochelle, N.Y.: Arlington House, 1959), 1968 edition, 228–9.

18. Ludwig von Mises, *Bureaucracy* (New Haven: Yale University Press, 1944), 1969 edition (New Rochelle, N.Y.: Arlington House), 10.

19. *Economic Report of the President, Transmitted to the Congress, February 1993, together with the Annual Report of the Council of Economic Advisors*, op. cit., 435.

20. Ibid, 348.

21. Stephen E. Ambrose, *Eisenhower: The President* (New York: Simon & Schuster, 1984), II, 251, 301.

22. Ibid, 250–1.

23. See William E. Leuchtenburg, *In the Shadow of FDR: From Harry Truman to Bill Clinton* (Ithaca and London: Cornell University Press, 1993), 54.

24. See *The Eisenhower Diaries*, Robert H. Ferrell, ed. (New York: Norton, 1981), 231, 374, and Leuchtenburg, *In the Shadow of FDR*, op. cit., 50–57.

25. Jacob K. Javits, *Order of Battle: A Republican's Call to Reason* (New York: Atheneum Publishers, 1964), 55–6, 61.

26. Ibid, 304.

27. Peter Viereck, *Conservatism Revisited* (New York: Collier Books, 1949), 1962 edition, Book II, *The New Conservatism: What Went Wrong?*, 131.

28. Ibid, 17.

29. Russell Kirk, *The Conservative Mind: From Burke to Santayana* (Chicago: Henry Regnery Company, 1953), 67, 75, 81, passim.

30. Franklin D. Roosevelt, address delivered at the Democratic State Convention, Syracuse, N.Y., September 29, 1936, in *The Public Papers and Addresses of Franklin D. Roosevelt*, op. cit., V, 384.

31. Harold L. Ickes, "Academic Freedom," *School and Society*, June 8, 1935, cited in Arthur Schlesinger, Jr., *The Politics of Upheaval*, op. cit., 195.

32. Frances Perkins, "Eight Years as Madame Secretary," *Fortune*, September, 1941, 94.

33. John Adams to Thomas Jefferson, February 2, 1816, in Lester J. Cappon, ed., *The Adams-Jefferson Letters* (Chapel Hill: University of North Carolina Press, 1959), II, 463. The insight, of course, is biblical: "Every way of a man is right in his own eyes: but the Lord pondereth the hearts" (*Proverbs*, 21: 2).

34. Edmund Burke, *Reflections on the Revolution in France* (1790), *The Works of the Rt. Hon. Edmund Burke* (Boston: Little, Brown and Co., 1877), III, 419–420. John Adams was similarly insistent regarding the principle that tyranny could emanate from anywhere in the political or social spectrum: "The fund[a]mental Article of my political Creed," he told Jefferson, "is, that Despotism, or unlimited Sovereignty, or absolute Power is the same in a Majority of a popular Assembly, an Aristocratical

Counsel, an oligarchical Junto and a single Emperor." John Adams to Thomas Jefferson, November 13, 1815, in Cappon, op. cit., II, 456.

35. Ibid, 396.

36. Thomas Paine, "Common Sense," in *Complete Writings*, op. cit., I, 6.

37. Woodrow Wilson, address to the U.S. Senate, July 10, 1919, in Arthur S. Link, ed. *The Papers of Woodrow Wilson* (Princeton: Princeton University Press, 1990), LXI, 436, and address in Pueblo, Colorado, Sept. 25, 1919, in Link, ed., *Papers*, LXIII, 512–3.

38. Clarence Weinstock, "We Did Not Pant For War," in Theodore A. Wilson, ed., *World War II: Readings on Critical Issues* (New York: Charles Scribner's Sons, 1972), 1974 edition, 23.

39. Lincoln Steffens to Sam Darcy, April 28, 1934, in *The Letters of Lincoln Steffens*, Ella Winter and Granville Hicks, eds. (New York: Harcourt, Brace and Company, 1938), II, 983.

40. Lincoln Steffens to the Editor of the *New Republic*, August 1, 1934, in *Letters*, op. cit., 987–8.

41. Arthur Schlesinger, Jr., *The Vital Center: Our Purposes and Perils on the Tightrope of American Liberalism* (Boston: Houghton, Mifflin Co., 1949), Sentry edition, 1962, 165.

42. Ibid, 255–6.

43. Reinhold Niebuhr, *The Irony of American History*, op. cit., 173.

44. Walt W. Rostow, *The Stages of Economic Growth: A Non-Communist Manifesto* (London and New York: Cambridge University Press, 1960), 1962 edition, 162–3, 164.

45. Hubert H. Humphrey, *The Cause is Mankind: A Liberal Program for Modern America* (New York, Washington, London: Frederick A. Praeger, Publishers, 1964), 148, 149.

46. Ibid, 148–9.

47. Gabriel Kolko, *The Roots of American Foreign Policy* (Boston: Beacon Press, 1969), 29.

48. Richard Nixon, Annual Message to Congress on the State of the Union, January 22, 1971, in *Public Papers of the Presidents of the United States: Richard Nixon, 1971* (Washington, D.C.: U.S. Government Printing Office, 1972), 55.

49. Richard Nixon, "'A Conversation with the President,' Interview with Four Representatives of the Television Networks," January 4, 1971, in *Public Papers of the Presidents of the United States: Richard Nixon, 1971* (Washington, D.C.: U.S. Government Printing Office, 1971), 22. See also Russell E. Train, "The Environmental Record of the Nixon Administration," *Presidential Studies Quarterly*, Vol. XXVI, No. 1, Winter 1996, 185–96.

50. Richard Nixon, Annual Message to Congress on the State of the Union, January 22, 1970, in *Public Papers of the Presidents of the United States: Richard Nixon, 1970* (Washington, D.C., U.S. Government Printing Office, 1971), 13.

51. Ibid, 14.

52. Richard Nixon, Annual Message to Congress on the State of the Union, January 22, 1971, *Public Papers of the Presidents of the United States: Richard Nixon, 1971*, op. cit., 53.

53. For a useful discussion of these issues, see Alonzo L. Hamby, *Liberalism and its Challengers* (New York and Oxford: Oxford University Press, 1985), 1992 edition, 316–24, Stephen E. Ambrose, *Nixon: The Triumph of a Politician, 1962–1972* (New York: Simon and Schuster, 1989), 404–5, and William Leuchtenburg, *In the Shadow of FDR*, op. cit., 161–73.

54. Eugene McCarthy, quoted in "Losers Weepers — or Walkers?" *Newsweek*, September 9, 1968, 42.

55. Ibid, 42.

56. George McGovern, Acceptance Speech, July 13, 1972, in *An American Journey: The Presidential Campaign Speeches of George McGovern*, George McGovern, ed. (New York: Random House, 1974), 18.

57. Jimmy Carter, State of the Union Address, January 19, 1978, in *Public Papers of the Presidents of the United States: Jimmy Carter, 1978* (Washington, D.C.: U.S. Government Printing Office, 1978), I, 91.

58. Jimmy Carter, Inaugural Address, January 20, 1977, in *Public Papers of the Presidents of the United States: Jimmy Carter, 1977* (Washington, D.C.: U.S. Government Printing Office, 1977), I, 2.

59. Charles Peters, "A Neo-Liberal's Manifesto," *The Washington Post*, September 5, 1982, C-1.

60. Isaac Shapiro and Robert Greenstein, *Selective Prosperity: Increasing Income Disparities Since 1977* (Washington, D.C.: Center on Budget and Policy Priorities, 1991), vii, passim.

61. 1991 *Green Book*, Committee on Ways and Means, U.S. House of Representatives, 102nd Congress, First Session, Background Material and Data on Programs within the Jurisdiction of the Committee on Ways and Means, 1341.

62. Kevin Phillips, *The Politics of Rich and Poor: Wealth and the American Electorate in the Reagan Aftermath* (New York: Random House, 1990), 21.

63. 1991 *Green Book* op. cit., 482.

64. Kevin Phillips, *Boiling Point: Republicans, Democrats, and the Decline of Middle-Class Prosperity* (New York: Random House, 1993), xxi–xxii. See also, Richard Morin," America's Middle-Class Meltdown," *The Washington Post*, December 1, 1991, C-1, C-2.

65. George F. Will, "In Defense of the Welfare State," *The New Republic*, May 9, 1983, 21.

CHAPTER FIVE

1. See William S. Maddox and Stuart A. Lilie, *Beyond Liberal and Conservative: Reassessing the Political Spectrum* (Washington, D.C.: The Cato Institute, 1984), and John J. Fialka, "Cato Institute's Influence Grows in Washington as Republican-Dominated Congress Sets Up Shop," *The Wall Street Journal,* Dec. 14, 1994, A-16. The provenance of the Cato Institute's name is worthy of comment. The Institute disavows a direct connection with either of the two ancient Roman Senators who bore the "Cato" cognomen: the elder and younger Marcus Porcius Cato. Rather, the Institute's literature states that the organization "is named for *Cato's Letters,* pamphlets that were widely read in the American colonies in the early eighteenth century. . . ." But the pamphlets, written by the Radical Whigs John Trenchard and Thomas Gordon from 1720 to 1723, make it clear that the authors were inspired by the life of Cato the Younger (95 B.C. – 46 B.C.), the Roman leader who committed suicide at Utica after Julius Caesar's victory over Pompey the Great. Trenchard and Gordon revered Cato as a champion of liberty; in *Cato's Letter # 23* (April 1, 1721), they attributed the following declamation to Cato: "No, says Cato, I scorn to be beholden to tyranny. I am as free as Caesar; and shall I owe my Life to him, who has no Right even to my Submission [?]" This heroic image of Cato in early eighteenth-century England was to a large extent the result of an influential play, Joseph Addison's *Tragedy of Cato* (1713). But if the founders of the Cato Institute had consulted Roman sources instead of English eighteenth-century pamphlets,

they would have discovered that their indirect namesake was regarded even by his friends as a plodding dogmatist. Marcus Tullius Cicero, for instance, who eulogized Cato after his death, could not resist poking fun at his stubborn orthodoxies; see Cicero's speech *Pro Murena* (62 B.C.) in *Cicero: On Government,* Michael Grant, trans., Penguin Classics, 1993, 143, 145.

2. Progressive Policy Institute, Prospectus (Washington, D.C.: Progressive Policy Institute, undated), 1, 2, and David Osborne, "A New Compact: Sorting Out Washington's Proper Role," in Will Marshall and Martin Shram, eds., *Mandate for Change,* op. cit., 240–1.

3. See Mickey Kaus, "Paradigm's Loss," *The New Republic,* July 27, 1992, 17–8, and James P. Pinkerton, *What Comes Next: The End of Big Government and the New Paradigm Ahead,* op. cit., passim.

4. George F. Will, "Congealed in Traffic," *The Washington Post,* March 11, 1990, B-7.

5. Don Phillips, "Taking Different Roads on Highway Bill," *The Washington Post,* December 18, 1991, A-21.

6. See Jason DeParle, "Latest Plan to Cure Welfare Troubles Borrows W.P.A. Blueprints of 1930's," *The New York Times,* March 13, 1992, A-14. See also Allan C. Miller, "Brown Appeals for Aid Program to Rebuild Cities," *Los Angeles Times,* May 15, 1992, A-25.

7. Mickey Kaus, *The End of Equality* (New York: New Republic/Basic Books, 1992), 125, 132, 128. See also John Leo, "A New Deal for the Underclass," *U.S. News & World Report,* May 25, 1992, 29.

8. Bill Clinton, Acceptance Speech, Democratic National Convention, July

16, 1992, *The Washington Post*, July 17, 1992, A-26.

9. Ibid.

10. Ibid.

11. Ibid.

12. *President Clinton's New Beginning: The Complete Text, with Illustrations, of the Historic Clinton-Gore Economic Conference, Little Rock, Arkansas, December 14–15, 1992* (New York: Donald I. Fine, Inc., 1993), 35–7.

13. Statement of Charles A. Bowsher, Comptroller-General of the United States, *Major Issues Facing a New Congress and a New Administration*, Testimony before the Committee on Governmental Affairs, United States Senate, January 8, 1993, United States General Accounting Office (Washington, D.C.: U. S. Government Printing Office, 1993), 11.

14. *A Vision of Change for America*, February 17, 1993 (Washington, D.C.: U.S. Government Printing Office, 1993), 29–30.

15. George F. Will, "Get Ready for More Government," *The Washington Post*, February 25, 1993, A-23, "Stampede for Statism," *The Washington Post*, February 19, 1993, A-21, "It's the Infrastructure Myth That's Crumbling," *The Washington Post*, January 10, 1993, C-7, "Do Americans Want Big Government," *The Washington Post*, February 28, 1993, C-7.

16. Rush Limbaugh, *See, I Told You So* (New York: Pocket Books, 1993), 306.

17. William Claiborne, "Big-City Mayors Voice Frustration Over Failure of Stimulus Package," *The Washington Post*, May 26, 1993, A-6.

18. See Hobart Rowen, "It's Not Much of a Budget," *The Washington Post*, August 12, 1993, A-27.

19. Jimmy Carter and Gerald R. Ford, "This One Can't Wait," *The Washington Post*, September 21, 1993, A-19.

20. Howard Kurtz, "Company for 'Harry and Louise' in Debate on Health Care Reform," *The Washington Post*, February 13, 1994, A-3.

21. Bill Clinton, Address to Joint Session of Congress, September 22, 1993, *The Washington Post*, September 23, 1993, A-19, A-20.

22. E. J. Dionne, Jr., "The Government Albatross," *The Washington Post*, May 4, 1993, A-21.

23. E. J. Dionne, Jr., "Lost Threads of a Presidency," *The Washington Post*, August 2, 1994, A-15.

24. Ann Devroy, "GOP Taking Joy in Obstructionism: Clinton Agenda Dying on Hill," *The Washington Post*, October 7, 1994, A-1, A-16.

25. Dick Armey, *The Freedom Revolution* (Washington, D.C.: Regnery Publishing, Inc., 1995), 316.

26. Paul Starr, "State of the Union? Someday, Paralyzed," *The New York Times*, January 24, 1995, A-19.

27. Richard Kogen, "High Cost of a Balanced Budget Amendment," *The Washington Post*, February 27, 1995, A-19.

28. Stephen Barr, "Economic Advisers Placed on Block," *The Washington Post*, June 24, 1995, A-6.

29. Gary Lee, "'Contract' Leaves Bad Taste with Food Safety Advocates," *The Washington Post*, March 9, 1995, A-19.

30. "Gingrich's Plan Sounds Fishy to Business," *Fortune*, March 20, 1995, 24.

31. Kathleen Day, "Budget Cuts Slow Agencies Fighting New Bacteria Strains," *The Washington Post*, June 27, 1995, A-1, A-6.

32. Kathy Sawyer, "Report Forecasts Poor Funding for Civilian Science: Group Says Congressional Plan Would Drastically Reduce Spending on Applied Research," *The Washington Post*, August 29, 1995, A-5. See also Elizabeth

Corcoran, "Hill Panel Votes to Halt Chip Research Funding," *The Washington Post*, July 26, 1995, G-1.

33. John Harris, "Clinton Assails GOP Plans for National Parks," *The Washington Post*, August 26, 1995, A-4.

34. Tom Kenworthy and Gary Lee, "Divided GOP Falters on Environmental Agenda," *The Washington Post*, November 24, 1995, A-1, A-10.

35. John F. Harris, "Administration Launches Assault on GOP Budget Plans," *The Washington Post*, May 11, 1995, A-12.

36. Ibid.

37. E. J. Dionne, Jr., "So Far From Victory," *The Washington Post*, April 4, 1995, A-23.

38. E. J. Dionne, Jr., "No Reason to be Smug," *The Washington Post*, January 23, 1996, A-15.

39. Paul Taylor and Thomas B. Edsall, "Disoriented Democrats Search for Direction," *The Washington Post*, June 25, 1995, A-1, A-4.

40. See David S. Broder, "The Power of Our Discontent," *The Washington Post*, September 6, 1995, A-21.

41. See "The Right Way to Balance the Budget," paid advertising by the Concord Coalition, *The Washington Post*, November 19, 1995, C-7, and Robert Kuttner, "Return of the Mugwump," *The Washington Post*, December 26, 1995, A-23.

42. Bill Clinton, State of the Union Address, January 23, 1996, *The Washington Post*, January 24, 1996, A-13.

43. James P. Pinkerton, *What Comes Next: The End of Big Government and the New Paradigm Ahead* (New York: Hyperion, 1995), 313–7.

44. George F. Will, "Maybe the Moon," *The Washington Post*, August 13, 1995, C-7.

45. George F. Will, "Road Work Ahead," *The Washington Post*, April 25, 1996, A-31.

46. "Campaign '96: Transcript of the First Presidential Debate," *The Washington Post*, October 7, 1996, A-8.

47. Edward Walsh, "Dole Casts Clinton as Liberal Masked by Rhetoric," *The Washington Post*, September 23, 1996, A-11.

48. "The Record is Relevant," excerpts from Washington Post Interview with President Clinton, *The Washington Post*, August 25, 1996, A-19.

49. E. J. Dionne, Jr., "Three of a Kind," *The Washington Post*, June 11, 1996, A-17.

50. Rick Weiss, "President Orders Overhaul of Meat Safety Inspections," *The Washington Post*, July 7, 1996, A-1, A-10, Peter Baker, "Clinton Announces Registry of Nation's Sex Offenders," *The Washington Post*, August 25, 1996, A-16, John F. Harris, "Clinton Backs Crime Victims' Amendment," *The Washington Post*, June 26, 1996, A-1, A-7, Roberto Suro, "U.S. Government to Assume Primary Responsibility for Airport Security," *The Washington Post*, September 6, 1996, A-3.

51. Helen Dewar and Judith Havemann, "Water, Wage Bills Pass as Congress Recesses," *The Washington Post*, August 3, 1996, A-1, A-8, Helen Dewar and Eric Pianin, "Pragmatism Drives Legislative Frenzy," *The Washington Post*, August 4, 1996, A-1, A-24, Dan Morgan, "GOP Congress's Budget Deep Freeze Begins to Melt," *The Washington Post*, July 22, 1996, A-1, A-10.

52. John F. Harris and Dan Balz, "Beyond Victory, There's History," *The Washington Post*, August 25, 1996, A-18.

53. President Clinton's Acceptance Speech to the Democratic National Convention, August 29, 1996, *The Washington Post*, August 30, 1996, A-36.

54. In March 1997 Clinton directed federal agencies to supplement efforts of the private sector in hiring welfare recipients. But budgetary constraints put a clear limitation on the scope of this directive. The *Washington Post's* coverage of the announcement reported that "experts on government hiring" insist that "some daunting obstacles to hiring welfare recipients remain, in part because of limited resources and a federal government being reduced." See Pierre Thomas, "Clinton Orders Welfare Hiring by U.S. Agencies," *The Washington Post*, March 9, 1997, A-1, A-11.

CHAPTER SIX

1. William Kristol and David Brooks, "What Ails Conservatism," *The Wall Street Journal*, September 15, 1997, A-22.

2. See Eric Pianin, "Rep. Kasich Decries Highway Bill as Pork," *The Washington Post*, March 28, 1998, A-4.

3. For the latest in a long line of analyses regarding the tension in conservative thought between authoritarian and libertarian tendencies, see Godfrey Hodgson, *The World Turned Right Side Up: A History of the Conservative Ascendancy in America* (Boston and New York: Houghton Mifflin Company, 1996).

4. "Crime and Justice," *The Washington Post*, May 4, 1996, B-3.

5. Robert J. Dole, Acceptance Speech, Republican National Convention, August 15, 1996, *The Washington Post*, August 16, 1996, A-37.

6. Marc Fisher, "The Color of Anger," *The Washington Post*, October 29, 1996, E-1, E-2. See also C. Eric Lincoln, *Coming Through the Fire: Surviving Race and Place in America* (Durham: Duke University Press, 1996), and Arthur Schlesinger, Jr., *The Disuniting of America* (New York and London: W.W. Norton and Company, 1992).

7. Richard D. Kahlenberg, "A Sensible Approach to Affirmative Action," *The Washington Post*, December 2, 1996, A-21. For a fuller treatment of the issue see Richard D. Kahlenberg, *The Remedy: Class, Race, and Affirmative Action* (New York: Basic Books, 1996).

8. Edwin L. Dale, "When Will It be Safe to Balance the Budget?" *The New York Times Magazine*, January 24, 1965, 14.

9. *Economic Report of the President, Transmitted to the Congress*, February 1993, op. cit., 435.

10. See Lawrence Mishel, Jared Bernstein, John Schmitt, *The State of Working America, 1996–97* (Washington, D.C.: Economic Policy Institute, 1997).

11. See Jessica Mathews, "Beware the 'Loose Nukes,'" *The Washington Post*, October 31, 1995, A-13, and Jessica Stern, "Terrorism Multiplied," *The Washington Post*, July 17, 1996, A-19..

12. See Robert Kuttner, "Cutting the Deficit Won't Cure the Economy," *The Washington Post*, July 31, 1992, A-23, and Hobart Rowen, "Growth and the Myth of the Deficit," *The Washington Post*, October 8, 1992, A-21.

13. Arthur Schlesinger, Jr., *The Cycles of American History* (Boston: Houghton Mifflin Company, 1986), 37.

14. Felix Rohatyn, "The Budget: Whom Can You Believe?" *The New York Review of Books*, August 10, 1995, 49.

15. David Alan Aschauer, *Public Investment and Private Growth: The Economic Benefits of Reducing America's*

"Third Deficit" (Washington, D.C.: Economic Policy Institute, 1990), 1, passim. See also Fred R. Bleakley, "Infrastructure Dollars Pay Big Dividends," *The Wall Street Journal*, August 12, 1997, 2.

16. Don Phillips and Alice Reid, "Clinton Proposes $175 Billion Road Bill," *The Washington Post*, March 13, 1997, A-4.

17. Eric Pianin, "Clinton Says Highway Bill Threatens Budget Accord," *The Washington Post*, March 29, 1998, A-4. See also Bud Shuster, "Once, Conservatives Knew the Value of Transportation," *The New York Times*, July 17, 1999, A-25.

18. Robert Novak, "Big-Government Conservatism," *The Washington Post*, September 25, 1997, A-25.

19. Felix G. Rohatyn, "Self-Defeating Myths About America," *The Washington Post*, July 6, 1992, op. cit.

20. Robert Kuttner, "No Market for Civility," *The Washington Post*, January 9, 1996, A-15.

21. Gerald F. Seib, "The Real Issue: Can Americans Hang Together?" *The Wall Street Journal*, October 25, 1995, A-16.

22. David Brooks, "A Return to National Greatness: A Manifesto for a Lost Creed," *The Weekly Standard*, March 3, 1997, 17, 20. See also George F. Will, "Conservative Challenge," *The Washington Post*, August 17, 1997, C-7.

23. Michael Lind, *The Next American Nation: The New Nationalism and the Fourth American Revolution* (New York: The Free Press, 1995), 301, 377.

24. E.J. Dionne, Jr., *They Only Look Dead: Why Progressives Will Dominate the Next Political Era* (New York: Simon & Schuster, 1996), 298.

25. E.J. Dionne, Jr., "The Liberal Revival: Why the Times are Ripe for a New Progressive Era," *The Washington Post*, February 4, 1996, C-1, C-4.

26. E.J. Dionne, *They Only Look Dead*, op. cit., 12.

Index

THE PERICLES INSTITUTE

THE PERICLES INSTITUTE IS A NON-PARTISAN, non-profit, and politically independent organization established to foster the principle of enlightened governmental stewardship at all levels, but especially the national level. Particularly in times of divided government, the Institute seeks to build a new consensus among Americans of all political persuasions — a consensus on behalf of governmental action in fields such as public infrastructure, workforce retraining, public safety, and scientific research that are vital to America's continued greatness.

Named in honor of the statesman who guided Athenian democracy during its golden age in the fifth century, B.C., the Institute will showcase the legacy of Periclean governance by American statesmen, both Republicans and Democrats, who have understood that well-conceived and well-executed governmental policies can empower individuals, communities, and the private sector.

The Pericles Institute is the *only* organization that seeks to bring conservatives and liberals together on behalf of wise activist governance in areas that command public support. With America facing national and global challenges in the twenty-first century that will require the utmost in social unity, economic strength, and cultural cohesion, the need for a revival of Periclean principles is clear. The Pericles Institute is a tax-exempt organization under Internal Revenue Code section 501(c)(3).